A BIBLIOGRAPHY OF

GEORGE MOORE

George Moore, 1932, a drawing by Francis Dodd, reproduced by permission of the National Portrait Gallery, London.

A BIBLIOGRAPHY OF

GEORGE
MOORE

BY

EDWIN GILCHER

NORTHERN ILLINOIS UNIVERSITY PRESS

DEKALB, ILLINOIS

IN MEMORY OF

ALLAN WADE

(1881–1955)

BIBLIOGRAPHER OF YEATS

AND SCHOLAR EXTRAORDINARY

Contents

Preface

It seems unlikely that any other author of modern times revised and rewrote to the extent that George Moore did, and it was the discovery, more than thirty years ago, of the textual differences in various editions of his books that led to the notes which have grown through several stages into the present bibliography.

Two previous bibliographies, published nearly fifty years ago, do not approach completeness, nor take more than casual note of revised texts. Both limit consideration to English editions and do not always agree in regard to dates and priority of issue.

The first, by I. A. Williams,[1] is hardly more than a check list; it contains brief descriptions of thirty-nine titles by Moore and two books about him, plus a listing of five books with prefaces or introductions which he contributed to works by other authors. The second, by Henry Danielson,[2] gives more detailed collations of fifty-two editions, including some limited editions, and seven books containing prefaces or introductions, concluding with a list of sales prices of the various volumes.

A third and more comprehensive bibliography was planned by A. J. A. Symons, who had the active, but not too helpful assistance of Moore in the project. It was intended for inclusion in the monumental *A Bibliography of the Writers & Illustrators of the Eighteen Nineties,*[3] which was never published, although some parts of it reached proof stage.

1. *Bibliographies of Modern Authors, No. 3, George Moore,* London and New York, 1921 (B19).

2. "George Moore, A Bibliography [1878–1921]," printed as an appendix to *A Portrait of George Moore in a Study of His Work,* by John Freeman, London, and New York, 1922.

3. It was first announced in a prospectus issued in 1925 and again in a double-page advertisement in THE BOOK-COLLECTOR'S QUARTERLY, II, 1931. Another advertisement in number X of the same periodical announced, shortly after Moore's death in 1933, a separate bibliography of his works by Symons, "giving particulars of revised editions, notes on the texts, collations of all first editions, etc.," but this too was never published.

A more recent bibliography, appended to an exhaustive study in French, *George Moore: L'Homme et L'Oeuvre (1852–1933)*[4] by Jean C. Noël, approaches completeness, but omissions in detailing revised and American editions, as well as in the listing of contributions and periodical printings, partially mar its usefulness.

All three of the published bibliographies, Williams, Danielson, and Noël, and in one instance Symons, have served as guides in the preparation of the present work, while the excellent *Life of George Moore*[5] by Joseph Hone has been a constant aid, as will be seen by the many references to it in the following pages.

Moore is reported to have said, "Just as I believe that the worst of all sins is bad writing, so I believe that the highest virtue is found in corrections, in an author's revisions. If you wish to estimate the true value of an author's art, study his revisions." [6]

Until comparatively recently, however, few scholars have taken serious note of the revisions Moore made in his works. A pioneer study is Royal A. Gettmann's "George Moore's Revisions of *The Lake*, 'The Wild Goose,' and *Esther Waters*" in PMLA, June 1944, which, because of the lack of sufficient bibliographical information at the time it was written, does not note all of the revisions that would have bolstered its thesis that Moore's rewritings were not just the work of his declining years, as has been stated by many commentators in writing of his books.

Since Professor Gettmann's study there have been a number of unpublished doctoral dissertations which have to a greater or lesser degree dealt with Moore's revisions, but unfortunately they are not readily available, although they can be had in microform copies.

The 1954 Stanford University dissertation of William A. Perkins, "George Moore's Realistic Novels: Roots, Achievements, Influence," lists, although not always correctly, and briefly comments on the revisions of the books discussed in his thesis.

John Denny Fischer's 1959 University of Illinois dissertation, "*Evelyn Innes* and *Sister Teresa* by George Moore: A Variorum Edition," is also a study of the revisions, including those specially made for German translations, in the two books (A22 and A25).

The revisions in *A Modern Lover* (A5), *A Mummer's Wife* (A6), *A Drama in Muslin* (A9), *A Mere Accident* (A10), *Spring Days* (A13), *Mike Fletcher* (A14), *Vain Fortune* (A16), and *Esther Waters* (A19) are thoroughly detailed in Jay Jernigan's 1966 Kansas State University dissertation, "George Moore's 'Re-Tying of Bows': A Critical Study of the Eight Early Novels and Their Revisions." Mr. Jernigan has incorporated the ma-

---

4. See B60.
5. See B44.
6. Quoted by William Lyon Phelps in *Autobiography with Letters* (B49).

terial in one section of his dissertation into an article, "The Bibliographical and Textual Complexities of George Moore's *A Mummer's Wife*" in the *Bulletin of the New York Public Library*, June 1970.

Susan Marie Dick's 1967 Northwestern University dissertation, "*Confessions of a Young Man* by George Moore: A Variorum Edition," details the many revisions and additions from the original periodical publication, including the French translations, to the revised 1918 edition text of the book (A12). A revised version of Miss Dick's dissertation is being published by McGill-Queen's University Press in Montreal.

The most recent study which notes revisions is *George Moore in Transition: Letters to T. Fisher Unwin and Lena Milman, 1894–1910*, edited with a commentary by Helmut E. Gerber (A66). It takes into account the rewriting in Moore's books from *Celibates* (A21) through *The Lake* (A27), particularly the involved revisions of the stories in *The Untilled Field* (A26).

In the present bibliography, primarily based on my own collection (but with every description checked against as many other copies as possible), it has been my intention not only to describe fully all of Moore's works in first editions, both English and American (except those utilizing sheets or plates of the English edition), but also all subsequent editions containing substantial revisions,[7] briefly noting the extent of the rewriting and listing subsequent editions of a particular text. In addition, for the benefit of collectors detailed descriptions are given of all illustrated, signed, and limited editions, even in those cases where an earlier text is reprinted or previously used plates are utilized.

The first section, which is by far the longest, contains descriptions of all titles associated with Moore, including early works excluded by him from the canon of the Carra and Uniform editions,[8] his translation of *Daphnis and Chloe*, the *Anthology of Pure Poetry*, which he edited, several volumes of letters, and occasional printings and pamphlets.

In the few instances where a book was rewritten and republished under

7. In some cases arbitrary decisions have had to be made regarding the amount of revision required to constitute a new text, and generally the addition of brief new prefatory material has not been considered sufficient to warrant a separate primary notation.

8. These are the two major collected editions, each with titles not in the other and each, at the time of publication, including the latest revised text (with two exceptions) of the books Moore hoped to save from oblivion. See A36-n2 for the titles of the 21-volume Carra Edition published 1922–24 in the United States, and A6-n9 for those in the 20-volume Uniform Edition published 1924–33 in England. Also see A13-n4 for an earlier abortive uniform collected edition in which only two volumes were published; A29-n1 for thirteen titles issued in England in a uniform binding; A13-n5 for eleven titles issued in the United States in the Brentano Uniform Edition; and A21-n1 for thirteen titles issued in uniform continental editions by Tauchnitz.

a new title, it is listed as a distinct publication with a new number and with cross references to and from its original listing.

Contributions to books by others are listed in the first part of the second section, with title-pages transcribed, brief collations of the volumes, and notations of Moore's contributions. Books which reprint letters or excerpts of letters not intended by Moore for publication are included in the second part, but only by title and author with no description of the volume.

Entries in the first section and in the two parts of the second are numbered in chronological order of original publication of the particular title, with a prefixed capital **A** denoting books in the first section and a prefixed capital **B** those in the second.

Lower case subletters after each number denote the text, **a** being used for the one first printed,[9] although in a few cases this is not the earliest, due to Moore's habit of making extensive revisions at proof stage. Subletters **b**, **c**, **d**, etc., are used for subsequent printings of different texts. Further printings from the same type or plates, or by photo-lithographic reproduction, are indicated by numbers suffixed to the text subletter. A prefixed number to the text subletter indicates a reprinting of that text from a different setting of type.[10] Each text is considered by itself, so that a recent reprint of an early text will be listed before a later text published prior to the reprint.

The third section is devoted to periodical publications, with entries unnumbered but listed in chronological order of first appearance. Some, but by no means all, of the numerous interviews, which in many cases were extensively revised or actually written by Moore, have been included. Articles signed by others, but known to have been written by Moore, and others containing otherwise unpublished material by him are also included.

Translations published in periodicals and book form, numbered separately and chronologically by countries, are in the fourth section.

The final section, Miscellanea, is devoted to brief accounts of titles sometimes attributed to Moore, but actually not by him, and of works known to have been written by him, but which apparently have never been published. A Postscript of acknowledgements and the Index complete the volume.

9. In the case of *Hail and Farewell*, which is a single work in spite of the fact that each of its three volumes was originally published in a different year, there is a single entry number (A31), with roman secondary numbers used to differentiate *Ave* (A31:I), *Salve* (A31:II), and *Vale* (A31:III), until the two-volume edition, when the use of a single number (A31-c) is resumed.

10. For example, the first edition of *Spring Days* is A13-a; the first American edition, which is reset, is A13-2a; the revised second English edition is A13-b; the Colonial and second American editions, both of which use sheets of the second English edition, are A13-b2 and A13-b3, respectively; and the Tauchnitz and Carra editions, both of which use the second edition text, but are printed from new settings of type, are A13-2b and A13-3b, respectively.

In the transcription of title-pages no attempt has been made, perhaps unwisely, to differentiate type sizes and families, but all upper and lower cases have been so transcribed, with line ends indicated, as is customary, by short vertical lines, and editorial comment [*in italics*] is enclosed in brackets.

As closely as the extreme deckle edges in some of the volumes being collated permit, page sizes are given to the nearest eighth of an inch, and binding colors are described as accurately as possible without resorting to manufacturers' identifying letters or numbers, or esoteric names and shades. Due to common usage, the terms "bound" and "binding" are used rather than the correct "cased" and "casing."

Catalogues noted as being "inserted" are publishers' advertisements on different paper, but which are sewn in with the rest of the gatherings in the process of binding.

As dust jackets and slip cases can in no sense be considered an integral part of the books they serve to protect and can easily be switched from copy to copy, they are not noted in the descriptions, with the one exception of the first edition of *Ulick and Soracha* (A51-a) where a special jacket is mentioned in the publisher's note.

Colophons, notices of limitation, copyright notices, printers' imprints, etc., are quoted in full. Titles of stories, poems, and articles are printed in roman with quotation marks. Names of periodicals are printed in capitals and small capitals. Book titles, except where they must be printed otherwise in transcriptions or quotations, are given in italics.

Moore is referred to throughout the text as GM. All information not of primary concern to a description is relegated to notes. References to Williams or Danielson are to their respective bibliographies, those to Hone to his biography, and those to Noel to his extended study. Quotations from letters to Edouard Dujardin, John Eglinton, Lady Cunard, and T. Fisher Unwin are from the published correspondence (A54, A62, A65, and A66).

The use of the term "first edition" is generally restricted to the first impression of the first printing, and an attempt has been made in the use of the terms "edition," "state," "issue," "impression," etc., to conform to the definitions given by John Carter in *ABC for Book-Collectors*, London, 1952; as well as keeping in mind the words of wisdom on the use of these terms by Percy H. Muir in *Points 1874–1930*, London and New York, 1931, and by Fredson Bowers in *Principles of Bibliographical Description*, Princeton, 1949. Some bibliographical purists, however, may object to the listing as separate editions those printings where there has been a substantial resetting of type, even though a large portion of the original setting is retained.

As far as possible, assignments of priority are based on sound bibliographical evidence, although in a few instances arbitrary decisions have been made on other evidence, subject to correction as more facts are discovered. Consistency of presentation has been the goal, but because of the extended time the work has been in preparation it is feared that this has not always been achieved.

Although it has been my intention to make this bibliography comprehensive, unfortunately there remain some unresolved problems, and certain items have had to be noted as "not located" or "not seen."

Among the unlocated is a Mandrake Press edition of *We'll to the Woods No More* by Edouard Dujardin, with a preface by GM, mentioned by James Joyce in a letter[11] to Harriet Shaw Weaver, dated 18 March 1930. This may never have been published, as no other reference to such an edition has been found.

Another book, published but not located, is *The Young George Moore*, by Earl F. Fisk, designed and printed by the author as a Christmas book in an edition of thirty copies, Green Bay, Wisconsin, 1922. Even the author's widow has not been able to supply information regarding the location of a copy of this book, which may or may not contain something by GM to warrant its inclusion in this bibliography.

There are bound to be some omissions, particularly in the section devoted to periodical appearances, as it has not been possible to locate and check files of all the papers and magazines, especially those of the 1880s and 1890s, that might contain contributions by GM.

Taking into consideration unresolved problems and possible omissions, I have decided to heed the advice of Henry R. Wagner, who wrote in *Bullion to Books*,[12] "In bibliographic work, after one has accumulated ninety-five per cent of the information he desires, he finds the remaining five per cent almost impossible to obtain. No sooner has the bibliography appeared on the market than somebody comes forth to announce that he or she has a book not mentioned in it, and after a while these sometimes amount to quite a disreputable number. Nevertheless, it is not worth while to try to get all; you are likely to die while waiting to obtain the last two or three per cent. Better publish what you have and let the other fellow add to it."

Folly Farm   EDWIN GILCHER
Cherry Plain, New York

11. *Letters of James Joyce*, edited by Stuart Gilbert, London, and New York, 1957.
12. Published by the Zamorano Club, Los Angeles, California, 1942.

I

Books and Pamphlets

A1

Flowers of Passion

a First edition:

FLOWERS OF PASSION. | [*decorative rule*] | BY | GEORGE MOORE. | [*decorative rule*] | LONDON: | PROVOST & CO., 36, HENRIETTA STREET, | COVENT GARDEN. | [*short rule*] | 1878.

Published autumn 1877 at 5/-

7⅜ x 6; [A]², B-H⁸, I² (tipped in); pp [2], ii, 116, comprising: title-page as above, verso blank, not paginated; tipped in ERRATA slip (1½ x 6, four lines with heading), verso blank, not paginated; table of CONTENTS pp [i]-ii; DEDICATION, verso blank, pp [1-2]; text pp [3]-114; publisher's advertisements pp [115-16]; cream endpapers; all edges trimmed, gilt on some copies, others plain;[1] bound in black cloth, back cover plain, gilt design of skull and crossbones in front of lyre with broken strings, all entwined with vines, on front cover, gilt lettered up the spine FLOWERS OF PASSION

Contents:

"Dedication: To L——"; "Ode to a Dead Body"; "Ginevra"; "Annie"; "Bernice"; "Sonnet: Night Perfume"; "Rondo"; "Ballad of a Lost Soul"; "Sonnet: The Corpse"; "A Page of Boccace"; "Sonnet: The Suicide"; "Serenade"; "Sonnet: The Lost Profile"; "Song"; "Sonnet: Unattained"; "The Balcony"; "Sonnet: Love's Grave"; "Serenade"; "Sonnet: Summer"; "Sonnet: Laus Veneris"; "Rondel"; "Sonnet: In Church"; "Sonnet: Summer on the Coast of Normandy"; "A Night in June"; "Sonnet: La Charmeuse"; "Song: The Assignation"; "Sonnet: To a Lost Art"; "Hendecasyllables";

---

1. No priority established, probably issued simultaneously; the presumably early, but undated, presentation copy from GM to his mother, now in the Fayant collection at Cornell University, has plain edges.

"Song"; "Le Succube" (from the French of Catulle Mendes); and "A Sapphic Dream."

Flowers of Passion was never reprinted and according to Hone (p 69), following highly unfavorable reviews and on the advice of a friend, Mrs. William Rossetti, GM withdrew the book, which had been published at his expense. Five of the poems are reprinted in *Pagan Poems* (A3), three in revised form.

A2

Martin Luther

a Regular edition:

MARTIN LUTHER: | A Tragedy, | IN FIVE ACTS. | BY | GEORGE MOORE, | Author of "Flowers of Passion," | AND | BERNARD LOPEZ, | COLLABORATEUR DE | SCRIBE, MÉRY, AUGUSTE | LEFRANC, THÉOPHILE GAUTIER, | ALEXANDRE DUMAS PÈRE, VICTOR | SÉJOUR, ALBOIZE, CHARLES DESNOYER, | GÉRARD DE NERVAL, DUPENTY, LAURENCIN, | GRANGÉ, HIPPOLYTE COGNIARD, LELARGE, | DELACOUR, VARIN, CHARLES NAR-REY, ROCHEFORT | PÈRE, DUMANOIR, CLAIRVILLE ET SAINT-GEORGES. | [*rule*] | London: | REMINGTON AND CO., | 5, ARUN-DEL STREET, STRAND, W.C. | [*short rule*] | 1879. | [All Rights Reserved.]

Published at 5/-

7⅛ x 4¾; [A]⁶, B-M⁸, N² (tipped in); pp [2], x, 180, comprising: blank page, with four-line "Acting Rights" notice within single-rule box in center of verso, not paginated; title-page as above, verso blank, pp [i-ii]; two-line quotation from Saint Gregory the Great, verso blank, pp [iii-iv]; DRAMATIS PERSONAE, with AUTHOR'S NOTE on verso, pp [v-vi]; SONNET DÉDICACE, p [vii]; ODE DÉDICACE pp [viii]-x; PREFACE pp [1]-38; text of play, pp [39]-179, with: Printed by REMINGTON & CO., 5, Arundel Street, Strand, W.C. at foot of p 179; p [180] blank; endpapers brown where facing; all edges trimmed, stained carmine on some copies, others plain; bound in bluish-gray cloth over beveled boards,¹ with conventional designs in black at top and bottom of front and back covers, lettered in gilt on front: MARTIN LUTHER | A Tragedy | and in center of back cover a black letter R within a circle; con-

---

1. Danielson lists "greenish-blue endpapers," bound in "red bevelled cloth," with "Bernardo" for "Bernard" on spine, and with a binder's label pasted inside back cover, lettered: Bound by Burn & Co. The copy described was from the collection of Sir Lucas King, and there seems to be no record of any other copy so bound.

ventional gilt decorations and black and gilt rules at top and bottom of spine which is gilt lettered MARTIN | LUTHER | A Tragedy | [rule] | GEORGE | MOORE | AND | BERNARD | LOPEZ | REMINGTON

Contents:

"Sonnet Dédicace à Algernon Charles Swinburne," signed "George Moore"; "Ode Dédicace à Algernon Charles Swinburne," signed "Bernard Lopez"; "Preface," which purports to be the correspondence between the two authors during the period of their collaboration;[2] *Martin Luther*.

GM says, in the Prefatory Letter to the Williams bibliography, "Lopez . . . supplied me with the scenario of *Martin Luther*, or, shall I say, with instructions regarding the disposition of the acts."

a2 Theater (?) impression:[3]

8⅜ x 5½; [A]² (tipped in), [a]¹ (tipped in between [A]₁ and [A]₂), [B]⁴, C-T⁴; pp [vi], 144, comprising: blank page, with notice of "Acting Rights" within single-rule box in center of verso, pp i-ii; title-page as in regular impression (a above), verso blank, pp [iii-iv]; DRAMATIS PERSONAE, with AUTHOR'S NOTE on verso, pp [v-vi]; text of play pp [1]-141; pp [142-44] blank; endpapers dark green where facing; all edges trimmed; bound in semi-limp black cloth, back cover blind stamped[4] with letter R within a circle, conventional designs blind stamped on front cover, which is gilt lettered MARTIN LUTHER | A Tragedy | BY | GEORGE MOORE & | BERNARD LOPEZ and spine lettered up in gilt: MARTIN LUTHER A Tragedy

Contents:

Text of play same as in regular edition (a above), printed from same setting of type, but with prefatory matter omitted and with page numbers and signature letters changed.

The "Sonnet Dédicace" is reprinted in the "Preface" of the 1904 edition

2. In *Portraits: Real and Imaginary*, London, and New York, 1924, Ernest Boyd says, "These eighteen letters may be cited as the authentic precursor of the prefaces subsequently made famous by Bernard Shaw. They are an amusing dissertation upon the art of playwriting in general and on *Martin Luther* in particular, with two interludes, consisting of a dramatization of an incident which occurred during Moore's journey to London from Paris, and a dream in five cantos about the decadence of the English stage."

3. Presumably this impression was issued to send to theater managers in an effort to secure a production, but as far as can be determined *Martin Luther* has never been produced. It may be the blank verse play submitted to Henry Irving by GM, who recalled the incident in "Bye, Bye Buchanan" in THE HAWK, 19 November 1889.

4. The blind stamping on back and front covers and the first two lines of gilt lettering on the front cover are done with the same dies used for the binding of the regular impression.

of *Confessions of a Young Man* (A12-c), and in section XI of the 1917 and subsequent editions (A12-d et seq.)

A3
Pagan Poems

a First edition:

PAGAN POEMS. | BY | GEORGE MOORE. | LONDON: | NEWMAN AND CO., | 43, HART STREET, BLOOMSBURY, W.C. | [*short rule*] | MDCCCLXXXI.

Published March 1881 at 6/-

7¼ x 4¾; [ ]² (tipped in), 1-10⁸, 11² (tipped in); pp iv, 164, comprising: title page[1] as above, verso blank, pp [i-ii]; table of CONTENTS, pp [iii]-iv; text, pp 1-164;[2] endpapers brown where facing; all edges trimmed; bound in dark blue cloth, spine gilt lettered PAGAN | POEMS | [*rule*] | GEORGE | MOORE | NEWMAN

Pagan Poems is found in three forms: (1) As above, with title-leaf an integral part of first gathering, and with the author's initials, *GM*, in ink in his autograph, written across the lower right hand corner of the publisher's imprint on the title-page.[3] (2) As above, except title-leaf has been re-

1. The title-page of a presentation copy "To Oscar Wilde" is pictured in A. Edward Newton's *Amenities of Book-Collecting*, 1918, and again in the sale catalogue of the Newton collection, sold at the Parke-Bernet Galleries, New York, 14–16 May 1941.

2. Some copies have the 3 in page number 53 imperfect, and in other copies it has been incorrectly replaced by a 5. This seems to have no significance in denoting priority, as each form has been noted in copies with, and in copies without, the title-leaf (see below). A. Edward Newton in "Conversations in the Library at 'Oak Knoll' " in *This Book-Collecting Game*, 1928, mentions an errata slip in his copy of *Pagan Poems*, but as no such slip, nor any other reference to one has been noted, it seems probable that Mr. Newton may have confused *Pagan Poems* with *Flowers of Passion* (A1), which does have an errata slip.

3. In a copy now in the Fountain Lawn Library of Dr. Lafayette Butler of Hazleton, Pennsylvania, there is an inscription on the verso of the title-leaf, "To A J A Symons, From George Moore who recognizes this copy to be one of the 20 copies that he received from the publisher Newman before he withdrew from business and tore out the title pages from the whole edition. GM" Actually he underestimated the number of copies left unmutilated, as there are more than twenty presentation copies with the original title-leaf in libraries and private collections, and there are also some copies, uninscribed except for the author's initials, that have the title-leaf as a part of the gathering. One such copy, in the Chapin Library at Williams College in Williamstown, Massachusetts, seems at first glance to have no initials after the pub-

moved. (3) As above, but sophisticated with a new title-leaf of a slightly different paper, skillfully tipped on stub of original leaf. The cancel title-page is printed from an almost imperceptibly different setting of type, and does not have the author's initials inked in after publisher's imprint. These leaves were fabricated and inserted by an unknown hand at a later date.

Contents:

"A I. d'A"; "Sonnet: Spleen"; "Ode to a Beggar Girl"; "À une Poitrinaire"; "A Parisian Idyl"; "Sappho"; "Sonnet: The Corpse," revised from *Flowers of Passion* (A1); "Ballad of a Lost Soul," revised from *Flowers of Passion*; "Sonnet: Chez Moi"; "A Love Letter"; "Sonnet: Used Up"; "La Maitresse Maternelle"; "Bernice," revised from *Flowers of Passion*; "A Joyous Death"; "The Portrait"; "A Night of June," reprinted from *Flowers of Passion*; "In the Morning"; "The Temple of Time"; "Sonnet"; "Ballad of a Lover of Life"; "Ambition"; "A Page of Boccace," reprinted from *Flowers of Passion*; "Sonnet: Une Fantaisie Parisienne"; "The Temptation"; "The Hermaphrodite"; and "A Modern Poem" (the lyric on pp 152-54 of this long poem is a revision of "The Love of the Past" in THE SPECTATOR, 11 December 1880).

Pagan Poems was never reprinted, but individual poems were used by GM in other books and several seem to be the first working of ideas later utilized by him in books and stories. A revised version of "À une Poitrinaire" is used in chapter X of *Mike Fletcher* (A14); it is again reprinted, minus its title, in section XI of the 1904 and subsequent editions of *Confessions of a Young Man* (A12-c et seq.); and it finally appears in "A Waitress" in *Memoirs of My Dead Life* (A29). A further revision of the first sixteen lines of "Ballad of a Lost Soul" is used in act III of *The Strike at Arlingford* (A18). "Ballad of a Lover of Life" is reprinted in a revised form as "The Ballade of Lovelace" in *Ballades and Rondeaus* (B4); and a further revision, "The Ballade of Don Juan Dead," is used in chapter II of *Mike Fletcher*. The lyric on pp 152-54 of "A Modern Poem" is reprinted as "The Sweetness of the Past" in section IX of *Confessions of a Young Man*. Malcolm Brown in *George Moore: A Reconsideration* suggests "A Parisian Idyl" as being the possible genesis of "The Lovers of Orelay" in *Memoirs of My Dead Life* and "A Modern Poem" as that of *A Drama in Muslin* (A9). "La Maitresse Maternelle" seems to be the genesis of *A Modern Lover* (A5), and the song on pp 73-74 of this duo-drama was revised as "Nuit de Septembre" and printed in PALL MALL GAZETTE, 15 January 1895, in THE BOOKMAN, October 1895, and reprinted in section XI of the 1904 and subsequent editions of *Confessions of a Young Man*.

---

lisher's imprint on the title-page, but a close inspection shows that they were once present and have been carefully removed by some previous owner or overzealous librarian who apparently failed to realize their significance.

A4

Les Cloches de Corneville

a First edition:

LES CLOCHES DE CORNEVILLE. | LYRICS BY | GEORGE AND
AUGUSTUS MOORE. | [*double rule*] | FOR PRIVATE CIRCULATION
ONLY.

Printed circa 1883[1]

7⅛ x 4⅞; [ ][12]; pp 24; comprising: title-page as above, verso blank,
pp [1-2]; text pp [3]-23; p [24] blank; issued in gray paper wrappers, lettered in black on front cover from same type setting used for title-page.

Contents:

Translation of Louis Claireville's lyrics for Robert Planquette's comic
opera, *Les Cloches de Corneville*.[2] The only located copy, formerly in the
library of George R. Sims, is in my collection.

Portions of these lyrics, with slight emendations, are used in chapters XV
and XVI of *A Mummer's Wife* (A6).

A5

A Modern Lover

a First edition:

A MODERN LOVER. | BY | GEORGE MOORE. | IN THREE
VOLUMES. | VOL. I. [II.] [III.] | LONDON: | TINSLEY BROTHERS,
8, CATHERINE ST., STRAND. | 1883.

Published early summer at 31/6

7⅜ x 4⅞; Vol. I: [A]² (tipped in), B-R⁸; pp [iv], 256, comprising:
title-page as above, with PRINTED BY | KELLY AND CO., PRINTERS,
GATE STREET, LINCOLN'S INN FIELD; | AND KINGSTON-ON-
THAMES. in center of verso, pp [i-ii]; table of CONTENTS, verso blank,
pp [iii-iv]; text pp [1]-252; pp [253-56] blank;

1. Probably printed for use by the cast in a production at the Folies Dramatiques
(Novelty Theatre renamed), London, 29 March 1883, with "Libretto by Messrs.
Claude Templar and George and Augustus Moore," which ran for only ten days,
according to J. M. Glover's letter, "George Moore as Librettist," in THE OBSERVER,
8 April 1923.

2. In the sale of Viscount Esher's library at Sotheby's, 18 November 1946, Lot
1351 was a copy of *"Les Cloches de Corneville, Opera Comique in three acts.*
Original wrappers, 8vo, J. Williams, n.d." listed as being the Moore translation. This
attribution, however, was an error, as it is actually the standard version by H. B.
Farnie and R. Reece and is credited to them in later Williams printings.

Vol. II: [A]^2 (tipped in), B-Q^8: pp [iv], 240, comprising preliminaries as in Vol. I, pp [i-iv]; text pp [1]-239; p [240] blank;

Vol. III: [A]^2 (tipped in), B-Q^8, P^1 (tipped in); pp [iv], 210, comprising: preliminaries as in Vols. I and II, pp [i-iv]; text pp [1]-210; followed by an inserted undated 32-page publisher's catalogue;[1] cream endpapers;[2] top edges untrimmed, fore and bottom edges trimmed; bound in light greenish-blue cloth,[3] back covers plain, front covers diagonally lettered in black: 1883 | A MODERN LOVER | George Moore [*facsimile of signature*] and spines gilt lettered A | MODERN | LOVER | [*short rule*] | VOL. I. [II.] [III.] | GEORGE MOORE | TINSLEY BROS.

There are two states: (1) Gathering P of Vol. III is as noted above, consisting of a single leaf, followed by an inserted 32-page catalogue; the front covers of all three volumes have the date 1883 set at about a 51-degree angle, with the lower edge of the 1 in the date lower than the word LOVER on the spines, with the figures slightly more than an inch from both the spine and the top edges. (2) Gathering P of Vol. III is a quarter sheet, consisting of a folding of two leaves, the second (pp [211-12]) being blank, generally with no inserted catalogue[4] following; the front covers of all three volumes have date 1883 set at about a 43-degree angle, and it is completely above the word LOVER on the spines; the figures are about ¾ inch from the spine and about ⅝ inch from the top edges.

Contents:

Previously unpublished, but basically the same theme as the poem, "La Maitresse Maternelle," in *Pagan Poems* (A3).

1. Which lists, on p 18 under the heading NOVELS RECENTLY PUBLISHED, *A Story of Three Women.* By George Moore in three volumes. This may have been an earlier title of *A Modern Lover*, although there seems to be no other reference to it, other than the possible faint echo in *Lewis Seymour and Some Women* (A36), the title of the final version.

2. A copy of Volume II in the first binding state has been noted with white endpapers.

3. A set in plum-colored cloth with a variant stamping in black on the front covers was listed by Charles Rare Books in their 1964 spring catalogue. The cover stamping on this set agrees with the copy of Volume II described and pictured as "A" by John Carter in *Binding Variants, 1820–1900*, p 142, which has an ornamental design on the front cover instead of the usual lettering, "has a title-page of very slightly different setting from the normal, and pp 161-239 are on proof paper, with various small differences." These may have been trial bindings, as may have been at least two sets bound in black diagonal fine-ribbed cloth, lettered in gold on the front cover as well as on the spine. One of these sets was Lot 132 in the sale of Viscount Esher's library at Sotheby's, 18 November 1946, which had a 16-page undated catalogue inserted at the end of Volume III. A set in a similar binding, acquired 24 January 1944, is in the Beinecke Library at Yale University.

4. At least one copy has been noted with a catalogue inserted between the two leaves of gathering P.

b Second edition:

A MODERN LOVER. | BY GEORGE MOORE, | AUTHOR OF A "MUMMER'S WIFE." | SECOND EDITION. | LONDON: | VIZE-TELLY & CO., 42 CATHERINE STREET, STRAND, | 1885.

Published April at 3/6

7³⁄₁₆ x 4⁷⁄₁₆; a ¹⁶, B-K ¹⁶; pp 320, comprising: leaf of PRESS NOTICES of A MUMMER'S WIFE, pp [1-2]; half-title, verso blank, pp [3-4]; title-page as above, with "Perth: | S. COWAN AND CO., STRATHMORE PRINTING WORKS." in center of verso, pp [5-6]; table of CONTENTS pp [7]-8; text pp [9]-319; p [320] blank; followed by a 20-page inserted publisher's catalogue dated APRIL, 1885.; endpapers medium gray where facing; all edges trimmed; bound in bluish-gray cloth, publisher's mono-gram device in brown in center of back cover, front cover stamped in brown, with decorative border at top and bottom and lettered A MODERN LOVER | [*decorative rule*] | GEORGE MOORE. and double brown rules at top and bottom of spine, which is gilt lettered A | MODERN | LOVER | [*rule*] GEORGE | MOORE. | VIZETELLY & CO.

Contents:

Text slightly revised throughout, with some additions. The most impor-tant changes are: chapter XIII, "Enfin," six pages added at end; chapter XVI, "Scandal," two pages inserted in middle; chapter XVIII, "Mother and Mistress" (in first edition "Motherly Love"), four pages inserted in middle; chapter XIX, "Success," last half rewritten; chapter XXIII, "Dif-ficulties Overcome," ending changed by insertion of a section from chapter XXIV, "The Bridal Dress"; chapter XXX, "A Private View," four pages added near end as substitution for a shorter passage.

Subsequent impressions issued by Vizetelly at 2/- in a variety of bind-ings, variously listed on title-page as "Third Edition," "Fourth Edition," etc. The Vizetelly plates also were used for at least two other impressions issued by other publishers:

b2 — An American edition, bearing the notation "Privately Printed for the trade, London," published in Realistic Series, Classic Publishing Company, Chicago, n.d. (Stein Co.'s Library).

b3 — Seventh Edition, Walter Scott Limited, London, March 1893.

2b First American printing:

A MODERN LOVER | A REALISTIC NOVEL | BY | GEORGE MOORE | Author of "An Actor's Wife," "A Drama in Muslin." | The Pastime Series. Issued Monthly. By Subscription $3.00 per annum. Vol. 36, Jan. | 1890. Entered at Chicago Post Office as second-class matter. | [*owl device*] | CHICAGO: | LAIRD & LEE PUBLISHERS | 1890.

Published January ⁵ at 25¢

5. So stated on title-page, but not necessarily the actual date of publication as

7⅜ x 5; [1]⁸, 2-19⁸, 20⁸; pp 308, comprising: publisher's advertisements pp [1-3]; illustration p [4]; title-page as above, with table of CONTENTS on verso, pp [5-6]; text pp [7]-306; publisher's advertisements pp [307-8]; all edges trimmed; wire stapled; issued in gray paper wrappers, with publisher's advertisement on back, notation of series, subscription rate, number, and postal information as on title-page printed in black in two lines at top of front cover, followed by black rule and lithographed cover design in gray and red, incorporating: The | LIBRARY | of | REALISTIC FICTION | and medallion portrait of Emile Zola at top and publisher's name and medallion portraits of Alexandre Dumas Fils and George Moore at bottom, with panel in center lettered in red: A MODERN LOVER | BY GEORGE MOORE | Author of "An Actor's Wife," etc. | ILLUSTRATED | and lettered in black down the spine: A MODERN LOVER — MOORE

Contents:

The text of the second English edition (b above) was used for this unauthorized reprint, and the plates of this edition were used for at least three other impressions:

2b2 — Columbia Series, issued in dark blue, elaborately decorated cloth, Laird and Lee, Chicago, circa 1892–93.

2b3 — Stein, Chicago, 1899, listed in *The United States Catalog*, but no copy located.

2b4 — L. Lipkind, New York, circa early 1900s, issued in orange wrappers and printed in 16s, although retaining the signings in 8s.

A Modern Lover was rewritten and republished in 1917 as *Lewis Seymour and Some Women* (A36).[6]

A6

A Mummer's Wife

a First edition:

VIZETELLY'S ONE-VOLUME NOVELS. | [rule] | III. | A MUMMER'S WIFE. | BY GEORGE MOORE, | AUTHOR OF "A MODERN

---

these various series, issued in the United States at this period, were required by postal law to date publications in monthly sequence to maintain periodical mailing rates, and frequently the dates had little connection with reality.

6. The sonnet by GM, shown in a reproduction of the autograph manuscript in Volume X of *The Ashley Library: A Catalogue of Printed Books, Manuscripts and Autograph Letters* is the one used at the close of both *A Modern Lover* and *Lewis Seymour and Some Women*.

LOVER." | [*publisher's device*] | LONDON: | VIZETELLY & CO., 42, CATHERINE STREET, STRAND. | 1885.

Published autumn 1884 [1] at 6/-

7⅛ x 4¾; A [4] (+[A]₃), B-EE [8]; pp 440, comprising: blank page, with advertisement of other titles in VIZETELLY'S ONE-VOLUME NOVELS [2] within single-rule box on verso, pp [1-2]; half-title, verso blank, pp [3-4]; title-page as above, with LONDON: | PRINTED BY J.S. VIRTUE AND CO., LIMITED, | CITY ROAD. in center of verso, pp [5-6]; dedication TO MY FRIEND, | JAMES DAVIS, | I DEDICATE THIS BOOK, IN ACKNOWLEDGEMENT OF A | LITERARY DEBT., verso blank, pp [7-8]; three-line quotation from Victor Duruy, verso blank, pp [9-10]; text pp [11]-438, with printer's imprint repeated in one line at foot of p 438; publisher's advertisements pp [439-40]; followed by an inserted 20-page catalogue of publisher's advertisements; all edges trimmed; end-papers gray where facing; bound in brown cloth, publisher's monogram device in red on back cover, decorative border in red at top and bottom of front cover and spine, front cover lettered in red A MUMMER'S WIFE | [*fancy gilt rule*] | GEORGE MOORE. with gilt ornaments above and below, and spine gilt lettered A | MUMMER'S | WIFE | [*rule*] | GEORGE | MOORE | VIZETELLY & CO

There are two [3] issues of the first edition: (1) As above, with inserted catalogue dated SEPTEMBER, 1884. (2) As above, with addition of a tipped-in slip at the half-title lettered "Notice. | This book has been placed in the Index Expurgatorius | of the 'Select' Circulating Libraries of Messrs. Mudie and | W. H. Smith & Son." All copies seen with this slip have the inserted catalogue dated DECEMBER, 1884.

Contents:

Previously unpublished, except for the lyric fragments on pp 247-52 slightly revised from *Les Cloches de Corneville, Lyrics by George and Augustus Moore* (A4).

Subsequent impressions are listed as "Second," "Third," "Fourth," etc., "Edition" on title-page. [4]

1. Reviewed in the ACADEMY, 29 November; also the P.S. O'Hegarty copy, formerly owned by Sir Henry Norman, is dated "November 1884" and has a further endorsement by Sir Henry "From the Author."

2. This series was inaugurated at GM's suggestion as a way of breaking the monopoly of the circulating libraries whose rejection automatically doomed the sale of any Victorian novel published as a three-decker at 31/6. GM's proposal, to circumvent this control by appealing directly to book-buyers rather than book-borrowers through the publication of one-volume novels at a price far below that of the three-volume sets, was the first nail driven into the coffin of the three-decker.

3. It is possible there is also a prepublication state with the title-leaf ([A]₃) an integral part of the gathering, but no copy of such a state has been located, nor has any reference been found regarding the reason why the original leaf was cancelled.

4. The rebound British Museum Library copy of the "Third Edition" has the date

b Second edition, revised:

VIZETELLY'S ONE-VOLUME NOVELS. | [*rule*] | III. | A MUM-
MER'S WIFE. | BY GEORGE MOORE, | AUTHOR OF "A MODERN
LOVER." | SIXTH EDITION. | [*publisher's device*] | LONDON: | VIZE-
TELLY & CO., 42, CATHERINE STREET, STRAND. | 1886.

Published autumn [5] 1885 at 3/6

7⅛ x 4¾; [a]² (tipped in), A-L¹⁶, M² (tipped in); pp x, [7]-356, comprising: half-title, with advertisement for two books BY THE SAME
AUTHOR on verso, pp [i-ii]; title-page as above, with "Perth: | S. CO-
WAN & CO., STRATHMORE PRINTING WORKS." on verso, pp [iii-
iv]; dedication, with three-line quotation from Victor Duruy on verso, pp
[v-vi]; PREFACE TO THE SIXTH EDITION pp [vii]-ix; p [x] blank;
text pp [7]-352; publisher's advertisements pp [354-56]; endpapers gray
where facing; all edges untrimmed; bound in gray cloth,[6] publisher's monogram device in brown on back cover, front cover stamped in brown with
decorative border at top and bottom and lettered A MUMMER'S WIFE |
[*decorative rule*] | GEORGE MOORE. and brown double rules at top and
bottom of spine, which is gilt lettered A | MUMMER'S | WIFE | [*rule*] |
GEORGE | MOORE. | VIZETELLY & CO

Contents:

Text shows minor revisions, and there is an added "Preface" by the author
wherein he says of the text, "Redundant words have been taken out, and
sentences have been recast."

Subsequent Vizetelly printings are indicated on the title-page as "Seventh," "Eighth," "Ninth," etc., "Edition," with corresponding changes in
the Preface text in each to conform with the "edition" number on the title-
page. The Vizetelly plates also were used later for at least one other impression by another publisher:

b2 — Twentieth Edition, Walter Scott Limited, London, March 1893, with
the Preface and ten lines[7] at the end of chapter IX omitted.

2b First American edition, unauthorized and retitled:

AN ACTOR'S WIFE | A REALISTIC NOVEL | BY | GEORGE
MOORE | Author of "A Modern Lover," "A Drama in Muslin," | "A
Mere Accident," Etc. | THE PASTIME SERIES. ISSUED MONTHLY.
BY SUBSCRIPTION $3.00 PER ANNUM. VOL. 28, | JUNE, 1889.

---

stamp "14 April '85," and its copy of the "Fourth Edition" has the inserted catalogue
dated "April 1885."

5. There is a note in THE BAT, 17 November 1885, regarding the new Preface to
this edition.

6. The format of this edition matches the 1885 Vizetelly "Second Edition" of *A
Modern Lover* (A5-b).

7. These are the concluding lines of the passage quoted by GM in *Literature at
Nurse* (A7) as having been the subject of objections by the circulating libraries.

ENTERED AT CHICAGO POSTOFFICE AS SECOND-CLASS MAT-
TER. | [*device of owl on lower horn of crescent moon*] | CHICAGO: |
LAIRD & LEE PUBLISHERS

Published June [8] 1889 at 25¢

7⅜ x 5; [1][8], 2-28[8]; pp. 448, comprising: publisher's advertisements,
with illustration captioned "His big blue eyes beamed with amazement" on
verso, pp [1-2]; title-page as above, with publisher's advertisements on
verso, pp [3-4]; text pp [5]-440; publisher's advertisements pp [441-48];
all edges trimmed; wire stapled; issued in gray wrappers, with publisher's
advertisements on back cover, notation of series, subscription rate, volume
number, and postal information as on title-page, printed in black in two
lines at top of front cover, followed by black rule and lithographed design
in gray and red, incorporating: The | LIBRARY | of | REALISTIC | FIC-
TION and medallion portrait of Emile Zola at top, and publisher's
name and medallion portraits of Alexandre Dumas Fils and George Moore
at bottom, with center panel lettered in red AN ACTOR'S WIFE | BY
GEORGE MOORE | Author of "A Modern Lover," etc. | ILLUSTRATED
and lettered in black down spine AN ACTOR'S WIFE —— MOORE

Contents:

The text is an unauthorized reprinting of the 1886 Vizetelly "Sixth Edition" (b above), with dedication, Victor Duruy quotation, and "Preface"
omitted, and title Americanized.

Another impression was issued in a slightly larger format (7½ x 5¼),
with date 1889 added after publisher's title-page imprint, in orange wrappers, and without illustrations, despite the statement "Illustrated" on cover.
The plates of this edition also were used for:

2b2 — The Popular Series, issued in an elaborately decorated brown cloth
binding, Laird and Lee, Chicago, 1889.

3b First authorized American edition:

A MUMMER'S WIFE | BY | GEORGE MOORE | AUTHOR OF "THE
CONFESSIONS OF A YOUNG MAN," "ESTHER WATERS," ETC.
| [*comedy-tragedy device*] | New York | BRENTANO'S | Union Square |
1903

Published May at $1.50

7⅝ x 5⅛; [ ][4], [1][8], 2-28[8], [29][8], 30[2] (tipped in); pp [viii], 468, comprising: blank leaf pp [i-ii]; title-page as above with printer's device of
PRESS OF J J LITTLE & CO | ASTOR PLACE NEW YORK U S A
in center of verso, pp [iii-iv]; dedication, verso blank, pp [v-vi]; quotation
from Victor Duruy, verso blank, pp [vii-viii]; text pp [1]-467; p [468]
blank; white endpapers; top edges trimmed, fore and bottom edges un-

---

8. So stated on title-page and cover, but not necessarily the actual date of publication (see A5-n5).

trimmed; bound in medium blue cloth, back cover plain, front cover blind stamped with double box, conventional design in lower, lettered in white in upper box: A Mummer's | Wife | [rule] and in lower box: by George Moore | and spine lettered in white: A | Mummer's | Wife | [rule] | Moore | BRENTANO'S

Contents:

Authorized reprint of the text of the Scott impression of the second edition (b2 above), again with "Preface" omitted. The plates of this edition also were used for:

3b2 — Brentano Uniform Edition, New York, 1917. This edition was almost immediately superseded in the series by a revised text (c below).

c Third American (second Brentano Uniform) edition, revised:

A MUMMER'S WIFE | BY | GEORGE MOORE | [orange diamond-shaped publisher's device] | NEW YORK | BRENTANO'S | 1917

Published 6 November at $1.50

$7\frac{7}{8}$ x $5\frac{3}{8}$; [1]^8, [ ]^1 (tipped in between [1]$_2$ and [1]$_3$), 2-30^8; pp xii, 466, comprising: blank leaf pp [i-ii]; half-title, with list of eight WORKS OF GEORGE MOORE | NEW AND REVISED EDITION | In Uniform Binding | in a single-rule box on verso, pp iii-iv; title-page as above, with COPYRIGHT 1917 | BY | BRENTANO'S in center of verso, pp [v-vi]; A DEDICATION TO ROBERT ROSS pp vii-xi; p [xii] blank; text pp 1-465; p [466] blank; free and paste-down rear endpapers part of final gathering, conjugate with 30$_2$ and 30$_1$, not paginated; front endpapers white; top edges trimmed and stained dark green, fore and bottom edges untrimmed; bound in green-ribbed cloth, front and back covers plain, gilt decorations at top and bottom of spine, which is gilt lettered A | MUMMER'S | WIFE | GEORGE | MOORE | BRENTANO'S

Contents:

Text completely revised and the preface, the "A Dedication to Robert Ross," is entirely new.

2c First English edition of second revision:

A MUMMER'S WIFE | BY GEORGE MOORE | [publisher's wind mill device, flanked by letters W and H, within single-rule box] | LONDON | WILLIAM HEINEMANN

Published April 1918 at 6/-

$7\frac{1}{2}$ x $4\frac{7}{8}$; [a]^4, [b]^1 (tipped in), A-2H^8 (signature letter B is on its side), [21]^1 (tipped in); pp x, 506, comprising: half-title, with list of seventeen WORKS BY GEORGE MOORE on verso, pp [i-ii]; title-page as above, with LONDON: WILLIAM HEINEMANN. 1918 at foot of verso, pp [iii-iv]; A DEDICATION TO ROBERT ROSS pp v-ix; p [x] blank; text pp [1]-505, with BILLINGS AND SONS, LTD., PRINTERS, GUILDFORD, ENGLAND at foot p 505; p [506] blank; white endpapers; top and fore edges trimmed, bottom edges untrimmed; bound in dark blue cloth, publisher's monogram device in blind in lower right corner of back cover, front cover blind stamped with large elongated paneled design enclosed within a double-rule box, and spine gilt lettered A | MUMMER'S | WIFE | GEORGE | MOORE | [*enclosed within single-rule box, with double rule and scallop-shaped design at top and bottom*] | HEINE-MANN

There are two states of the binding: (a) As above. (b) As above, except publisher's device in lower right corner of back cover is a windmill and not a monogram.

Contents:

Text revised as in third American edition (c above). Sheets of this edition were used for:

2c2 — Heinemann's Colonial Library, London, 1918; issued in red cloth binding. This final revised text was used for five other editions:

3c — Carra Edition, Volume II, Boni and Liveright, New York, 1922. A reproduction of a photograph of GM by Alvin Langdon Coburn is tipped in as a frontispiece and is protected by a tissue guard sheet. The pages of this edition, with preliminary matter omitted, were reproduced, slightly enlarged, by photo-offset lithography for:

3c2 — Black and Gold Library, Authorized Edition, Liveright Publishing Corp., New York, January 1966, with new "Foreword" by Walter James Miller, and frontispiece reproducing the Jack Yeats portrait of GM, also used as a frontispiece in the Carra Edition of *Muslin* (A34-3a).

4c — Uniform Edition, Heinemann, London, October 1933. In addition to "A Dedication to Robert Ross," the posthumous *A Communication to My Friends* (A60) is included as an introduction, this being the first[9] volume of the Uniform Edition. Reissued in a different binding as:

4c2 — Ebury Edition, Heinemann, London, March 1937.

9. Not the first title published, but the earliest according to date of original publication, in the Uniform Edition, which was to be the canon by which GM wished to be remembered. In addition to *A Mummer's Wife*, the series includes *Muslin* (A34-4a); *Confessions of a Young Man* (A12-2e); *Esther Waters* (A19-4c); *The Untilled Field* (A26-2e); *The Lake* (A27-3d); *Memoirs of My Dead Life* (A29-e); *Hail and Farewell* in three volumes (A31-3c); *The Brook Kerith* (A35-b); *A Story-Teller's Holiday* in two volumes (A37-2b); *Avowals* (A38-b); *Héloïse and Abélard* (A40-3b); *Conversations in Ebury Street* (A46-b); *Daphnis and Chloe* (A49-4a); and *Peronnik the Fool* (A50-2b) in one volume; *Celibate Lives* (A52-a); *The Passing of the Essenes* (A55-b); and *Aphrodite in Aulis* (A56-2b). It should be noted that the volumes vary in size, including thickness and height, and that the position of the spine labels differs from volume to volume. In some cases remainder sheets and in others the plates of the Uniform Edition were used when the titles were reissued in dark blue buckram binding in the Ebury Edition, which since 1942 has been called the Uniform Edition by the publishers.

5c — Washington Square Press, New York, February 1967, reset reprinting, including "Foreword" by Walter James Miller, of Black and Gold Library edition (3c2) above.

See D:Du-1 for a Dutch, D:Fr-3 and D:Fr-8 for French translations.

A7
Literature at Nurse

a First edition:

PRICE THREEPENCE | [*rule*] | Literature | at Nurse | OR | CIRCU-LATING MORALS | BY GEORGE MOORE | AUTHOR OF "A MUMMER'S WIFE," "A MODERN LOVER," ETC. | "They stand there, Respectable; and — what more? Dumb idols; with a skin | of delusively-painted waxwork, inwardly empty, or full of rags and bran. . . . | Such bounties, in this as in infinitely deeper matters, does Respectability shower | down on us. Sad are thy doings, O Gig; sadder than those of Juggernaut's Car: | that, with huge wheel, suddenly crushes asunder the bodies of men; thou in thy | light-bobbing Long-acre springs, gradually winnowest away their Souls!" | [*seven dots*] | "One day the Mudie mountain, which seemed to stand strong like the other rock | mountains, gave suddenly, as the icebergs do, a loud-sounding crack; suddenly, | with huge clangour, shivered itself into ice dust; and sank, carrying much along | with it." — Carlyle's Essays. | LONDON | VIZETELLY & CO., 42 CATHERINE STREET, STRAND | 1885

8⅜ x 5½; [ ]^{12}; pp 24, comprising: title-page[1] as above, with an advertisement for "New and Cheaper Edition" of A MODERN LOVER in center of verso, pp [1-2]; text pp [3]-22; PRESS NOTICES of A MUMMER'S WIFE pp [23-24]; all edges trimmed; issued without wrappers, sewn with single stitch of thread.

Contents:

An attack upon the "select" circulating libraries, particularly Mudie's, which imposed strait-laced moral standards upon English literature by an arbitrary exercise of censorship in banning books from their discreet shelves. The high cost of books, particularly the usual three-volume novel at 31/6, permitted the libraries, by financial pressure, to dictate the success or failure of a book, regardless of its critical reception. GM, incensed at this restriction of literary freedom and at Mudie's refusal to adequately stock *A Modern Lover* (A5) and *A Mummer's Wife* (A6), issued this pamphlet,

1. Pictured in *This Book-Collecting Game*, by A. Edward Newton, 1928.

citing passages from books circulated by the library that he considered far more risqué than the passage in *A Mummer's Wife* which gained that book's refusal as an immoral publication.

Literature at Nurse was never republished, but the essence of the article, according to GM as quoted by Hone (p 378), is incorporated in the "Address to the Jury" in chapter III of *Avowals* (A38), which is a revised version of "Freedom of the Pen: A Conversation with George Moore," by John Lloyd Balderston, in FORTNIGHTLY REVIEW, October 1917, and of its rewritten form, this time signed by GM, "Literature and Morals," in CENTURY MAGAZINE, May 1919.

A8
La Ballade de l'Amant de Coeur

a First edition:

La Ballade de l'Amant de Coeur | [*rule*] | A | Mes Frères d'Armes, | Burges | et | Pot

Printed circa mid-1880s [1886 ?]

8⅛ x 5⅛; [ ]²; pp [4], comprising: title-page as above, p [1]; text pp [2-3]; p [4] blank.

Contents:

The *Ballade* is signed "Pagan," and although GM's name is not given on the leaflet, a revised version is included in section XI of the fourth American edition of *Confessions of a Young Man* (A12-d) as "La Ballade d'Alfred, Alfred aux Belles Dents,"[1] and in the fourth English and all subsequent editions (A12-2d et seq.) is transferred to section XIV, with further slight revisions and with some meager details of its writing, but none of its printing.

The only located copy of this leaflet is in the Frank Fayant collection[2] and is the same one listed in the 1930 Maggs Brothers Catalogues 531 and 538. Accompanying the leaflet is a letter from GM's brother, Colonel Maurice Moore, stating GM's authorship, with the possible collaboration of another brother, Augustus, whom he identifies as "Burges" of the title. Colonel Moore also identifies "Pot" as Pot Stephens and adds that "Pagan"[3] was GM's pen-name in those days.

1. GM apparently worked on revisions for a number of years, as there is extant an autograph manuscript of a portion of the *Ballade*, dated 2-11-10, showing changes and revisions.

2. Now in the Cornell University Library at Ithaca, New York.

3. In *Old Pink 'un Days*, London, 1924, J. B. Booth states that GM wrote for

A9

A Drama in Muslin

a First edition:

VIZETELLY'S ONE-VOLUME NOVELS. | [*rule*] | XV. | A DRAMA IN MUSLIN | A Realistic Novel. | BY GEORGE MOORE, | Author of "A Mummer's Wife," "A Modern Lover," etc. | WITH A FRONTISPIECE FROM A DRAWING BY J.E. BLANCHE. | [*publisher's device*] | LONDON: | VIZETELLY & CO., 42, CATHERINE STREET, STRAND. | 1886. | [THE RIGHT OF TRANSLATION IS RESERVED.] Published June at 6/-

7⅜ x 4¾; [A]^2 (tipped in), [a]^1 (tipped in), B-X^8, Y^4, [Z]^1 (tipped in); pp [vi], 330, comprising: half-title, with list of VIZETELLY'S ONE-VOLUME NOVELS on verso, pp [i-ii]; inserted frontispiece on heavier paper, recto blank, illustration in blue on verso, lettered at foot IN THE CONVENT GARDEN, not paginated; title-page as above, verso blank, pp [iii-iv]; author's note, verso blank, pp [v-vi]; text pp 1-329, with CHAS. STRAKER AND SONS, BISHOPSGATE AVENUE, LONDON, E.C.; AND REDHILL. at foot p 329; p [330] blank; followed by an inserted 24-page publisher's catalogue dated APRIL, 1886.; endpapers flowered where facing; top edges untrimmed, fore and bottom edges trimmed; bound in light blue cloth, publisher's monogram device in blind in center of back cover, single-rule border in blind at outer edges of both back and front covers, latter lettered in dark blue: Vizetelly's One-Volume Novels. | A DRAMA | IN MUSLIN. | BY GEORGE MOORE, | Author of "A Mummer's Wife." | and spine gilt stamped [*double rule*] | A | DRAMA | IN | MUSLIN | [*dark blue ornament*] | GEORGE | MOORE | [*dark blue ornament*] | VIZETELLY & CO. | [*double rule*]

Contents:

Previously serialized in weekly installments in COURT AND SOCIETY REVIEW, 14 January through 1 July 1886; revised and slightly expanded for book publication.

Subsequent Vizetelly impressions are listed as "Second," "Third," "Fourth," etc., "Edition"^{1} on title-page, and the frontispiece, when present, is printed in black. The "Sixth Edition," without frontispiece, was issued

---

THE BAT as "Shifter, the Pagan," but nothing so signed has been located in that periodical. In the issues of 2 and 9 February 1886, however, he is referred to as "George Pagan Moore," a fact that might help date the leaflet.

1. In the "Second Edition" the inserted publisher's catalogue is dated April, 1886. as in first edition, and in the "Third Edition" it is dated November, 1885.

in 1888.[2] The plates were used by another publisher for at least one other impression:

a2 — Seventh edition,[3] Walter Scott, Ltd., London, 1893.

A Drama in Muslin was rewritten and republished as *Muslin* (A34).

See D:Du-2 for Dutch and D:Ru-1 for Russian translations. A French translation, *Une Drame dans la Mousseline*, announced "En preparation" in the 1925 Stock edition of *Confessions d'un Jeune Anglaise* (D:Fr-10), was never published. Professor Roger Lhombreaud kindly checked with Stock regarding this title and was shown a contract dated 1924 for publication of the book, but was told it had been annulled in 1926, although no one could tell him why.

A10

A Mere Accident

a First edition:

VIZETELLY'S ONE-VOLUME NOVELS. | [*rule*] | XXVI. | A MERE ACCIDENT. | BY | GEORGE MOORE, | AUTHOR OF "A MUMMER'S WIFE," "A MODERN LOVER," "A DRAMA IN MUSLIN," ETC. | [*publisher's device*] | LONDON: | VIZETELLY & CO., 42 CATHERINE ST., STRAND. | BRENTANOS: [*sic*] NEW YORK, WASHINGTON, AND CHICAGO. | 1887. | [*rule*] | (The Right of Translation is reserved.)

Published late June or early July at 3/6

7⅜ x 4¾; [A]⁴, B-S⁸, T⁴; pp [iv], 284, comprising: publisher's advertisements pp [i-ii]; half-title, with advertisement of MR. GEORGE MOORE'S REALISTIC NOVELS. on verso, pp [iii-iv]; title-page as above, verso blank, pp [1-2]; dedication "TO | My Friends at Buckingham.," verso blank, pp [3-4]; text pp [5]-282, with TURNBULL AND SPEARS, PRINTERS, EDINBURGH. at foot p 282; publisher's advertisements pp [283-84];[1] endpapers green where facing; top edges un-

2. In a format matching the 1885 Vizetelly "Second Edition" of *A Modern Lover* (A5-b) and the 1885 Vizetelly "Sixth Edition" of *A Mummer's Wife* (A6-b).

3. In format matching the 1893 Scott editions of *A Modern Lover* (A5-b3) and *A Mummer's Wife* (A6-b2). Although the Scott edition is called the "Seventh Edition," an "8th Edition, with a frontispiece," but with no publisher noted, is advertised on the inserted leaf in the front of some copies of the first edition of *Mike Fletcher* (A14-a, state 2), and a "Ninth Edition," Vizetelly, 1890, is listed in *The English Catalogue*.

1. In some copies there is a 32-page inserted catalogue dated MARCH, 1887. bound in following p [284], with *A Mere Accident* listed on the first page "To be

trimmed, fore and bottom edges trimmed; bound in light brown cloth, publisher's monogram device in blind in center of back cover, single-rule border in blind at outer edges, single-rule border in blind at outer edges of front cover which is lettered in dark brown: Vizetelly's One-Volume Novels. | A MERE | ACCIDENT. | BY GEORGE MOORE, | Author of "A Mummer's Wife." and spine gilt stamped [double rule] | A | MERE | ACCIDENT | [dark brown ornament] | GEORGE | MOORE | [dark brown ornament] | VIZETELLY & CO | [double rule]

Further impressions,[2] called "Editions" on title-pages, were issued in 1889 and 1891 at 2/- and in July 1895 at 1/-, the latter advertised as the "Fifth Edition."

A rewritten version of *A Mere Accident* was included in *Celibates* (A21) as "John Norton."

See D:Fr-7 for French and D:No-3 for Norwegian translations.

A11
Parnell and His Island

a First edition:

Parnell | and his | Island | BY | GEORGE MOORE | AUTHOR OF | 'A MUMMER'S WIFE,' 'DRAMA IN MUSLIN' ETC. | LONDON | SWAN SONNENSCHEIN, LOWREY, & CO. | PATERNOSTER SQUARE | 1887

Published June at 3/6 in cloth and 2/6 in wrappers

7⅛ x 4¾; [A]² (tipped in), B-R⁸; pp [iv], 256, comprising: title-page as above, with PRINTED BY | SPOTTISWOODE AND CO., NEW-STREET SQUARE | LONDON in center of verso, pp [i-ii]; table of CONTENTS, verso blank, pp [iii-iv]; text pp [1]-254, with printer's imprint repeated at foot of p 254; publisher's advertisements pp [255-56]; white endpapers; all edges trimmed; issued simultaneously in two styles: (a) Bright green cloth, back cover plain, front cover lettered in black within double-rule black border: Parnell | and his | Island | BY | GEORGE MOORE | [publisher's device] | THREE AND SIXPENCE and lettered up spine: Parnell and his Island. — George Moore. (b) Light cream wrap-

---

Ready during April"; however, in a letter dated 17 May 1887, GM wrote to Dujardin "'A Mere Accident' is to appear at the end of next month." The earliest review noted is in PALL MALL GAZETTE, 19 July 1887.

2. *A Mere Accident* is listed in *Shifting Love* (A13-2a), the unauthorized American edition of *Spring Days*, as being one of the books issued in The Lakeside Series, but no copy of this printing nor any other reference to it has been located.

pers, with publisher's advertisement on back cover, lettered in black on front cover within fine double-rule border: Parnell | and his | Island | BY | GEORGE MOORE | [rule] | HALF-A-CROWN: CLOTH, THREE-AND-SIX | [rule] | LONDON | SWAN SONNENSCHEIN, LOWREY & CO. | PATERNOSTER SQUARE | 1887

Reissued in both binding styles, June 1891.

Contents:

"Dublin — The Castle, The Shelbourne Hotel, The Kildare Street Club, Mrs. Rusville"; "An Irish Country House"; "The House of an Irish Poet"; "The Landlord"; "The Tenant Farmer"; "The Priest"; "The Patriot"; "A Castle of Yesterday"; "A Castle of To-day"; "An Eviction"; "A Hunting Breakfast"; "Conclusion." Revised from text previously used for translations in LE FIGARO, Paris, 31 July, 7, 14, 21, 28 August, and 4 September 1886 (D:Fr-4), and in *Terre d'Irlande* (D:Fr-5).

A12
Confessions of a Young Man

a First edition:

CONFESSIONS OF A | YOUNG MAN. | BY | GEORGE MOORE, | Author of "A Mummer's Wife," "Parnell and His Island," etc., etc. | [*publisher's device*] | LONDON: | SWAN SONNENSCHEIN, LOWREY, & CO., | PATERNOSTER SQUARE. | 1888.

Published February at 6/-

7⅜ x 5¾; [ ]¹ ᵒʳ ² (tipped in), 1-22 ⁸, 23 ⁴; pp [ii] or [iv], 360, comprising: (sometimes) half-title,[1] verso blank, pp [i-ii]; inserted frontispiece on heavier paper, recto blank, etched portrait of GM by WS (William Strang) on verso, not paginated; protective tissue guard sheet, not paginated; title-page as above, verso blank, pp [iii-iv] or [i-ii]; text pp 1-357; pp [358-60] blank; endpapers dark gray-green where facing; top edges untrimmed, fore and bottom edges trimmed; bound in gray cloth, back cover blank, front cover has design in dark blue of a young woman with her right knee on a chair and holding up her right hand to a gas wall bracket, lettered in blue across the top CONFESSIONS OF A | YOUNG MAN and lettered diagonally in gilt across lower right corner GEORGE MOORE and spine gilt lettered CONFESSIONS | OF A | YOUNG MAN | BY | GEORGE MOORE | SONNENSCHEIN

1. This leaf, as indicated in collation, does not appear in all copies, and its presence or absence, however, does not seem to indicate any priority of issue, as copies in both states have been noted with and without the advertising slip (see below) which, when present, does indicate a later issue.

There are two issues of the first edition:[2] (1) As above. (2) As above, with the addition of an inserted slip (5 x 4) tipped in between front endpapers, advertising *Parnell and His Island.*

Contents:

Chapters I and II originally published in TIME, London, July 1887. Chapters III and IV originally published in TIME, August 1887. Chapters V and VI originally published as "Extracts from a diary, 1875," in TIME, September 1887. Chapter VII "Synthesis of the Nouvelle Athenes" and chapter VIII "Extracts from a Letter" originally published in TIME, October 1887. Chapter IX originally published in TIME, November 1887; the poem "The Sweetness of the Past" in this chapter previously published as "The Love of the Past" in the SPECTATOR, 11 December 1880, and used as a part of the long poem "A Modern Poem" in *Pagan Poems* (A3); and the poem "Nostalgia" previously anonymously published as "Looking Back" in the SPECTATOR, 15 October 1881. Chapter X previously unpublished. Chapter XI "Thoughts in a Strand Lodging" previously unpublished except for two translations from Mallarmé originally published in the unsigned article, "Les Decadents," in COURT AND SOCIETY REVIEW, 19 January 1887. Chapter XII previously unpublished.

Later in 1888 a second impression was issued identical with the first, except that the words "Second Edition" were added on the title-page flanking the publisher's device. Sheets of the first edition, in two lots of 500 sets each,[3] were used for an American edition:

a2 — Brentano's, Chicago, New York and Paris, 1888; issued at $1.00 in gray cloth binding similar to English edition and at 50¢ in pink wrappers.

2. According to Howard S. Mott, a book dealer of Sheffield, Massachusetts, there is also a preliminary state of *Confessions of a Young Man.* In a note contributed to THE PAPERS OF THE BIBLIOGRAPHICAL SOCIETY OF AMERICA, Vol. 36 (First Quarter 1942), he wrote: "A few copies of this book exist with an unflattering photographic frontispiece of the author. It is said that Moore objected to this (understandably) and the etched frontispiece by William Strang was substituted after about twenty copies with the earlier frontispiece had been released." Mr. Mott informs me that he once briefly owned a copy of this state, which he had purchased at the dispersal of the Frank Dearden library, that the source of his information regarding it was from a note in that copy, and that the present location of it is unknown to him. No other independent reference to this preliminary state has been found, nor has a copy been located, but the possibility that such a state was in fact issued is substantiated by a letter (Ms. 3888, No. 2 in the National Library of Ireland, quoted by Susan Dick in her doctoral dissertation, "*Confessions of a Young Man* by George Moore: A Variorum Edition") from GM to a Mr. Wigram, an editor for Swan Sonnenschein, Lowrey & Co., in which he says, "I think it would be well to print my portrait in the confessions. It would attract attention for I have a photograph that is very like the author of the confessions."

3. According to GM in a letter to the editor of the ATHENAEUM, 8 December 1888, and in an interview in PALL MALL GAZETTE, 27 January 1889.

2a First American printing:

CONFESSIONS OF A | YOUNG MAN | BY | GEORGE MOORE | [*rule*] | SECOND EDITION | [*rule*] | BRENTANOS [*sic*] | NEW YORK, CHICAGO, WASHINGTON AND PARIS

Published late 1888 at 50¢

7⅛ x 4¾; pp [ii], 200, comprising: title-page as above, verso blank, pp [i-ii]; text pp [1]-199; p [200] blank; no endpapers; issued in grayish-green wrappers, publisher's advertisements on verso of front cover which is lettered on recto GEORGE MOORE | [*rule*] | CONFESSIONS | OF A YOUNG MAN | [*rule*] | (AUTHORIZED EDITION.) | [*rule*] | BRENTANOS [*sic*] | NEW YORK, CHICAGO, | WASHINGTON, PARIS. [*all within single-rule border*][4]

Contents:

Same as first edition (a above), but with spellings Americanized. According to GM's letter in the ATHENAEUM, 8 December 1888, this edition was not authorized, despite statement on cover. Plates of this edition were used for further impressions in 1901, 1906, 1907, and 1911. They were also used for:

2a2 — Brentano Uniform Edition, New York, 1915. In 1917 this edition was superseded in the series by a revised text (d below). The first edition text also was used for:

3a — Modern Library, No. 16, New York, 1917, with an "Introduction" by Floyd Dell, and in later impressions it has as a frontispiece a reproduction of the Henry Tonks drawing of GM and the facsimile inscription by him, also used as a frontispiece to the first editions of *Sister Teresa* (A25-a). After the title was dropped from the series the plates were used for:

3a2 — Carlton House, New York, circa 1943.

4a — Haldeman-Julius Publications, Girard, Kansas, 10 June 1927; issued in a paperbound, center wire stapled edition, in a format larger (8⅜ x 5⅜) than the firm's Little Blue Books (see A43).

b Second English edition, revised:

CONFESSIONS OF A | YOUNG MAN. | BY | GEORGE MOORE, | Author of "A Mummer's Wife," "Parnell and His Island," etc., etc. | THIRD [*publisher's device*] | EDITION | LONDON: | SWAN SONNENSCHEIN & CO., | PATERNOSTER SQUARE. | 1889.

Published at 3/6

7⅜ x 4¾; [ ]⁶, 1-24⁸, 25² (tipped in); pp [2], x, 388, comprising: blank leaf, not paginated; half-title with COPYRIGHT IN GREAT BRITAIN AND THE UNITED | STATES OF AMERICA. in center of verso, pp

---

4. Page size and other data from only located copy, in Yale University Library, which is rebound with only front wrapper retained. Also issued in cloth at $1.00, according to *The United States Catalog*, 1888.

[i-ii]; inserted etched portrait of GM (by Walter Sickert), with tissue guard sheet; title-page as above, verso blank, pp [iii-iv]; thirteen-line dedication À JACQUES BLANCHE in French, verso blank, pp [v-vi]; PREFACE pp [vii]-x; text pp 1-387; p [388] blank; off-white endpapers; top edges untrimmed, fore and bottom edges trimmed; bound in olive green cloth, stamped in black on front cover with same design and lettering as first edition (a above), except author's name is omitted, back cover blank, and spine lettered in black as on first edition, with addition of a double rule at top and bottom.

Contents:

The dedication and "Preface" are new, the narrator's name is changed from "Edward Dayne" to "George Moore," five pages are added to chapter I, five to chapter II, three to chapter III, and two pages rewritten in chapter XI, and a new chapter of seventeen pages, in the form of a dialogue between "Conscience and I," is inserted as the penultimate chapter.

A new impression was issued at 2/- in November 1892 as the "Fourth Edition," in light green paper-covered boards, with stamping of previous editions on front cover and spine, and with a commercial advertisement on the back cover.

c Third English edition, revised:

CONFESSIONS OF | [*in green*] | A YOUNG MAN [*in green*] | By GEORGE MOORE. 1886. | Edited and Annotated by GEORGE MOORE, 1904. | London: T. WERNER LAURIE [*publisher's name in green*] | Clifford's Inn [*two printer's ornaments*] 1904

Published November at 6/-

7½ x 4⅜; a⁸, A-T⁸; pp xvi, 304, comprising: blank leaf, except for signature at bottom of recto, pp [i-ii]; half-title with publisher's device in lower right corner, verso blank, pp [iii-iv]; title-page as above, verso blank, pp [v-vi]; thirteen-line dedication À JACQUES BLANCHE, verso blank, pp [vii-viii]; PREFACE TO A NEW EDITION OF | "CONFESSIONS OF A YOUNG MAN" pp ix-xvi; text pp 1-303, with "Colston & Coy, Limited, Printers Edinburgh." at foot of p 303; publisher's advertisement p [304]; white endpapers; top edges trimmed and stained green, fore edges trimmed, bottom edges untrimmed; bound in medium green cloth, back cover plain except for single-rule border in blind at outer edge, front cover gilt lettered CONFESSIONS of | a YOUNG MAN | BY GEORGE MOORE at top and publisher's monogram in blind at bottom all within single-rule border in blind at outer edge, and spine gilt lettered CONFESSIONS | of a | YOUNG MAN | [*rule*] | GEORGE MOORE | T. WERNER LAURIE with heavy gilt-rule border at top and bottom.

Contents:

The text is the same, with slight revisions, omissions, and additions, as the revised second English edition (b above), with a new eight-page

"Preface," also published in DANA, November 1904, and includes an untitled sonnet in French originally printed as "Sonnet Dédicace à Algernon Charles Swinburne" in *Martin Luther* (A2). Among the additions to the text there is, in section XI, an untitled poem, a revision of "À une Poitrinaire" from *Pagan Poems* (A3), and two poems in French, "Nuit de Septembre" and "Pour un Tableau de Lord Leighton," the first originally published as a portion of the duo-drama "La Maitresse Maternelle" in *Pagan Poems* and republished under its present title in PALL MALL GAZETTE, 15 January 1895, and again in THE BOOKMAN, October 1895, and the second is a revision of "Les Dormeuses" in PALL MALL GAZETTE, circa February 1896.

Copies of this edition were issued in the United States in a bright red cloth binding:

c2 — Mitchell Kennerley, New York, with a slip (1 x 3⅝) lettered in black with name of American publisher pasted over the Laurie imprint on the title-page. Sheets of the Laurie edition with half-title and title-page (in black) reset, were used for:

c3 — Bell's Indian and Colonial Library, No. 591. George Bell and Sons, London, 1904. Reissued in 1906. The revised text of these printings also was used for:

2c — Collection of British and American Authors, Vol. 3812, Bernhard Tauchnitz, Leipzig, 1905.[5]

d Fourth edition (second Brentano Uniform) revised:

CONFESSIONS OF | A YOUNG MAN | BY | GEORGE MOORE, 1886 | EDITED AND ANNOTATED | BY GEORGE MOORE 1904 | AND AGAIN IN 1916 | [*diamond-shaped publisher's device*] | NEW YORK | BRENTANO'S | 1917

Published at $1.50

7⅞ x 5⅜; [1]⁸, 2-18⁸; pp [6], viii, 274, comprising: half-title, with list of WORKS OF GEORGE MOORE | NEW AND REVISED EDITION within single-rule box on verso, not paginated; title-page as above, with COPYRIGHT, 1917, BY BRENTANO'S on verso, not paginated; dedication À JACQUES BLANCHE, verso blank, not paginated; PREFACE, pp i-viii; text pp 1-271; pp [272-74] blank; white endpapers; top edges trimmed and stained green, fore and bottom edges untrimmed; bound in

---

5. In a letter to Lady Cunard (dated "Spring 1905" by the editor) GM wrote, "I did not send you the *Confessions* because I am waiting for the Tauchnitz edition. The English edition is detestable — thoroughly detestable. I have written to Leipzig to ask if they will print a few copies on Holland paper (I suppose I should say Dutch paper). The ordinary edition will arrive here on Wednesday or Thursday — you shall have your copy on Friday." No Dutch paper copy, nor any other reference to such copies, has been located.

green ribbed cloth, back and front covers plain, gilt decorations at top and bottom of spine, which is gilt lettered CONFESSIONS | OF A | YOUNG | MAN | GEORGE | MOORE | BRENTANO'S

Contents:

The text shows many minor revisions and additions from the 1904 edition (c above), and a slight alternation is made in the French of the first sentence of the dedication, here "et jái [sic] eu l'idée" in place of "et j'étais inspiré" of the 1889 and 1904 texts. The "Preface" is new, but again includes the letter from Walter Pater first published in the "Preface" to the 1904 edition. The dedicatory sonnet to Swinburne from *Martin Luther* reprinted in the 1904 "Preface" is transferred to section XI. An addition to the same section is "La Ballade d'Alfred, Alfred aux Belles Dents" which is a revised version of *La Ballade de l'Amant de Coeur* (A8). A third untitled translation from Mallarmé added to section XIV was originally published as "The Future Phenomenon" in the third number of THE SAVOY, July 1896. The text pages of this edition were reproduced by photo-offset for a padded, paperbound edition:

d2 — Capricorn Books, No. 20, G. P. Putnam's Sons, New York, 1959, with an Introduction by Robert M. Coates.

2d Fourth English edition, revised:

CONFESSIONS OF | A YOUNG MAN | BY | GEORGE MOORE. 1886 | EDITED AND ANNOTATED BY GEORGE MOORE, 1904 | AND AGAIN IN 1916 | [*publisher's device of windmill, flanked by letters* W *and* H, *within single-rule box*] | LONDON | WILLIAM HEINEMANN
    Published April 1918[6] at 6/-

7⅜ x 4¾; [ ]⁸, A-O⁸, pp [2], xiv, 224, comprising: blank leaf, not paginated; half-title, with list of WORKS BY GEORGE MOORE on verso, pp [i-ii]; title-page as above, with LONDON: WILLIAM HEINEMANN, 1917 at foot of verso, pp [iii-iv]: dedication À JACQUES BLANCHE, verso blank, pp v-[vi]; PREFACE pp vii-xiii; p [xiv] blank;[7] text pp [1]-224, with BILLING AND SONS, LTD., PRINTERS, GUILDFORD, ENGLAND at foot of p 224; followed by an inserted 16-page publisher's catalogue; white endpapers; top and fore edges trimmed, bottom edges untrimmed; bound in dark blue cloth, with large elongated paneled design enclosed within double-rule border in blind on front cover, publisher's monogram device in blind in lower right corner of back cover, spine gilt

---

6. Although dated 1917 on verso of title-leaf, the date is as given here and subsequent impressions carry the notation on verso of title-leaf "First published, April 1918," which is also the date given in *The English Catalogue*.

7. Florian J. Shasky has a copy of this edition with an errata slip tipped in between pp [xiv] and [l], correcting several errors carried over from the revised Brentano edition (d above). All were corrected before the plates of this edition were used for the expanded 1926 edition (2d2 below).

stamped CONFESSIONS | OF A | YOUNG | MAN | GEORGE | MOORE [*enclosed within single-rule border with scallop-shaped design at top and bottom*] | HEINEMANN

Contents:

Further minor revisions and deletions in texts, including correction of the error in the French of the first sentence of the dedication, and with "La Ballade d'Alfred . . ." transferred to section XIV, which is the dialogue between "Conscience" and "I."

2d2 Fifth English edition, expanded:

In February 1926 Heinemann issued an enlarged edition in the same format as the fourth English edition (2d above), using the plates of that edition, with an additional leaf (pp [xv-xvi]) tipped in between [ ]$_8$ and A$_1$ having an author's NOTE on recto, and five additional gatherings, P-T^8, of new text (pp [225]-301), printer's imprint transferred from p 224 to p [302], and pp [303-4] blank.

Contents:

Same as previous Heinemann edition, with additions: "Note" by GM, explaining the inclusion of the new material; "Mummer Worship" reprinted from *Impressions and Opinions* (A15); "A Visit to Medan," retitled reprinting of "My Impressions of Zola" from 1913 edition of *Impressions and Opinions* (A15-b); "An Actress of the Eighteenth Century" reprinted from *Impressions and Opinions*; "Le Revers d'un Grand Homme" reprinted from *Impressions and Opinions*; "Epistles to the Cymry" originally published in FORTNIGHTLY REVIEW, September 1914.

The plates of this expanded edition were used for two further printings:

2d3 — Travelers' Library, No. 76, Heinemann, London, March 1928; reprinted April 1928, and again in 1929.

2d4 — Windmill Library, Heinemann, London, July 1933. The expanded text also was used for:

3d — Penguin Books, No. 185, Harmondsworth, Middlesex, January 1939. The second (September 1939) and subsequent printings include a short biographical note of GM by Osbert Burdett, previously used on the jacket of the Penguin edition of *Esther Waters* (A19-6c)

e — Carra Edition,[8] Volume IX, Boni and Liveright, New York, 20 June[9] 1923. In this edition, *Confessions of a Young Man* is included in the same volume as *Avowals*, and although it is listed first on title-page and spine label, it is printed after the later book on pp [287]-489. There is a tipped-in

8. Although a detailed collation is not given, this edition is given a separate textual letter as it is the first printing of the final text.

9. According to Library of Congress copyright records, but the Boni and Liveright trade edition of *Avowals* (A38-3a2) has a note on the verso of the title-leaf, "First issued in Carra Edition, May, 1923."

frontispiece, protected by a tissue guard sheet which is lettered in red at bottom of verso GEORGE MOORE | From a sketch by Manet[10]

Contents:

The text is slightly revised and "Vers d'Album"[11] is added in section X. This final text, with the addition of the five articles added in the expanded fifth English edition (2d2 above), was used for:

2e — Uniform Edition, Heinemann, London, June 1933. Reissued in a different binding as:

2e2 — Ebury Edition, Heinemann, London, June 1937. This final expanded text also was used for:

3e — Digit Books, G465, Brown, Watson Limited, London, 1961.

See D:Cz-3 for Czech, D:Fr-9 and D:Fr-10 for French, D:It-1 for Italian, and D:Ja-1 for Japanese translations.

A13

Spring Days

a First edition:

VIZETELLY S [sic] ONE-VOLUME NOVELS. | [rule] | XXIX. | SPRING DAYS. | A REALISTIC NOVEL. | A PRELUDE TO "DON JUAN." | BY | GEORGE MOORE, | AUTHOR OF "A MUMMER'S WIFE," "A MODERN LOVER," "A DRAMA IN MUSLIN," | "A MERE ACCIDENT," ETC. | [publisher's device] | LONDON: | VIZETELLY & CO., 16 HENRIETTA STREET, | COVENT GARDEN. | 1888.

Published late August or early September at 6/-

7⅜ x 4⅞; [ ]² (tipped in), [A]⁸, B-Z⁸, 2A² (tipped in); pp [iv], 372, comprising: half-title, with advertisement for four of GM's REALISTIC NOVELS on verso, pp [i-ii]; title-page as above, verso blank, pp [iii-iv]; dedication TO | MY FRIEND, | FRANK HARRIS., verso blank, pp [1-2]; PREFACE pp [3-4] (p [4] misnumbered iv); text pp [5]-371, with TURNBULL AND SPEARS, PRINTERS, EDINBURGH. at foot of p 371; p [372] blank; followed by inserted 32-page publisher's catalogue dated APRIL, 1888.; endpapers dark green where facing; all edges untrimmed; bound in dull pinkish-brown cloth, publisher's monogram in blind in center of back cover, front cover lettered in black SPRING DAYS |

---

10. Same as frontispiece of the expanded edition of *Modern Painting* (A17-b). Original is in Metropolitan Museum of Art in New York.

11. This bit of verse also printed (p 110) in *Letters to Dujardin* (A54).

A REALISTIC NOVEL | GEORGE MOORE and spine gilt lettered SPRING | DAYS | A REALISTIC | NOVEL | GEORGE MOORE | VIZETELLY & CO. with double rules in black at top and bottom.

Contents:

Extensively revised from serial version published in THE EVENING NEWS, London, 3 April through 31 May 1888.

Further impressions issued in various colored cloths and decorated paper-covered boards, frequently printed on thinner paper, and generally without inserted catalogue.

2a First American edition, unauthorized and retitled:

SHIFTING LOVE | A REALISTIC NOVEL | A PRELUDE TO "DON JUAN" | BY | GEORGE MOORE | Author of "AN ACTOR'S WIFE," "A MODERN LOVER," "A DRAMA | IN MUSLIN," "A MERE ACCIDENT," ETC. | [rule] | CHICAGO: G. E. WILSON, PUBLISHER. | 1891

Published 10 March [1] at 25¢

7½ x 5¼; [1]⁸, 2-17⁸, 18⁴; pp 280, comprising: half-title, verso blank, pp [1-2]; title-page as above, verso blank, pp [3-4]; text pp 5-276, with four inserted illustrations, not paginated, facing pp 49, 112, 193, 249; publisher's advertisements pp [277-79]; p [280] blank; all edges trimmed; issued in gray paper wrappers,[2] back cover blank, picture of a girl reclining in a hammock and being sketched by a mustached artist sitting on a three-legged stool is on front cover, which is lettered in red at top SHIFTING | LOVE, and in blank below illustration G. E. WILSON, | 314 STATE STREET, CHICAGO. | Wilson's Library of Fiction Issued Monthly, by subscription $3.00 per annum. No. 1, March 10, 1891. | Entered at Chicago Postoffice as second-class matter. | and lettered down the spine in black SHIFTING LOVE – – MOORE.

Contents:

Same as first edition (a above), with dedication omitted. This is an unauthorized edition, and it is presumed that its plates were used for:

2a2 — SHIFTING LOVE, Stein, Chicago, 1899.[3]

b Second English edition, revised:

SPRING DAYS | BY | GEORGE MOORE | LONDON | T. WERNER LAURIE | CLIFFORD'S INN

1. According to date on cover, but not necessarily actual date of publication (see A5-n5).

2. Also issued in cloth, according to an advertisement (p [279]) for The Lakeside Series, but no copy has been located.

3. Listed in *The United States Catalog*, and although no copy has been located it seems reasonable to assume that the Wilson plates were used for this edition, as about this period Stein used their plates for republication of several books by other authors.

Published June 1912 at 6/-

7⅞ x 5⅛; [ ]⁶, A-U⁸, X² (tipped in); pp xii, 324, comprising: half-title with publisher's device in lower right corner, and advertisement for three books BY GEORGE MOORE within single-rule box on verso, pp [i-ii]; title-page as above, verso blank, pp [iii-iv]; PREFACE pp v-x; fly-title, verso blank, pp [xi-xii]; text pp 1-320; with PRINTED AT THE EDINBURGH PRESS, 9 and 11 YOUNG STREET. at foot of p 320; advertisement on verso of half-title repeated,[4] p 321; pp [322-24] blank; white endpapers; top edges trimmed, fore and bottom edges untrimmed; bound in dark green cloth, front and back covers plain, spine gilt lettered SPRING | DAYS | GEORGE | MOORE | WERNER | LAURIE

Contents:

The text is slightly revised, and in the "Preface," which is entirely new, GM, after explaining how he tried to supress "the worst book I ever wrote," gives an account of the circumstances that led to its reprinting. The plates of this edition were used for two other issues:

b2 — A Colonial edition, printed on thinner paper, T. Werner Laurie, London, circa 1912;

b3 — Brentano Uniform Edition,[5] New York, November 1912. The revised text also was used for:

2b — Collection of British and American Authors, Volume 4364, Bernhard Tauchnitz, Leipzig, October 1912.

3b — Carra Edition, Volume IV, Boni and Liveright, New York, 1922. There is a tipped-in frontispiece, protected by a tissue guard sheet lettered in red at foot of recto GEORGE MOORE | From a sketch by J. B. Yeats | In the collection of John Quinn, Esq. The sketch is dated "August 1st, 1905."

4. This is the "slight mistake . . . in pagination" noted by GM in the "Preface" to the revised edition of *Impressions and Opinions* (A15-b), the second and only other volume in a projected uniform edition of his collected works. A. J. A. Symons noted (in a fragment of his uncompleted bibliography now in my collection) that "in size, binding material and style of lettering" the two volumes "faithfully" resemble the first editions of Walter Pater (an author greatly admired by GM).

5. *Spring Days* was the first volume issued in the "Brentano Uniform Edition of the Early Works of George Moore," which as it was expanded to eleven volumes, dropped the word "Early" from its name. The series also included *Impressions and Opinions* (A15-b2); *Celibates* (A21-2a2); *Muslin* (A34-a2); *Confessions of a Young Man* (A12-2a2), which was replaced by a revised text (A12-d); *A Mummer's Wife* (A6-3b2), which almost immediately was replaced by a revised text (A6-c); *Sister Teresa* (A25-2a3); *Lewis Seymour and Some Women* (A36-a); *The Brook Kerith* (A35-2a3); *Esther Waters* (A19-2b3), which also was replaced by a revised text (A19-c3); and *The Untilled Field* (A26-2a2).

A14

Mike Fletcher

a First edition:

MIKE FLETCHER. | A NOVEL. | BY | GEORGE MOORE, | AUTHOR OF | "A MUMMER'S WIFE," "CONFESSIONS OF A YOUNG MAN," ETC. | London: | WARD AND DOWNEY, | 12, YORK STREET, COVENT GARDEN. | 1889. | [All rights reserved.]

Published December at 6/-

7⅜ x 4⅞; [A] ^{2} (tipped in), [a] ^{1} (tipped in between [A] $_1$ and [A] $_2$), B-U ^{8}; pp [vi], 304, comprising: half-title, verso blank, pp [i-ii]; title-page as above, verso blank, pp [iii-iv]; dedication TO | MY BROTHER AUGUSTUS, | IN MEMORY OF | MANY YEARS OF MUTUAL ASPIRATION AND LABOUR., verso blank, pp [v-vi]; text pp [1]-304; endpapers gray flowered where facing; all edges untrimmed; bound in medium blue cloth, publisher's monogram in blind in center of back cover, conventional stylized design in brown on front cover and spine, front cover gilt stamped MIKE FLETCHER | [*rule*] | GEORGE MOORE and spine gilt stamped MIKE | FLETCHER | [*rule*] | GEORGE | MOORE | WARD & DOWNEY

There are two states of the first edition: (1) As above. (2) As above, with an additional leaf of press notices of MR. GEORGE MOORE'S REALISTIC NOVELS tipped in between the half-title leaf ([A]$_1$) and the title-leaf ([a]$_1$).

Contents:

Previously unpublished,[1] except for the poems "The Ballade of Don Juan Dead" in chapter II and "A une Poetrenaire" [*sic*] on pp 252-53 which had been originally published in *Pagan Poems* (A3), and parts of chapter III revised from the unsigned article, "An Evening at Alphonse Daudet's," in THE BAT, 1 March 1887.

In 1899 Ward and Downey reissued *Mike Fletcher*, with date and "All rights reserved" notice at foot of title-page omitted. In this issue the first gathering is [A] ^{4} (sewn in) comprising: blank leaf pp [i-ii]; half-title, verso blank, pp [iii-iv]; title-page, verso blank, pp [v-vi]; dedication, verso blank, pp [vii-viii]; white endpapers; all edges trimmed; bound in light green cloth, back cover plain, front cover gilt lettered MIKE | FLETCHER | George Moore | and spine gilt lettered MIKE | FLETCHER | GEORGE MOORE | 1899

---

1. William A. Perkins, in his unpublished 1954 Stanford University doctoral thesis "George Moore's Realistic Novels," suggests (p 268) that *Mike Fletcher* may be a reworking of the discarded novel "The Aristocracy of Vice" (M3) which "would explain the author's private admission later that in *Mike Fletcher* he had taken his 'first steps'"; as well as making "understandable his introduction of verses from *Pagan Poems* into the novel."

2a First American edition:

MIKE FLETCHER. | A Novel. | BY | GEORGE MOORE, | AUTHOR OF | "A MUMMER'S WIFE," "CONFESSIONS OF A YOUNG MAN," ETC. | [*rule*] | PRESS OF | THE MINERVA PUBLISHING COMPANY, | 10 WEST 23D STREET, NEW YORK. | 1889.

Published 12 July 1890[2] at 50¢

7 x 4¾; [1-19][8], wire stapled; pp [ii], 302, comprising: blank leaf, pp [i-ii]; title-page as above, with "Copyright, 1889. | BY | THE MINERVA PUB. CO. | [*rule*] | All Rights Reserved." in center of verso, pp [1-2]; PREFACE, verso blank, pp 3-[4]; text pp 5-302; no endpapers; all edges trimmed; issued in cream wrappers,[3] publisher's advertisements on recto and verso of back wrapper, verso of front wrapper blank, recto lettered in blue against a line drawing in red of Minerva standing at the base of a columned classical structure with an owl peering down at her: PRICE 50 CENTS. | Entered at Post Office, New York, at second-class rates. | [*at upper left*:] MINERVA SERIES. No. 17 | Issued monthly. | [*at upper right*:] DECEMBER, 1889. | Subscription Price, | $6.00 per Year. | [*in center*:] MIKE | FLETCHER | BY | GEORGE MOORE | [*in base of column, in red*:] MINERVA PUBLISHING CO. | 10 WEST 23[d] ST. | NEW YORK and spine lettered down in dark blue MIKE FLETCHER

Contents:

"Preface" by T. T. Timayenis, the publisher. Text same as first edition (a above). This edition was authorized[4] and is an almost line by line resetting of the Ward and Downey edition, with a few slight differences and some misprints corrected. The poem in chapter X is called "A une Potrinaire" [*sic*].

A15
Impressions and Opinions

a First edition:

IMPRESSIONS | AND OPINIONS | BY | GEORGE MOORE | AUTHOR OF 'A MUMMER'S WIFE;' | 'A MODERN LOVER;' 'CONFESSIONS | OF A YOUNG MAN,' ETC. | [*fleuret*] | LONDON | Published by DAVID NUTT | in the Strand | 1891

2. According to the *United States Catalog Cumulative Index* 1890; the wrapper, however, gives "December, 1889," but this is not necessarily the actual date of publication (see A5-n5).

3. Also advertised as being issued in cloth, but no copy has been located and it is not so listed in *The United States Catalog*.

4. See "My Friendship with George Moore, Three Thousand Miles Away," by the Marquise Clara Lanza, in THE BOOKMAN (New York), July 1918.

Published March at 5/- (1,000 copies printed in February, of which 528 were bound in March)

6⅞ x 4½; [ ]⁴, A-X⁸, Y⁴, Z¹ (tipped in); pp [viii], 346, comprising: half-title, verso blank, pp [i-ii]; title-page as above, verso blank, pp [iii-iv]; author's note,[1] verso blank, pp [v-vi]; table of CONTENTS, verso blank, pp [vii-viii]; text pp [1]-346, with "Printed by T. and A. CONSTABLE, Printers to Her Majesty, | at the Edinburgh University Press." at foot p 346; followed by inserted 12-page catalogue of publisher's announcements (6⅜ x 4); white endpapers; all edges untrimmed; bound in red or dark green cloth, back cover plain, gilt decorations across top and bottom of front cover, same decorations at top and bottom of spine which is gilt lettered IMPRESSIONS | AND | OPINIONS | GEORGE | MOORE | DAVID NUTT [*publisher's name in decoration at foot of spine*]

There are three[2] states of the first edition: (1) As above, with page number 180 perfect and with final page of inserted publisher's announcements

1. "Since their first appearance in the Reviews | these papers have all been revised, and in | some cases entirely rewritten. The article on | Balzac, first printed in the 'Fortnightly,' has | been increased to nearly three times its ori- | ginal length. 'Mummer-Worship' has been | redeemed from certain emendations introduced | into it by Mr. Quilter. For these discarded | trifles the curious are referred to the pages of | the 'Universal Review.' Other articles have | been printed from the 'Magazine of Art' | and the 'St. James's Gazette.'" The "discarded trifles" of "Mummer-Worship" are four paragraphs, not too different from the rest of the article. The first is omitted from the text, as printed here, after the continued paragraph on p 157; the second before the last paragraph on p 163; and the other two following the continued paragraph on p 176.

2. In addition there is another which can be called an "advance" or "pre-publication" state. According to a note in THE SPEAKER, 18 April 1891, "The first edition of Mr. Moore's new book [*Impressions and Opinions*] had to be recalled on account of a printer's error." This was the misprint AUTHOR OF 'A HUMMEROUS [*sic*] WIFE' on the title-page. These copies are lettered ESSAYS | GEORGE | MOORE on the spine. At least three of these copies survive, each with an undated presentation inscription on the title-page, one of which is pictured in *This Book-Collecting Game* by A. Edward Newton, who had two copies in his collection. Both were sold at the Newton Sale at the Parke-Bernet Galleries, New York, 16 May 1941. One, bound in blue, is inscribed to "W. Henley from George Moore," and the other, bound in yellow, is inscribed "To Madge and Ellen Dixon from their friend George Moore." A third copy, bound in blue and inscribed "To Frank Harris from his friend George Moore," was sold in the H. Bertram Smith sale at the same galleries, 10 December 1941. As two of the recipients, Henley and Harris, were journalists, it seems probable that these copies were rushed through the press and hastily bound for review purposes. Another copy lettered ESSAYS on the spine and without the publisher's name in the gilt decoration at the bottom, listed in *The Modern Library Collected by Viscount Esher at Watlington Park* (privately printed 1930) and now in my collection, does not have the error on the title-page. It is bound in green, has page number 180 perfect, but has no inserted advertisements, and presents a puzzling problem as the final gathering is a folding [Z² (tipped in)] as in the third state noted below.

listing but a single title, *Poliphili Hypnerotomachia*, edited by Andrew Lang, and noted as being "In the Press." (2) As above, with page number 180 perfect, with final page of inserted announcements listing four titles, the final one being *Impressions and Opinions*, and with the Lang title dated 1890 and priced at £1 1s.[3] (3) As above, except final gathering is a folding, Z^2 (tipped in), with Z_2 being a blank leaf; the figure 1 is missing from page number 180, and copies of this state are most frequently bound in red, though sometimes seen in green.

Contents:

"Balzac" expanded from "Some of Balzac's Minor Pieces" published in FORTNIGHTLY REVIEW, October 1889. "Turgueneff" originally published in FORTNIGHTLY REVIEW, February 1888. "A Great Poet" originally published in THE HAWK, 25 February 1890. "Two Unknown Poets" originally published as "Notes and Sensations" in THE HAWK, 23 September 1890. " 'Le Rêve' " originally published as "M. Zola 'On the Side of the Angels' " in ST. JAMES'S GAZETTE, 2 November 1888. "Le Revers d'un Grand Homme" originally published in THE HAWK, 28 January 1890. "An Actress of the Eighteenth Century" originally published in THE HAWK, 22 July 1890. "Mummer-Worship" revised from its original publication in THE UNIVERSAL REVIEW, September 1888. "Our Dramatists and Their Literature" originally published in FORTNIGHTLY REVIEW, November 1889, and here augmented with the addition of "Is 'Judah' Literature?" from THE HAWK, 26 August 1890, and "The Secret of Immortality" from THE HAWK, 29 April 1890. "Note on 'Ghosts' " originally published as "Le Théâtre Libre" in THE HAWK, 17 June 1890. "Théâtre Libre" originally published as "The New Théâtre Libre" in THE HAWK, 24 June 1890. "On the Necessity of an English Théâtre Libre" originally published as "The New Théâtre Libre" in THE HAWK, 8 July 1890. "Meissonier and the Salon Julian" originally[4] published in FORTNIGHTLY REVIEW, July 1890, and here augmented with an added passage of "From the Naked Model" published in THE HAWK, 24 December 1889. "Art for the Villa" originally published in MAGAZINE OF ART, July 1889. "Degas" originally published in MAGAZINE OF ART, November 1890. "The New Pictures in the National Gallery" incorporates passages, revised, from "Buy the Tryon" in THE HAWK, 4 March 1890.

The English Catalogue lists an edition of *Impressions and Opinions*, Walter Scott, London, April 1895, but no copy with a Scott imprint has been located. Stereotyped plates[5] of the first edition were used for the first American edition:

3. The only review copy noted is of this state.
4. The unsigned article, "Cheap Tripping to Parnassus" in THE BAT, 28 December 1886, has striking similarities to this article and may have been its genesis.
5. With page number 180 perfect as in first and second states of first edition, but

33

a2 — Charles Scribner's Sons, New York, 1891.

b Second English edition, revised:

IMPRESSIONS | AND OPINIONS | BY | GEORGE MOORE | LONDON | T. WERNER LAURIE, LTD. | CLIFFORD'S INN | 1913

    Published February at 6/-

    7⅞ x 5⅛; [a]² (tipped in), [b]⁴, A-P⁸, Q⁴; pp [2], x, 248, comprising: blank leaf not paginated; half-title with publisher's device in lower right corner, and three-line notice of *Spring Days* in single-rule box on verso, pp [i-ii]; title-page as above, verso blank, pp [iii-iv]; PREFACE pp v-viii; table of CONTENTS, verso blank, pp ix-[x]; text pp 1-247; "Printed at | The Edinburgh Press, | 9 and 11 Young Street." in center p [248]; white endpapers; top edges trimmed, fore and bottom edges untrimmed; bound in green cloth,⁶ back and front covers plain, spine gilt stamped IMPRESSIONS | AND | OPINIONS | GEORGE | MOORE | T. WERNER | [*dot*] LAURIE [*dot*] | L^TD

    Contents:

    Text revised from first edition (a above) with the following additions and substitutions: "Preface" previously unpublished. "My Impressions of Zola" revised from original publication in ENGLISH ILLUSTRATED MAGAZINE, February 1894, replaces " 'Le Rêve'." "Une Rencontre au Salon" originally published in FORTNIGHTLY REVIEW, November 1912, replaces "Art for the Villa."

    Sheets of this edition, with cancel half-title and title-leaves, were used for:

b2 — Brentano Uniform Edition, New York, 1913.

    When revising his works for inclusion in the Heinemann Uniform Edition GM "decided that *Impressions and Opinions* could not be admitted into the canon."⁷ He had already included "Degas" in the Carra Edition of *Modern Painting* (A17-b4), and "Mummer-Worship," "My Impression of Zola" (retitled "A Visit to Medan"), "An Actress of the Eighteenth Century," and "Le Revers d'un Grande Homme" were salvaged for inclusion in the 1926 and subsequent editions of *Confessions of a Young Man* (A12-2d2 et seq.). Also "Balzac" served as the basis of chapter III, and "A Great Poet" and "Two Unknown Poets" were the inspiration for chapters XII and XIII of *Conversations in Ebury Street* (A46).

---

with single quotation marks present at the beginning of final two lines on page 85, and the figure 6 present in page number 256, all of which are missing in the three states of the first edition.

    6. Matching the 1912 edition of *Spring Days* (A13-b; see Note 4).

    7. From the prefatory "Note" to the 1926 and subsequent editions of *Confessions of a Young Man* (A12-2d2 et seq.).

A16

Vain Fortune

a First edition:

VAIN FORTUNE. | BY | GEORGE MOORE, | Author of "A Mummer's Life [*sic*]," "Impressions and Opinions," "Confessions of a | Young Man," "A Modern Lover," etc. | WITH ELEVEN ILLUSTRATIONS BY MAURICE GREIFFENHAGEN. | LONDON: | HENRY AND CO., | BOUVERIE STREET, E.C.

Published October 1891 at 6/-

7⅝ x 5⅛; [ ]² (tipped in), 1-19⁸; pp [iv], 304, plus five inserted plates with tissue guards, facing title-page and pp 35, 101, 180, and 293,¹ comprising: inserted frontispiece, not paginated; title-page as above, with "Printed by Hazell, Watson & Viney, Ld., London and Aylesbury." at foot of verso, pp [i-ii]; author's note, verso blank, pp [iii-iv]; text pp 1-296, with printer's imprint repeated at foot of p 296; publisher's advertisements pp [297-304]²; endpapers navy blue where facing; all edges trimmed; bound in dark red cloth, back cover plain except for double-rule border in blind at outer edge, front cover plain except for gilt double-rule border at outer edge, spine gilt lettered VAIN | FORTUNE | GEORGE | MOORE | HENRY & Cᵒ

There are three issues of the first edition: (1) As above. (2) As above, except endpapers where facing are brown and the error on the title-page is corrected by an overprint of a W on the L changing "Life" to "Wife." (3) Remainder sheets, with brown endpapers, but with title-page error uncorrected, were issued in 1893 by Walter Scott in a brown cloth binding, front and back covers plain, lettered in gilt on spine as in previous issues, except publisher's imprint at foot is changed to "Walter Scott, Ltd."

Contents:

Revised from serialization in the weekly LADY'S PICTORIAL, 4 July through 17 October 1891, where the author's identity was hidden under the *nom de plume* of Lady Rhone.³ Several illustrations by Maurice Greiffenhagen accompany each installment, and it was from these that those used in the book were selected.

1. Other illustrations printed with text on pp 84, 106, 174, 202, 264, and 273. The frontispiece "The great critics had each a separate audience" shows the stalls of a theatre during intermission of a play, and two of the three standing critics appear to be Oscar Wilde and GM.

2. An advertisement for *Vain Fortune* on p [303] repeats the title-page error of "Life" for "Wife."

3. Allan Wade, in his unpublished "Notes for George Moore's Bibliographer," said of this, "Would the chaste readers of The Lady's Pictorial in 1891 really have shuddered at the thought of a novel by George Moore? And was it a recollection that some of Balzac's 'Oeuvres de Jeunesse' had been published by 'Lord R'Loone', which led Mr. Moore to take 'Lady Rhone' as his nom-de-plume?"

a2 Limited edition:

VAIN FORTUNE. | BY | GEORGE MOORE, | Author of "A Mummer's Wife," "Impressions and Opinions," "Confessions of a | Young Man," "A Modern Lover," etc. | WITH ELEVEN ILLUSTRATIONS BY MAURICE GREIFFENHAGEN. | LONDON: | HENRY AND CO., | BOUVERIE STREET, E.C.

Published October 1891 at 1/5/-

10 x 7¼; all particulars same as regular edition (a above), with addition of a single leaf ([ ]¹) tipped in after free front endpaper, having half-title on recto and notice of limitation as below on verso; all printed on heavier paper, watermarked with various marks including "The Huth Library"; endpapers tan floral design where facing, free endpapers lined with white paper; all edges untrimmed; bound in white cloth over beveled boards, back cover plain, front cover gilt lettered, angled up from left to right, VAIN | FORTUNE in upper center and horizontally GEORGE MOORE in lower right corner, and spine gilt lettered VAIN | FORTUNE | GEORGE | MOORE | HENRY & C°

Notice of limitation:

"Only One Hundred and Fifty Copies of this Large Paper Edition | have been Printed, of which this is | No. . . . ."

There are two issues of the limited edition: (1) As above, unnumbered and unsigned, for although these were advertised (p [303]) as being "Numbered and Signed by the Author" apparently none were so issued. (2) Remainder sheets reissued by Walter Scott, Ltd., London, 1893, top edges gilt, bound in dark red buckram, back and front covers plain, spine gilt stamped VAIN | FORTUNE | A REALISTIC | NOVEL | [*rule*] | GEORGE MOORE. These copies are numbered in ink on limitation page, and rubber stamped in blue below the number: For WALTER SCOTT, LIMITED | Marion T. Scott [*signed in ink*] DIRECTOR

Contents:

Same as first edition (a above), printed from same plates, but with misprint on title-page corrected; the same misprint, however, in the advertisement on p [303] is not corrected.

2a First American edition:

VAIN FORTUNE. | BY | GEORGE MOORE, | Author of "A Mummer's Wife," "Impressions and Opin- | ions," "Confessions of a Young Man," "A Modern Lover," etc. | NEW YORK: | P.F. COLLIER, PUBLISHER. | 1892.

Published 23 February⁴ at 25¢

7 x 4½; [1-18]¹² (wire stapled); pp 192, comprising: title-page as above,

4. Publication date taken from front cover, but not necessarily the actual date of publication (see A5-n5).

with commercial advertisements on verso, pp [1]-2; text pp 3-189, with four-line commercial advertisement at foot p 189; publisher's advertisements pp [190-92] (numbered 5-7); no endpapers; all edges untrimmed; issued in gray-green wrappers, with commercial advertisements on lower half p [1] and on pp [2-4], spine plain, top half of front cover lettered in black ONCE A WEEK | [*dot*] LIBRARY [*dot*] | Issued Weekly. Entered at the Post-Office at New York as second-class matter. | [*double rule*] | VOL. VIII., No. 19. FEBRUARY 23, 1892. [*brace*] Subscription Price $3.00 | Single Copies 25 Cents. | [*double rule*] | VAIN FORTUNE | By GEORGE MOORE. | P.F. COLLIER, PUBLISHER, 523 WEST THIRTEENTH St., NEW YORK [*half-page commercial advertisement noted above*]

Contents:

Text same as first edition (a above).

New impression 1895.

b Second American edition, revised:

VAIN FORTUNE | BY GEORGE MOORE | AUTHOR OF "A MUM-MER'S WIFE," "IMPRESSIONS AND | OPINIONS," "A DRAMA IN MUSLIN," ETC. | NEW YORK | CHARLES SCRIBNER'S SONS | 1892

Published April at $1.00

$7\frac{3}{16}$ x $4\frac{5}{8}$; [1]^8, 2-18^8 (signed on recto of leaf 3); pp [iv], 284, comprising: half-title, verso blank, pp [i-ii]; title-page as above, with COPY-RIGHT, 1892, BY | CHARLES SCRIBNER'S SONS in center and: Press of J. J. Little & Co. | Astor Place, New York | at foot of verso, pp [iii-iv]; text pp [1]-283; p [284] blank; white endpapers; all edges trimmed; bound in brown cloth, back cover plain, front cover lettered in mauve outlined in black within decorative frame: VAIN | FORTUNE and spine gilt lettered VAIN | FORTUNE [*title within decorative frame*] | GEORGE | MOORE | SCRIBNERS

Contents:

In the "Prefatory Note" to the 1895 edition (c below) GM wrote, ". . . when Messers. Scribner proposed to print the book in America, I stipulated that I should be allowed to rewrite it. They consented, and I began the story with Emily Watson, making her the principal character instead of Hubert Price."

c Second English edition, revised:

VAIN FORTUNE | A NOVEL BY | GEORGE MOORE | WITH FIVE ILLUSTRATIONS By | MAURICE GREIFFENHAGEN | NEW EDI-TION | COMPLETELY | REVISED | LONDON: WALTER SCOTT, LTD. | PATERNOSTER SQUARE | 1895

Published March at 3/6 in an edition of about 700 copies

$7\frac{5}{16}$ x $4\frac{7}{8}$; [a]^4, A-R^8, S^4; pp viii, 280, (plus five inserted plates facing title-page and pp 28, 48, 116, 194) [5], comprising: half-title, with list of nine titles BY THE SAME AUTHOR. within single-rule box on verso, pp [i-ii]; title-page as above, with "Edinburgh: T. and A. CONSTABLE, Printers to Her Majesty" at foot of verso, pp [iii-iv]; PREFATORY NOTE pp v-vii; p [viii] blank; text pp 1-[272] with "Printed by T. and A. CONSTABLE, Printers to Her Majesty | at the Edinburgh University Press" at foot p [272]; publisher's advertisements pp [273-80]; followed by inserted 16-page catalogue of publisher's advertisements; endpapers black where facing; bound in dark red cloth, back cover plain, double-rule border in blind at outer edges of front cover which is gilt lettered VAIN FORTUNE | A NOVEL BY | GEORGE MOORE | WITH FIVE ILLUSTRATIONS By | MAURICE GREIFFENHAGEN and spine gilt lettered VAIN | FORTUNE | A REALISTIC | NOVEL | [rule] | GEORGE MOORE | NEW EDITION | WALTER SCOTT

There are three issues of this edition: (1) As above. (2) As above, except for binding, which is green, back cover plain, single-rule border in blind at outer edges of front cover with wreath in blind in center, spine gilt lettered as above, but publisher's imprint at foot changed to SCOTT PUBLISHING CO. | LIMITED. (3) As above, except inserted illustrations other than frontispiece, gathering S (advertisements) and publisher's inserted catalogue are omitted; bound in dark red cloth, back and front covers plain, and spine gilt lettered as above, but with publisher's imprint changed to WALTER SCOTT | PUBLISHING CO.

Contents:

GM tells in the "Prefatory Note" of rewriting *Vain Fortune* and says "the inclusion of the hundred or more pages of new matter written for the American edition (b above) led me into a third revision of the story. But no more than in the second has the skeleton, or the attitude of the skeleton been altered in this third version, only flesh and muscle have been added, and, I think, a little life."

See D:Du-3 for Dutch translation. No trace has been found of the French translation by the Rosny brothers in REVUE HEBDOMADAIRE mentioned by Hone (p 174).[6]

5. The plates are five of the eleven illustrations used in first edition and are, respectively, the same as those facing pp 293 and 35, the frontispiece, the one facing p 101, and the one printed in the text on p 202 of that edition (a above).

6. Georges-Paul Collet in *George Moore et La France* (B57) also lists this translation and gives 1893 as the date of its publication. When questioned he stated that he had seen it; however, a search in the Boston Public Library of a file of REVUE HEBDOMADAIRE for that year failed to locate it; and nothing by GM is listed in the periodical's Table Générale for 1892–97.

A17
Modern Painting

a First edition:

MODERN | PAINTING | By GEORGE MOORE | LONDON | WALTER SCOTT, LIMITED | 24 WARWICK LANE | 1893

Published May at 6/-

7¼ x 4⅞; [a]² (tipped in), [b]¹ (tipped in), 1-16⁸; pp [vi], 256, comprising: half-title, with list of five titles BY THE SAME AUTHOR on verso, pp [i-ii]; title-page as above, with author's note on verso, pp [iii-iv]; table of CONTENTS, verso blank, pp [v-vi]; text pp 1-248, with THE WALTER SCOTT PRESS, NEWCASTLE-ON-TYNE at foot of p 248; publisher's advertisements, pp [249-56]; followed by a 16-page undated catalogue of publisher's advertisements on different paper from rest of book; endpapers black where facing; top edges gilt, fore and bottom edges trimmed; bound in dark red cloth, back and front covers plain, spine gilt lettered MODERN | PAINTING | GEORGE MOORE | WALTER SCOTT, LTD.

Contents:

Each section was originally published as an article, or is a combination of articles, all of which, with one exception, appeared in THE SPEAKER, where from 21 March 1891 to 23 November 1895 GM served as art critic.

"Whistler," from "Society of Portrait Painters" (11 July 1891), "Mr. Whistler: The Man and His Art" (26 March 1892), and "Mr. Whistler's Portraits" (2 and 9 April 1892). "Chavannes, Millet, and Manet" from "Art (Manet)" (16 July 1892), "Handling" (30 July 1892), and "A Hint for Manchester and Glasgow" (6 August 1892). "The Failure of the Nineteenth Century" from "The Subject" (14 November 1891), and "Curiosity in Art" (21 November 1891). "Artistic Education in France and England" from "More About Artistic Education" (6 February 1892). "Ingres and Corot" from "Corot" (20 August 1892), and "Values" (27 August 1892). "Monet, Sisley, Pissarro, and the Decadence" from "Decadence" (3 September 1892), and "The Division of Tones" (10 September 1892). "Our Academicians" from "Mr. G. F. Watts" (19 November 1892), and "The Royal Academy Exhibition, 1892" in FORTNIGHTLY REVIEW, June 1892. "The Organisation of Art" (17 September 1892). "Art and Science" (19 March 1892). "Royalty in Art" (12 December 1891). "Art Patrons" (27 June 1891). "Picture Dealers" (12 November 1892). "Mr. Burne-Jones and the Academy," two letters "To the Editor," one by R.I. (19 November), and the other by G.M. (26 November 1892). "The Alderman in Art" from "Rival Cities" (15 October 1892), and "The Alderman in Art" (22 and 29 October 1892). "Religiosity in Art" (28 November 1891). "The Camera in

Art" (16 May 1891). "The New English Art Club" from two articles of same title (26 November and 3 December), "The Glasgow School" (10 December), and "Mr. Brabazon" (17 December 1892). "A Great Artist" (4 April 1891). "Sex in Art" (18 and 25 June 1892). "The New Art Criticism" (25 March, 1 and 8 April 1893).

Later issues have endpapers dark green where facing, and the inserted catalogue of publisher's advertisements sometimes lists "Second Edition" [*sic*] of *Modern Painting* on p [1] and again on p [14] where *Esther Waters*, which was not published until March 1894, is also listed.

Sheets and binding syle of first edition, with publisher's imprint on title-page and spine changed, were used for an American edition:

a2 — Charles Scribner's Sons, New York, 1893. Copies are found with endpapers both black and dark green where facing.

b — Second edition, enlarged:

MODERN | PAINTING | By GEORGE MOORE | NEW EDITION, EN-LARGED | LONDON: | Walter Scott, Limited | Paternoster Square | 1897

Published autumn 1896

7¼ x 4⅞; [ ]⁴, 1-18 ⁸; pp [viii], 288, comprising: half-title with list of eight books BY THE SAME AUTHOR. on verso, pp [i-ii]; inserted plate of reproduction of "Portrait by Manet." and facsimile signature George Moore on verso, not paginated; title-page as above, with THE WALTER SCOTT PRESS, NEWCASTLE-ON-TYNE. on verso, pp [iii-iv]; dedication TO SIR WILLIAM EDEN, BART., with author's note as in first edition (a above) on verso, pp [v-vi]; table of CONTENTS, verso blank, pp [vii-viii]; text pp 1-288; followed by 16-page publisher's catalogue; white endpapers; top edges gilt, fore and bottom edges trimmed; bound in dark red cloth, back and front covers plain, spine gilt lettered MODERN | PAINT-ING | [*rule*] | GEORGE MOORE | NEW EDITION. | WALTER SCOTT, LTD.

Contents:

Text same as first edition, with additions reprinted from THE SPEAKER. "Nationality in Art," inserted between "A Great Artist" and "Sex in Art." "Mr. Steer's Exhibition" (3 March 1894). "Claude Monet" (15 June 1895). "Notes" — "Mr. Mark Fisher" (29 June 1895), "A Portrait by Mr. Sargent" from "A Portrait in the New Gallery" (6 May 1893), "An Orchid by Mr. James" (17 June 1893), "The Whistler Album" (16 December 1893), "Ingres" from "The National Gallery II" (16 September 1893). "Some Japanese Prints" from "The Genius of Japan" (10 February 1894). [Above eight articles inserted between "Sex in Art" and " The New Art Criticism."] "Long Ago in Italy."

Sheets of later impressions, with preliminaries reset, were used for editions issued by two American publishers:

b2 — Charles Scribner's Sons, New York, 1898; another impression 1900.

b3 — Brentano's, New York, circa 1913. The text of the expanded edition, with the addition of "Degas" from *Impressions and Opinions* (A15), was used for:

b4 — Carra Edition, Volume XIX, Boni and Liveright, New York, 1923. There is a tipped-in frontispiece, protected by a tissue guard sheet, which is lettered in red at foot of verso GEORGE MOORE | From a drawing by William H. Rothenstein

See D:Cz-2 for a presumed Czech translation.

A18

The Strike at Arlingford

a First edition:

THE STRIKE AT | ARLINGFORD | PLAY IN THREE ACTS | By GEORGE MOORE | LONDON | WALTER SCOTT, LIMITED | 24 WARWICK LANE | 1893

Published June at 5/-

7¼ x 4⅞; 1-11 ⁸, [12] ¹ (tipped in); pp 178, comprising: half-title, verso blank, pp [1-2]; title-page as above, verso blank, pp [3-4]; author's NOTE., verso blank, pp [5-6]; cast of CHARACTERS., verso blank, pp [7-8]; text pp [9]-175, with THE WALTER SCOTT PRESS, NEW-CASTLE-ON-TYNE. at foot p 175; p [176] blank; publisher's advertisements of works by GM pp [177-78]; endpapers dark olive green where facing; all edges trimmed, top edges gilt; bound in dark red cloth, back cover plain, front cover decorated with three gilt double-rule boxes, concentrically arranged, with center one embellished with scallops and fan-like decorations at corners,¹ spine gilt stamped: The | Strike at | Arlingford | PLAY IN THREE ACTS | [*rule*] | George Moore | [*all within single-rule border with scallop design at top and bottom*] | WALTER SCOTT

Contents:

Written for production by the Independent Theatre Society,² which presented the play 21 February 1893 "at the long since vanished Opera Comique in the Strand," according to Hone (p 182). Originally the play was written

1. The stamping on front cover is from a design by Albert Moore. GM was particularly pleased with it and the same design, in blind, was used on the front covers of the Heinemann standard binding, beginning in 1906 with the first edition of *Memoirs of My Dead Life* (A29-a).

2. Chapter I of *Ave* (A31:I-a) and Hone (pp 181-2) give details of the wager with G. R. Sims which led to the readying of the play for production.

in five acts [3] and later reduced to three with the assistance of Arthur Kennedy,[4] an old friend. The poem in act III, represented as being from a book of verse by John Reid, one of the principal characters, is a revision of the first sixteen lines of "Ballad of a Lost Soul" previously printed in both *Flowers of Passion* (A1) and *Pagan Poems* (A3).

Sheets and binding of this edition, with the addition of the American publisher's catalogue of imported books inserted at the end and their imprint substituted at foot of spine, were used for:

a2 — Charles Scribner's Sons, New York, 1893

GM's correspondence of this period mentions the play being translated into French by Edouard Dujardin, but no mention of a production or publication has been located.

A19
Esther Waters

a First edition:

ESTHER WATERS | A Novel | BY | GEORGE MOORE | LONDON | WALTER SCOTT, LTD. | 24 WARWICK LANE. PATERNOSTER ROW | 1894

Published March at 6/-

$7\frac{1}{4}$ x $4\frac{3}{4}$; [a]^1 (tipped in), [b]^2 (tipped in), 1-23^8, 24^6; pp [vi], 380, comprising: blank page, with list of six books BY THE SAME AUTHOR on verso, pp [i-ii]; title-page as above, verso blank, pp [iii-iv]; dedication "To My Brother | Major Maurice Moore, | I Affectionately Dedicate | this Book.", verso blank, pp [v-vi]; text pp 1-377, with THE WALTER SCOTT PRESS, NEWCASTLE-ON-TYNE. at foot of p 377; p [378] blank; publisher's advertisements of works by GM pp [379-80]; followed by 16-page undated catalogue of publisher's advertisements;[1] endpapers maroon where facing; all edges trimmed, top edges gilt; bound in dark green cloth, back and front

3. The manuscript of this version is in the Columbia University Library in New York.

4. In a letter to the Marquise Clara Lanza (quoted in "My Friendship with George Moore, Three Thousand Miles Away," by Madame Lanza in THE BOOKMAN, New York, July 1918) GM wrote, "It is a great play . . . but of course Kennedy has helped me a lot. Had it not been for him I could never have done it, for while I can describe a scene in a novel, I cannot write a scene in dialogue."

1. Listing the Scott Library pp [1-6]; Great Writers pp [7-10], The Contemporary Science Series pp [11-13], Books at 3/6 p [14], The England Library p [15], and Library of Humor p [16].

covers plain, spine gilt lettered ESTHER WATERS | A NOVEL | GEORGE MOORE | WALTER SCOTT

Contents:

Passages from the Life of a Workgirl, an early version[2] of chapters XX-XIII, XXV-XXVII, and XXIX was serialized in eleven installments in THE PALL MALL GAZETTE, 2-4, 6-7, and 9-14 October 1893. This version is divided into ten chapters and starts with the Bingleys after Esther has met William, been seduced, and is pregnant.

In May a second impression, advertised as "Second Edition," was issued, and this and subsequent impressions have the front cover lettered in gilt at top ESTHER WATERS | A NOVEL | GEORGE MOORE and a spray of flowers in gilt in lower left corner.[3] Copies of these impressions have endpapers where facing in various tones of deep blue.

Proofs of the Scott edition were submitted to, and rejected by, Harper's, Scribner's, and Appleton's for American publication. In June 1894, following the success of *Esther Waters* in England, copies of the second impression were imported for distribution in the United States and these can be distinguished by the rubber stamping, "Printed in Great Britain," on verso of title-leaf.

Two American editions were reproduced from sheets of the first edition; one (a2 below), contemporary with it, was duplicated by some early photo-lithographic process, and the other (a3 below) was reproduced sixty-four years later by photo-offset for a padded, paperbound edition:

a2 — Charles H. Sergel Company, Chicago, May or June[4] 1894, issued in cloth and also, according to contemporary advertisements, in wrappers, but no wrappered copy has been located.

a3 — Norton Library, No. 6, W. W. Norton & Company, Inc., New York, 1958, with an "Introduction" by Malcolm Brown and a short biographical sketch of GM, with his picture, on back cover. The first edition text was also used for:

2a — English Library, two volumes, Nos. 198 and 199, Heinemann and Balestier, Leipzig, 1894; a "Copyright Edition," similar in format to the Tauchnitz volumes, issued for continental circulation.

2. Differences between the serial and first edition texts are detailed by Jay Jernigan in an extended note, "The Forgotten Serial Version of George Moore's *Esther Waters*," in NINETEENTH-CENTURY FICTION, June 1968.

3. The "second issue" noted by Percy Muir in *Points 1874–1930* is actually this second impression, and it should be noted that the advertisements correctly cited by him for the "first issue" are also found in some copies of the second impression.

4. Noted by Lucy Monroe in "Chicago Letter" in THE CRITIC, 23 June, and reviewed in LITERARY WORLD (Boston), 30 June. Both refer to it as an "authorized edition," a doubtful statement, but one which may have been printed on the dust jacket or on the cover of the unlocated wrappered copies.

3a, 4a, and **5a** — In the United States the loss of copyright, due to there being no authorized American printing, simultaneous with the English first edition, coupled with the book's success in England, brought the pirate publishers swarming in and within a short time there were more than twenty reprints on the market. In addition to the Sergel edition (a2 above), there were printings from three distinct setting of type of 350,[5] 328,[6] and 322 [7] pages of text, respectively, with no positive priority established. Plates of these three settings were used for several years by a number of publishers who issued impressions in numerous bindings, both cloth and wrappers, and at various prices.[8]

b Second English edition, revised:

ESTHER WATERS | A NOVEL. | BY | GEORGE MOORE | LONDON: | WALTER SCOTT, LIMITED, PATERNOSTER SQUARE. | 1899

Published May at -/6

8¼ x 5½; A-F[16]; pp 182, x, comprising: page of commercial advertisements, with list of nine books "By the same Author." within single-rule box on verso, pp [1-2]; title-page as above, verso blank; pp [3-4]; dedication as in first edition (a above), verso blank, pp [5-6]; PREFACE., verso blank, pp [7-8]; text, two columns to the page, pp [9]-182, with WALTER SCOTT PRESS, NEWCASTLE-UPON-TYNE. at foot of p 182; publisher's advertisements pp i-x; no endpapers; wire stapled; issued in off-white wrappers, with commercial advertisements pp [2-4]; lettered in brown on front cover PRICE SIXPENCE [*underlined with rule*] | Esther Waters | A NOVEL | BY | GEORGE MOORE [*triangular printer's ornament*] | London: | WALTER SCOTT, LIMITED, | PATERNOSTER SQUARE. [*all within triple-rule border, heavy rule with fine on each side*] and lettered down the spine in brown ESTHER WATERS. GEORGE MOORE.

5. Including an issue in The Melburne Series, No. 23, E. A. Weeks & Company, Chicago, May [*sic* — see A5-n5] 1894; and one published by The Hennberry Company, Chicago, n.d.

6. Including issues in Hurst's Library, No. 7, 25 June 1894; Munro's Library of Popular Novels, No. 2, 7 July 1894; and Ogilvie's Peerless Series, No. 79, July 1894.

7. Including issues in Abbey Series, No. 53, W. B. Conkey Company, Chicago, n.d.; same, No. 123, Homewood Publishing Company, Chicago, n.d.; Rosebud Edition, Optimus Printing Company, New York, n.d.; Souvenir Edition, No. 10, Optimus, n.d.; Paragon Library, No. 2, Optimus (an advertisement for this edition describes *Esther Waters* as the *Uncle Tom's Cabin* of the white slaves of London); and also impressions issued by Henry Altemus, Philadelphia, 1895; Hurst; Conkey (differing from Abbey Series above), circa 1901 or later as *Sister Theresa* [*sic*] is listed on title-page.

8. In addition to the various impressions noted specifically with 350, 328, or 322 pages of text, references have been noted of additional printings, with no indication of the number of pages, including further impressions published by Hurst, and by Optimus, as well as those issued by Nobel; Hill; Stein, 1899; and Donahue, 1904.

Contents:

The text is revised and in part rewritten, the revisions being for the most part omission of passages, including much of chapter XXXIV, with only a few sentences added. In the "Preface," which is completely new, GM says, "The text of the original edition of *Esther Waters* was achieved largely on the proof-sheets . . . and on reading my book its general proportions, its architecture, seemed to me superior to the mere writing . . . and it has been love's labour to try to finish what I had left unfinished." [9]

2b First authorized American edition:

Esther Waters | A NOVEL | BY | GEORGE MOORE | REVISED AND ENLARGED EDITION | [*publisher's device in red*] | HERBERT S. STONE AND COMPANY | CHICAGO AND NEW YORK | MDCCCXCIX [*all within double-rule border*]

Published 9 December [10] 1899 at $1.50

7½ x 4¾; [1]⁴, [2]² (tipped in), [3]¹ (tipped in), [4-35]⁸: pp [4], x, 512, comprising: two blank leaves, not paginated; half-title, verso blank, pp [i-ii]; title-page as above, with COPYRIGHT 1899, BY | HERBERT S. STONE & CO | ALL RIGHTS RESERVED in center of upper half of verso, pp [iii-iv]; PREFACE pp v-ix; p [x] blank; text pp 1-508; PRINTED BY R. R. DONNELLEY | AND SONS COMPANY AT THE | LAKESIDE PRESS, CHICAGO, ILL. in center of p [509]; pp [510-12] blank; white endpapers; top edges trimmed and gilt, fore and bottom edges untrimmed; bound in dark blue cloth, flat spine, back and front covers silver stamped ESTHER WATERS | by [*tail of* y *circles around* b] GEORGE MOORE | [*two printer's fleurets*] | [*single fleuret*] [*all within single-rule border*] and spine silver stamped ESTHER | WATERS | by [*as on covers*] | GEORGE | MOORE | Stone | Chicago [*with rule at top and bottom of spine*]

Contents:

Text same as revised English edition (b above) with "Preface" enlarged. In 1901 a second impression was issued, in slightly smaller format, all

9. For a detailed account of the revisions see Appendix I of the edition edited by Lionel Stevenson (3b below).

10. According to Sidney Kramer in the historical portion of *A History of Stone & Kimball and Herbert S. Stone & Co., With a Bibliography of Their Publications*, University of Chicago Press, 1940, who says of this edition, "publication was delayed from April 10th, when 192 pages were deposited for copyright by Stone in the Library of Congress, until December 9, 1899, when the complete work was entered in the 'Weekly Record of New Publications' of PUBLISHER'S WEEKLY." In the bibliographical section, however, he states, ". . . published sometime in 1899; advertised as 'Ready May 12' in PUBLISHER'S WEEKLY." Mr. Kramer also says, in the historical section, "When a cheap edition of *Esther Waters* . . . was called for in England in 1899, Moore rewrote large sections . . . [and] in sending proofs of the new English edition (published in May 1896 [*sic*] by Walter Scott) to America, Moore rewrote again" a statement not borne out by a comparison of the two texts. The binding is pictured in Fig. 31 of the Kramer book.

edges trimmed, bound in bright red cloth, back cover plain, ornamental border and center design stamped in green on front cover, spine lettered in green as in first impression, but without rules at top and bottom.

In March 1906 the booklist and plates of Herbert S. Stone and Company, including *Esther Waters*, were sold to a New York firm which issued a new impression in a format similar to the original Stone edition:

2b2 — Duffield and Company, New York, July 1906; reprinted 1913. These Stone-Duffield plates again were used for:

2b3 — Brentano Uniform Edition, New York, 1917, which was replaced in the series in 1921 by a new impression with further textual revisions (c3 below). The revised second edition (b) text was used for a paperbound padded edition:

3b — Riverside Editions, B80, Houghton Mifflin Company, Boston, The Riverside Press, Cambridge, June 1963, with an "Introduction" and textual analysis by Professor Lionel Stevenson [11] of Duke University.

c Third English edition, revised:

ESTHER WATERS | AN ENGLISH STORY | BY | GEORGE MOORE | 19 [*publisher's windmill device*] 20 | [*rule, which also is base of device*] | LONDON: WILLIAM HEINEMANN

Published June 1920 at 7/6

7⅜ x 4¾; [A]⁴, B-2D⁸: pp [2], vi, 416, comprising: blank leaf,[12] not paginated; half-title, with list of books "By the Same Author" on verso, pp [i-ii]; title-page as above, verso blank, pp [iii-iv]; EPISTLE DEDICATORY | [*to*] MY DEAR ROLLESTON pp v-vi; text pp [1]-415, with BILLING AND SONS, LTD., PRINTERS, GUILDFORD, ENGLAND. at foot of p 415; p [416] blank [13] white endpapers; top and fore edges trimmed, bottom edges rough trimmed; bound in dark blue cloth, publisher's monogram in

11. Who, in explaining why the 1899 text was used for this edition, says, "It has seemed advisable . . . to allow Moore the advantage of his first revision, which was mainly confined to the elimination of errors and awkwardnesses, and at the same time to retain the freshness which was partly obliterated by the more sophisticated changes made twenty years later. The most important of the final changes are listed in the appendix along with the principal variations between the present text and its predecessor. In the text a few obvious misprints have been corrected by reverting to the readings of the first edition." The editorial analysis and the two appendices, detailing textual differences between the editions of 1894 and 1899 and the editions of 1899 and 1920, makes this the most scholarly and at the same time the closest to a variorum edition of any of GM's works so far issued for the general reader.

12. Some copies, possibly issued in advance for review purposes, are without this blank leaf, and its conjugate leaf ([A]₄), containing the "Epistle Dedicatory," is tipped in. The page size in these copies is smaller (7⅛ x 4¼); all edges are trimmed; the back and front covers are plain and the spine is gilt stamped ESTHER | WA-TERS | GEORGE | MOORE | HEINEMANN [*with double rule at top and bottom*]

13. Some copies have an inserted 56-page publisher's catalogue of "Books actually in print, AUTUMN, 1919."

blind in lower right corner of back cover, front cover blind stamped with large elongated paneled design enclosed within double-rule border, spine gilt stamped ESTHER | WATERS | GEORGE | MOORE [*all enclosed within thin single-rule border with scallop-shaped design at top and bottom*] | HEINEMANN

Contents:

The "Epistle Dedicatory" is new and text is completely revised.[14]

Further impressions issued in 1920, 1922, 1923, 1925, 1926,[15] 1928, 1929, 1931, and 1936, with some copies of the latter impression issued in three-quarter leather binding.

c2 Limited edition impression of third English edition:

ESTHER WATERS | BY | GEORGE MOORE | LONDON | PRIVATELY PRINTED FOR SUBSCRIBERS ONLY BY | Cumann Sean-eolais na h-Eireann [*in Gaelic characters*] | 1920

Issued[16] October

8¾ x 5¾; [A]⁴, [a]¹ (tipped in), B-2D⁸; pp [4], vi, 416, comprising: blank leaf, not paginated; half-title, with list of five books "By GEORGE MOORE" on verso, not paginated; title-page as above, verso blank, pp [i-ii]; notice of limitation as below, verso blank, pp [iii-iv]; EPISTLE DEDICATORY pp v-vi; text pp [1]-415, with BILLING AND SONS, LTD., PRINTERS, GUILDFORD, ENGLAND. at foot of p 415; p [416] blank; pale blue endpapers; top edges trimmed, fore and bottom edges untrimmed; blue paper covered board sides, matching endpapers, white parchment spine with white paper label lettered in brown: Esther | Waters | [*printer's ornament*] | GEORGE | MOORE | Privately | Printed

Notice of limitation:

This edition consists of 750 copies | numbered and signed. | This is No. . . . . . [*numbered in ink*][17] | George Moore [*signed in ink*]

Contents:

Text same as third English edition (c above), the plates of which were used for this impression.[18] Sheets of the regular edition, omitting the "Epistle Dedicatory," were used for:

14. For an account of the revisions see Appendix II of the edition edited by Lionel Stevenson (3b above).

15. Slight revisions of a comparatively few words were made for the 1926 impressions. Jay Jernigan, with the use of a Hinman collator, found "70 one or two word emendations . . . scattered throughout the book." This emended text was used for subsequent impressions and editions.

16. See A32-n1.

17. There were also nine "over" copies, numbered rather than marked "Out of Series" as is customary.

18. GM, in a letter to R. D. Main, published in the TIMES LITERARY SUPPLEMENT, 17 March 1921, explains why these plates were used, rather than having the text hand-set as in other of his works issued in limited editions.

c3 — Brentano Uniform Edition, New York, 1921, replacing the earlier text (2b3) originally used for the series. Sheets of a later impression of the English edition, this time including the "Epistle Dedicatory," were imported and issued in the series in 1931. The complete revised text was used for at least nine further editions:

2c — Carra Edition, Volume V, Boni and Liveright, New York, 1922. There is a tipped-in frontispiece, protected by a tissue guard lettered in red at foot of verso GEORGE MOORE | From a Painting by Mark Fisher, A.R.A.

3c — Black and Gold Library, Liveright, Inc., New York, 24 June 1932, which includes for the first time "A Colloquy: George Moore and Esther Waters," [19] a revision of "Esther Waters and Mr. Moore" published in THE OBSERVER, 21 February 1932.

4c — Uniform Edition, Heinemann, London, October 1932. Second impression 1936. Reissued in a different binding as:

4c2 — Ebury Edition, Heinemann, February 1938.

5c — Everyman's Library, No. 933, Dent, London, 1936, with an "Introductory Note" by C.D. Medley, GM's literary executor, and a list of GM's works with dates of first appearance in book form. Reprinted in 1951.

5c2 — Everyman's Library, 1962, partially reimposed and reissued in a larger format, with a new "Introduction" by Walter Allen replacing Medley's "Introductory Note."

6c — Penguin Books, No. 23, paperbound, London, 1936.

7c — Premier World Classics, No. d95, paperbound, Fawcett Publications, Inc., Greenwich, Conn., July 1960, with an "Introduction" by Bergen Evans, general editor of the series.

8c — The World's Classics, No. 594, Oxford University Press, London, 1964, with an "Introduction" by Graham Hough.

A dramatization of a portion of *Esther Waters* was published January 1913 as *Esther Waters: A Play in Five Acts* (A32).

See D:Da-1 for Danish; D:Fr-12 and D:Fr-26 for French; D:Ge-5 for German; D:It-3 and D:It-5 for Italian; D:Ru-2 for Russian; and D:Sw-1 for Swedish translations.

19. Also included in 4c, 4c2, 6c, 7c, and 8c.

A20

The Royal Academy 1895

a First edition:

"NEW BUDGET" EXTRAS. No. 1 | THE ROYAL ACADEMY | 1895 | [*wavy rule*] | Criticisms [*underlined with rule*] | BY GEORGE MOORE | Caricatures [*underlined with rule*] | BY HARRY FURNISS | Some of which appeared in THE NEW BUDGET | PRICE SIXPENCE | PUBLISHED AT THE OFFICE OF "THE NEW BUDGET" | 69 FLEET STREET, E.C. | 1895 | All rights reserved

Published May [1]

8 x 6; [ ]³²; pp 64, comprising: title-page as above, with commercial advertisement on verso, pp [1-2]; INDEX pp [3]-4; commercial advertisements pp [5-6]; "Criticisms" pp [7]-24; "Caricatures" pp 25-62; commercial advertisements pp [63-64]; no endpapers; all edges trimmed; wire stapled in center fold; issued in light green wrappers, with commercial advertisements pp [2-4], front cover printed in black: The New Budget Extra: No. 1 [*underlined with double rule*] | The Royal | ACADEMY [*these two lines in imitation of hand lettering*] | [*on left: reproduction of caricature on p 62, with date 1895 added on pedestal*] | No. 1701. HAMO THORNYCROFT, R.A. The New Woman Triumphant. | [*on right:*] Criticism [*underlined with double rule, lower one descending at right end*] | BY | GEORGE MOORE | [*three printer's ornaments*] | Caricatures [*underlined with double rule as above*] | BY | HARRY FURNISS | [*at bottom:*] PRICE SIXPENCE | PUBLISHING OFFICE: 69 FLEET STREET, E.C.

Contents:

The "Criticism" by GM first appeared as "The Royal Academy Exhibition" in THE NEW BUDGET, 9 May 1895.

A21

Celibates

a First edition:

CELIBATES | BY | GEORGE MOORE | LONDON: WALTER SCOTT, LTD. | PATERNOSTER SQUARE | 1895

Published June at 6/- in an edition of about 1,200 copies

7¼ x 4⅞; [ ]⁴, A-2M⁸; pp [viii], 560, comprising: half-title, with list of eight works BY THE SAME AUTHOR within single-rule box on verso,

---

1. Advertised as being "Now Ready" in THE NEW BUDGET, 16 May.

pp [i-ii]; title-page as above, verso blank, pp [iii-iv]; table of CONTENTS, verso blank, pp [v-vi]; sectional title, verso blank, pp [vii-viii]; text pp [1]-559, with sectional titles, versos blank, pp [313-14] and [453-54], and "Printed by T. and A. CONSTABLE, Printers to Her Majesty | at the Edinburgh University Press" at foot p 559; p [560] blank; followed by an 8-page gathering of publisher's advertisements (signed S on recto of first leaf); endpapers dark blue where facing; all edges trimmed, top edges gilt; bound in red ribbed cloth, back cover plain, front cover gilt lettered CELIBATES | BY | GEORGE MOORE and spine gilt stamped [*double rule*] | [*double rule*] | CELIBATES | BY | GEORGE MOORE | [*double rule*] | WALTER SCOTT | [*triple rule*]

Contents:

"Mildred Lawson," sections XIV-XVII revised from "An Art Student" in TODAY, Spring 1895; "John Norton," revised and condensed from *A Mere Accident* (A10); "Agnes Lahens," previously unpublished.

Sheets of this edition, including publisher's catalogue, were used for:

a2 — Colonial Edition, Scott Publishing Co., Ltd., London, 1895.

2a First American edition:

CELIBATES | BY | GEORGE MOORE | AUTHOR OF "ESTHER WATERS," ETC., ETC. | New York | MACMILLAN AND CO. | AND LONDON | 1895 | All rights reserved

Published July at $1.50

$7\frac{1}{16}$ x $4\frac{7}{8}$; B-2F^8, 2G^{10} (all signed on recto of leaf 5); pp viii, 460, comprising: half-title, with publisher's monogram on verso, pp [i-ii]; title-page as above, with "COPYRIGHT 1895, | BY MACMILLAN AND CO. | Norwood Press: | J.S. Cushing & Co. — Berwick & Smith. | Norwood, Mass., U.S.A." on verso, pp [iii-iv]; table of CONTENTS., verso blank, pp v-[vi]; sectional title, verso blank, pp [vii-viii]; text pp 1-453, with sectional titles, versos blank, pp [255-56] and [369-70]; p [454] blank; publisher's advertisements pp [455-58]; pp [459-60] blank; white endpapers; all edges trimmed; bound in grayish-green cloth, back cover plain, front cover gilt lettered within fancy decorative border of dark green CELIBATES | [*dark green ornament*] | GEORGE MOORE and spine gilt lettered CELIBATES | [*dark green ornament*] | MOORE | MACMILLAN & C° with fancy decorative border in dark green at top and bottom.

Contents:

Text same as first edition (a above).

Later issues have lettering on binding in black. Plates of this edition were used for:

2a2 — Brentano Uniform Edition, New York, 7 May 1915, which includes an "Introduction" by Temple Scott found in no other edition. The first edition text also was used for:

3a — Collection of British and American Authors,[1] Volume 3068, Bernhard Tauchnitz, Leipzig, 1895.

"Mildred Lawson" was rewritten as "Henrietta Marr" and included in *In Single Strictness* (A44), which was reissued as *Celibate Lives* (A52) with "Hugh Monfret" omitted. The latter story is a reworking, although not strictly a rewriting, of "John Norton."

See D:Cz-1 for Czech translation of "Mildred Lawson" and "John Norton"; D:No-1 and D:No-2 for Norwegian translations of "Agnes Lahens" and "John Norton"; and D:Ru-3 for a Russian translation of "Mildred Lawson." According to Stanislaus Joyce in *My Brother's Keeper*, New York, 1958 [p 98], James Joyce translated a "good part" of *Celibates* "into Italian while he was living in Trieste," but no record of publication has been located.

A 22

Evelyn Innes

a First edition:

EVELYN INNES [*red*] | BY | GEORGE MOORE | LONDON | T. FISHER UNWIN [*red*] | 1898

Published May at 6/- in an edition of 10,000 copies [1]

7⅞ x 4⅞; a[4], A-2G[8]; pp [viii], 480, comprising: blank page except for signature letter at foot, with list of twenty-five NOVELS AT SIX SHILLINGS EACH within single-rule box on verso, pp [i-ii]; half-title with publisher's monogram in center of verso, pp [iii-iv]; title-page as above with list of ten books BY THE SAME AUTHOR in center and "[All rights reserved.]" [2]

1. (A21). *Celibates* was the first of thirteen books by GM, issued in nineteen volumes, in this series. Other titles include *Evelyn Innes*, two volumes (A22-2a); *Sister Teresa*, two volumes (A25-2b); *The Untilled Field* (A26-b); *Confessions of a Young Man* (A12-2c); *The Lake* (A27-b); *Memoirs of My Dead Life* (A29-b); *Hail and Farewell*, three volumes (A31:I-3a, A31:II-3a, and A31:III-b); *Spring Days* (A13-2b); *The Brook Kerith*, two volumes (A35-3a); *Muslin*, two volumes (A34-2a); *The Coming of Gabrielle* (A39-b); and *Celibate Lives* (A52-3a).

1. (A22). According to an advertisement for the book in THE SATURDAY REVIEW, 11 June 1898; a later advertisement in the issue of 3 September gives the figure as 10,250 copies.

2. The final bracket is missing in some copies, possibly having been omitted in composition and corrected during printing, or vice versa. Its presence or absence, however, creates only a prepublication state and does not indicate any priority of issue. A variant of the first edition, noted in a single copy, has the first leaf (a₁) cancelled and has a remnant of a slip [3⅛ x ?], printed in red, tipped in before the publisher's catalogue. Another variant, a possibly unique copy, with the author's name

51

at foot of verso, pp [v-vi]; dedication TO | ARTHUR SYMONS AND W.B. YEATS | TWO CONTEMPORARY WRITERS | WITH WHOM | I AM IN SYMPATHY, verso blank, pp [vii-viii]; text pp [1]-480, with "Colston & Coy, Limited, Printers, Edinburgh." at foot of p 480; followed by an 8-page publisher's catalogue on same paper as rest of book; white endpapers; top edges gilt, all edges trimmed; bound in dark green ribbed cloth, front and back covers plain, spine gilt stamped EVELYN | INNES | GEORGE | MOORE [all within 2 x 1½-inch single-rule box] | T. FISHER UNWIN [type 1⅜ inches long, within ½ x 1½-inch single-rule box]

Contents:

Previously unpublished, although an "Editorial Note" by Arthur Symons in THE SAVOY, No. 3, July 1896, says, "arrangements are being made with Mr. George Moore for the serial publication of his new novel, 'Evelyn Innes'." The periodical, however, ceased publication before the story could appear in it. The complete first edition text was used for three other editions:

2a — Collection of British and American Authors, Volumes 3294 and 3295, Bernhard Tauchnitz, Leipzig, 1897.

3a — Carra Edition, Volume VI, Boni and Liveright, New York, 1923, with title spelled INNESS on spine label. There is a tipped-in frontispiece, protected by a tissue guard sheet, of a reproduction of S.C. Harrison's painting of GM.

4a — Benn's Essex Library, No. 1, Ernest Benn, Ltd., London, April 1929. The final revision of *Sister Teresa*, the continuation of *Evelyn Innes*, was used in this series (A25-3c), so that the reader passing from one to the other finds a disconnected narrative.

2a First American edition:

EVELYN INNES | BY | GEORGE MOORE | AUTHOR OF ESTHER WATERS | [publisher's device] | NEW YORK | D. APPLETON AND COMPANY | 1898

Published 2 June at $1.50

7⅜ x 4⅞; [1]⁸, 2-28⁸; pp [ii], 446, comprising: title-page as above, with COPYRIGHT, 1898, | BY D. APPLETON AND COMPANY. in center of verso, pp [i-ii]; text pp 1-435; p [436] blank; publisher's advertisements pp [437-46]; binder's flyleaves at front and back, white endpapers; all edges trimmed; bound in tan cloth, back cover plain, front cover stamped with reddish-brown decorative design, lettered in gilt in design EVELYN INNES | GEORGE | MOORE and spine gilt lettered EVELYN | INNES | [rule] | MOORE | [decorative design in reddish-brown] | APPLETONS

spelled MOOR on the spine, was listed in *Books of The "Nineties"* issued in 1932 by Elkin Mathews, Ltd., London, offering for sale the books collected by A. J. A. Symons in preparation for his never completed *Bibliography of the Writers & Illustrators of the Eighteen Nineties.*

Contents:

Text generally same as first edition (a above), but with a number of expurgations and deletions made by the publisher, and without some of the changes made by GM on the proofs of the first edition.

Later impressions issued in dark blue cloth. Plates of this edition were used for:

3a — Appleton Dollar Library,[3] D. Appleton and Company, New York, 1927.

b Second English edition:

Published August at 6/- in a format similar to first edition.[4]

$7\frac{7}{8}$ x $4\frac{7}{8}$; a^4, A-2G^8, 2H^2 (tipped in); pp [viii], 484, comprising: blank page except for signature letter at foot, with list of thirty-three NOVELS AT SIX SHILLINGS EACH within single-rule box on verso, pp [i-ii]; half-title with publisher's monogram on verso, pp [iii-iv]; title-page same as first edition (a above), with list of ten books BY THE SAME AUTHOR in center and "[All Rights Reserved.]" at foot of verso, pp [v-vi]; dedication as in first edition, verso blank, pp [vii-viii]; text pp [1]-482; "Colston & Coy., Limited, Printers, Edinburgh." in center of p [483]; p [484] blank; white endpapers; top edges gilt; all edges trimmed; bound in dark green ribbed cloth, back and front covers plain, spine gilt stamped EVELYN | INNES | GEORGE | MOORE [*all within 2 x 1*$\frac{5}{16}$*-inch single-rule box*] | T. FISHER UNWIN [*type slightly more than 1 inch long, within ½ x 1¼-inch single-rule box*]

Contents:

Text considerably revised from p 149 to end, with pp 149-50 containing new material, and other revisions on pp 184-86, 195, 244-45, 250, 252, 263-67, 302-3, and 340-41.

Cut down (7⅜ x 4⅝) sheets of this edition, without preliminary leaf with advertisements on verso, and with cancel undated title-page, printed in one color on heavier paper, verso blank, were issued in a horizontally ribbed purplish cloth, back and front covers plain, spine gilt lettered EVELYN | INNES | GEORGE MOORE

c Trial revised edition:

Twelve copies of what might be termed a "trial revised edition" of *Evelyn Innes* were prepared in October 1898, either by GM or under his supervision. These consisted of copies of the second edition (b above), corrected by the pasting over of certain pages with proofs of a revised text, and in some cases effecting deletions. Changes were made on pp 150-51, 184-88, 195, 239-40, 242, 244-45, 252, 263-67, 293-300, and 417-18. Also, in the

---

3. Also sometimes called Modern Literature Series.

4. Because of this similarity and identical title-page, and with no indication of a revised text, this edition is frequently confused with the first edition (a above), and is so listed by Danielson.

copies examined, various other changes are inked, or penciled, in Moore's handwriting, these varying from copy to copy.

Writing of this special "edition," in a letter to Edouard Dujardin dated 28 September 1898, GM said, "Next week at latest I hope to send you a copy of 'Evelyn Innes' with all the corrections — that is to say, the text of the third edition," and in a letter to William Butler Yeats dated 13 October 1898, he said, "At last I have finished 'Evelyn Innes' and I want to send you the revised edition; my revised edition exists only in an edition of 12 copies . . . I shall receive my little edition early next week and wish to send you a copy at once."

At about the same time GM wrote to Lady Cunard, "I have altered Evelyn Innes and enormously improved it — some of the alterations are in the second edition, but the more interesting alterations will not appear until the third edition. I will send you a copy, one of a dozen which I am having printed for myself. This little edition will be out next week."

GM again wrote Yeats, 28 October, saying, "I send you my revised Evelyn. You will find Ulick Dean rewritten everywhere. I wish you would compare page 184 to the end of the chapter with the original. Chapter 22 is entirely rewritten and in the intention of converting an episode into a symbol. Ulick's farewell letter did not satisfy me — I have written another — if the second does not satisfy you you must write a letter for Ulick yourself."

And on the fly-leaf of a copy sent 14 November to Edmund Gosse, GM wrote, "Here is one of my 12 copies of 'Evelyn Innes.' It contains all my emendations. If you, my dear critic, approve of these I propose to give them to the public in the next edition. The character of Ulick Dean you will find retouched everywhere."

When GM prepared the text for the third edition (d below), some of these "emendations" were used, but actually the rewriting was far more extensive.

d Third edition, revised:

EVELYN INNES | BY | GEORGE MOORE | POPULAR EDITION | LONDON | T. FISHER UNWIN | PATERNOSTER SQUARE, E.C.

Published 8 July 1901 at -/6

8⅜ x 5⅜; [1]^{16}, 2-6^{16}; pp 192, comprising: leaf of commercial advertisements, pp [1-2]; half-title, with publisher's advertisement for THREE POPULAR NOVELS within single-rule box on verso, pp [3-4]; title-page as above, with "All Rights Reserved" in center of verso, pp 5-6; PREFACE, verso blank, pp 7-[8]; text in double columns, pp 9-187, with "Mr. T. Fisher Unwin will publish shortly the sequel to this book under the title | 'SISTER TERESA.' Price Six Shillings." at bottom p 187; PRINTED BY MORRISON AND GIBB LIMITED, EDINBURGH in center p [188]; commercial advertisements p [189]; publisher's advertisements pp [190-92]; no endpapers; all edges trimmed; issued in bright green wrappers, with commercial advertisements pp [2-4]; front cover stamped in black: Evelyn Innes | By George Moore | 6d [*drawing of woman in evening dress and cape, within single-rule box indented at each side for price*] 6d | [*row of printer's ornaments*] | London: T. Fisher Unwin [*all within border of printer's ornaments, forming with row noted above a double compartment*], and lettered in black up the spine EVELYN INNES

Contents:

In the "Preface," which is new, GM explains the completely rewritten text, "I appreciated Mr. Unwin's idea of a sixpenny edition more than ever, for it has allowed me to remould *Evelyn Innes*. The story of course has not been altered, but the text is almost completely new. No one, perhaps, has rewritten a book so completely . . . the new version, notwithstanding many additions, is 90 pages shorter than the original." The first two paragraphs of the "Preface" are the same as the "Preface" printed with the first and Tauchnitz editions of *Sister Teresa* (A25-a and A25-b).

Reprinted January 1903.

e Fourth edition, revised:

EVELYN INNES | BY | GEORGE MOORE | AUTHOR OF "SISTER TERESA," "ESTHER WATERS," ETC. | Fourth Edition. Revised and Reset | LONDON | T. FISHER UNWIN | ADELPHI TERRACE | (All rights reserved)

Published April 1908 at -/6

8¾ x 5⅞; A-F^{16}; pp [ii], 190, comprising: commercial advertisements, pp [i-ii]; commercial advertisements, with publisher's advertisements for *Sister Teresa* on verso, pp [1-2]; half-title, with commercial advertisements on verso, pp [5-6]; text in double columns pp 7-172, [174, 176, 178, 180, 182, 184 (misnumbered 173-78)]; commercial advertisements pp [173, 175, 177, 179, 181, 183, 185-90]; no endpapers; all edges trimmed; issued in white paper wrappers, with commercial advertisements pp [2-4], front cover black, lettered in gray-green EVELYN INNES [*drawing of woman against striped background*] | M [*in a circle*] | GEORGE [*dot*] MOORE and lettered in black down spine EVELYN INNES GEORGE MOORE 6$^{D.}$

Contents:

As stated on title-page, this is a revised text, and GM explains that the book has undergone "a complete rewriting" in the entirely new "Preface" to the next edition which reprints this text:

2e — Adelphi Library,[5] T. Fisher Unwin, London, October 1908, including the new "Preface" which is found in no other edition.

See D:Ge-6 for a German translation. In letters to Dujardin of 12 October 1907 and 4 January 1908, GM speaks of recasting *Evelyn Innes* for Hach-

5. Matching the Adelphi Library edition of *Sister Teresa* (A25-c).

ette, the Paris publisher, and of sending proofs to be used for a translation, but no French translation has been located.

A23
The Bending of the Bough

a First edition:

The Bending of the Bough. | A Comedy in Five Acts. | By George Moore. [*double ornament*] | London | T. Fisher Unwin | Paternoster Square | 1900
    Published 21 February at 3/6
    7⅜ x 5; [1]¹⁰, 2-10⁸, 11⁶; pp xx, 156, comprising: half-title, with advertisement for *Evelyn Innes* within single-rule box on verso, pp [i-ii]; title-page as above, with "[All rights reserved.]" on verso, pp [iii-iv]; LIST OF CHARACTERS, verso blank, pp [v-vi]; PREFACE pp vii-xx; text pp [1]-153. with UNWIN BROTHERS, THE GRESHAM PRESS, WOKING AND LONDON. at foot p 153; pp [154-56] blank; white endpapers; all edges untrimmed; bound in blue ribbed cloth,[1] back cover plain, front cover gilt lettered THE BENDING OF THE BOUGH | GEORGE MOORE and spine gilt lettered THE | BENDING | OF THE | BOUGH | GEORGE | MOORE | T. Fisher Unwin
    Contents:
    "Preface" previously published in FORTNIGHTLY REVIEW, February 1900, and reprinted as a pamphlet (A24); *The Bending of the Bough*. As related in the "Preface," this is a rewriting of Edward Martyn's play, *The Tale of the Town*, and although only GM's name is on the title-page, William Butler Yeats also had a hand in the rewriting, as is shown in a letter[2] from him to AE (George Russell), where he says, "Moore told me he was going to tell you about *The Tale of a Town* — a great secret — and our changes in it. Moore has written a tremendous scene in the third act and I have worked on it here and there throughout. If Martyn will only consent, it will make an immense sensation and our theatre a national power." Martyn did consent, but with the stipulation that his name should not appear as either

1. There are extant at least two copies on a variant binding, one in dark red in the library of the American-Irish Historical Society in New York, and the other in brown in the collection of Dr. Ulrich Middeldorf; both have top edges gilt, front cover blind stamped with an elaborate decorative design, with the author's name in two lines in smaller type, and spine lettered as in usual binding.

2. Dated "Nov. [1899]" and published in *The Letters of W. B. Yeats*, edited by Allan Wade, London, and New York, 1955; previously published in DUBLIN MAGAZINE, July–September 1939.

author or co-author of the play,[3] which was produced by the Irish Literary Theatre at the Gaiety Theatre in Dublin, 19 February 1900.

In January, before the first edition was issued, GM requested that another 100 or 200 copies be printed,[4] incorporating changes made during rehearsals. This was done and copies of this second edition (b below) are scarcer than those of the first edition, and in consequence have sometimes been noted as examples of a rare first issue. The correct order of the two editions has been determined by a textual comparison of them with *The Tale of a Town*, which shows the progression of changes in the evolution of Martyn's play into *The Bending of the Bough*.

b Second edition, revised:

The Bending of the Bough. | A Comedy in Five Acts. | By George Moore. | London | T. Fisher Unwin | Paternoster Square | 1900

Published late February[5] at 3/6

7⅜ x 5; [1][10], 2-10[8], 11[2] (tipped in); pp xx, 148, comprising: half-title, with advertisement for *Evelyn Innes* within single-rule box on verso, pp [i-ii]; title-page as above, with "[All rights reserved.]" at foot of verso, pp [iii-iv]; LIST OF CHARACTERS, verso blank, pp [v-vi]; PREFACE pp vii-xx; text pp 1-145; "The Gresham Press | UNWIN BROTHERS, | WOKING AND LONDON." in center p [146]; blank leaf, pp [147-48]; white endpapers; all edges untrimmed; binding identical with first edition (a above).

Contents:

Text revised, incorporating many of the changes made for the American edition (c below), plus other revisions.

c First American edition, revised:

The | Bending of the Bough | A COMEDY IN FIVE ACTS | BY | GEORGE MOORE | HERBERT S. STONE & COMPANY | CHICAGO & NEW YORK | 1900 [*all against the silhouette of a tree in green*]

Published 21 April at $1.25

6¾ x 4¼; [1][4], [2-14][8], [15][4], [16][2] (tipped in); pp [4], xxvi, 198, comprising: two blank leaves, not paginated; half-title with "The Green Tree Library" at top, and with list of seven books in the series on verso, pp [i-ii]; title-page as above, with COPYRIGHT 1900 BY | HERBERT S. STONE & CO. in center of verso, pp [iii-iv]; LIST OF CHARACTERS, verso blank,

---

3. In 1902 Martyn published the play as originally written, with a prefatory note, "There was an adaption . . . made by George Moore, with my consent, for the Irish Literary Theatre performances." The original version was published with *An Enchanted Sea* at Kilkenny by Standish O'Grady and issued in London by T. Fisher Unwin.

4. In a letter to T. Fisher Unwin dated "23 January 1900."

5. In a letter dated "March 1st, 1900" GM wrote Unwin about buying a copy of the play and discovering it was the first edition, adding the hope that all of the second edition had not been sold.

pp [v-vi]; PREFACE pp vii-xxvi; text pp [1]-192; PRINTED BY R.R. DONNELLEY | AND SONS COMPANY AT THE | LAKESIDE PRESS, CHICAGO, ILL. in center p [193]; pp [194-98] blank; white endpapers; top edges gilt, fore and bottom edges untrimmed; bound in light green cloth, stamped with vertical purple lines and darker green outline of trees, both back and front covers gilt lettered THE | GREEN | TREE | LIBRARY | [ornament] and spine gilt lettered THE | BENDING | OF THE | BOUGH | BY | GEORGE | MOORE [lettering on spine and covers adjacent and all within single-rule purple box] [6]

Contents:

Text revised and is an intermediate state between the first and second editions (a and b above).

c2 — Second American edition:

In 1969 an edition of *The Bending of the Bough* was published as Vol. III, Irish Drama Series, edited by William J. Feeney, De Paul University, Chicago, with GM's "Preface" replaced by an "Introduction" by the editor detailing changes from Martyn's *The Tale of a Town* and the play's relationship to contemporary events in Ireland.

The text is a combination of the second Unwin (b above) and Stone (c above) editions with the textual variants in the latter printed in a different shade of ink and with the speeches remaining unchanged from Martyn's text indicated by an asterisk. Preference apparently is given to readings in Stone as the editor seems to indicate they are later, and in at least one instance in the first act four speeches present in the Unwin text are omitted.

A24

A Preface to "The Bending of the Bough"

a First separate edition:

A PREFACE | TO | "THE BENDING OF THE BOUGH" | By | GEORGE MOORE | [circular publisher's device, lettered around perimeter at top The Tucker Publishing Co. and at bottom New York enclosing a figure of the Goddess of Knowledge in a crouching position, with an ancient lamp in her left hand and her right hand on an open book which she appears to be reading, and with a scroll behind her lettered LIGHT, MORE LIGHT] | Office of Publication: | Rooms 2128-29-30-31, Park Row Building

Published 9 March 1900

8 x 5½; [ ][8]; pp 16, comprising: title-page as above, verso blank, pp

6. Binding of Green Tree Library shown in Fig. 24 (p 174) of *A History of Stone & Kimball and Herbert S. Stone & Company*, by Sidney Kramer, Chicago, 1940.

[1-2]; text pp 3-16; no endpapers; all edges trimmed; wire stapled in center fold; issued in olive wrappers, insides and back cover plain, front cover lettered in red within an ornamental design: The | Balzac | Library | A PREF-ACE | TO | "The Bending of the Bough" | By | GEORGE MOORE | [*publisher's monogram in the design*] | New York | The Tucker Pub. Co. | [*artist's lettered signature* Edward Dewsen 1900 *at bottom of design*] [*all of foregoing within single-rule border*] | [*in lower left corner:*] Six times a week | No. 7 — March 9, 1900 | [*and in lower right corner:*] Subscription, $10 a year

Contents:

Reprinted from FORTNIGHTLY REVIEW, February 1900; also previously printed with the play (A23). The text is apparently printed from type, but with no attempt to justify right margins. Copies of the pamphlets in this series were later gathered together and issued in four volumes by William Rickey, New York, n.d.[1]

A25

Sister Teresa

a First edition:

SISTER TERESA | BY | GEORGE MOORE | [*device of publisher's monogram on a shield, flanked by rampant lions*] | LONDON | T. FISHER UNWIN | PATERNOSTER SQUARE | 1901

Published 3 July at 6/-

7⅜ x 4⅞; a⁴, A-P⁸, [Q]⁴; pp vii, 248, comprising: blank leaf, except for signature letter at foot of recto, pp [i-ii]; half-title, with advertisements for A SIXPENNY EDITION OF | EVELYN INNES and THE BENDING OF THE | BOUGH within a single-rule three-compartment box on verso, pp [iii-iv]; inserted leaf of imitation Japanese vellum with reproduction of line drawing of GM (by Henry Tonks) and a facsimile inscription "Always yours | George Moore" on verso, not paginated; title-page as above, with "All Rights reserved" at foot of verso, pp [v-vi]; PREFACE pp vii-viii; text pp [1]-236, with "Colston & Coy. Limited, Printers, Edinburgh" at foot p 236; publisher's advertisements pp [237-47]; p [248] blank, white endpapers; top edges gilt; fore and bottom edges untrimmed; bound in dark green ribbed cloth,[1] back and front covers plain, spine gilt stamped SISTER | TERESA | BY | GEORGE | MOORE [*all within 2 x 1⁵⁄₁₆-inch single-rule box*] | T. FISHER UNWIN [*within 1⅜ x ½-inch single-rule box*]

1. (A24). Copies in the Fayant and the Gilcher collections.
1. (A25). Binding and format of this edition match the first and second editions of *Evelyn Innes* (A22-a, A22-b).

Contents:

The "Preface" is the same as the first two paragraphs of the "Preface" of the third English edition (A-22-d) of *Evelyn Innes*, and the text is a continuation of that novel. In the "Preface" GM says, "I will hope that it will be understood that this is really the second volume of a novel which is meant to be read under one name and within one cover, and which will perhaps be ultimately presented to the public under the single title of *Evelyn Innes*." Sheets of this edition, with verso of half-title and title-page reset, were used for:

a2 — Unwin's Colonial Library, London, 1901.

2a First American edition:

Sister Teresa | by | George Moore | [*publisher's device*] | Philadelphia | J. B. Lippincott Company | Mdcccci [*all within single-rule border*]

Published 3 August 1901 at $1.50

7½ x 4⅞; [1]^8, 2-23^8, [24]^8; pp 384, comprising: blank leaf pp [1-2]; half-title, verso blank, pp [3-4]; inserted glossy leaf with a reproduction of line drawing of GM (by Henry Tonks) and facsimile inscription "Always yours | George Moore" against an off-white background with hairline-rule border on verso, not paginated; title-page as above, with "Copyright, 1901 | By J. B. Lippincott Company" in center and "Electrotyped and Printed by | J. B. Lippincott Company, Philadelphia, U. S. A." at bottom of verso, pp [5-6]; text pp 7-378; pp [379-84] blank; white endpapers; all edges trimmed; bound in dark blue cloth, back cover plain, front cover gilt stamped with decorative design of double rules running both horizontally and vertically forming nine different sized compartments, with flower in upper left compartment, top center one gilt stamped SISTER TERESA | A NOVEL | By GEORGE MOORE, center one has elaborate design of smoking heart and swinging censer with initial H in lower left corner, right center one has flower at bottom, all other compartments plain, spine gilt lettered SISTER | TERESA | By | GEORGE MOORE | LIPPINC°TT

Contents:

Same as first edition (a above) but with "Preface" omitted. Plates of this edition were used for two further printings:

2a2 — Lippincott's Select Novels, Philadelphia, 4 June 1905, in wrappers at 50¢.

2a3 — Brentano Uniform Edition, New York, 11 November 1918. Copies later remaindered in medium blue cloth binding. The text of the first edition also was used for:

3a — Carra Edition, Volume VII, Boni and Liveright, New York, 1923. There is a tipped-in frontispiece, protected by a tissue guard sheet, of a reproduction of a painting of GM by William Orpen.

b Trial revised edition:

Twenty copies of what could be called a "trial revised edition" of *Sister Teresa*, similar to the twelve-copy special edition of *Evelyn Innes* (A22-c), seem to have been prepared for GM. In a letter[2] to Gosse, dated 30 July 1901, he wrote, "I intend to rewrite the first sixty or seventy pages. I am not attracted with the opening, and I send you a copy of 'Sister Teresa' containing a chapter and a few pages which do not appear in the current edition. I write as you know on the proof sheets and these additions were late for the press. The copy I am sending you is one of twenty copies." The copy presented to Gosse is not mentioned, however, in the Cox catalogue,[3] and no other copy definitely has been identified, although two copies of *Sister Teresa* in the University of Illinois Library, differing somewhat from the regular edition, may be examples of this special edition. Both are heavily annotated, possibly by GM for a subsequent edition, so much so that the binding of at least one has been broken by the insertion of many interleavings, and they agree in their changes with a set of proof pages in my possession of gathering M (pp 177-92) of an Unwin printing, showing changes[4] in this section corresponding with the "specially rewritten" text of the Tauchnitz edition:

2b — Collection of British Authors, Volumes 3535 and 3536, Bernhard Tauchnitz, Leipzig, November 1901.

c Second English, Adelphi Library, edition, rewritten:

SISTER | TERESA | BY | GEORGE MOORE | [*device*] | . . . LONDON . . . | T. FISHER UNWIN | ADELPHI TERRACE [*all within double-compartment frame, title being in the upper and the balance in the lower compartment, the complete frame resembling a classic door*]

Published June 1909 at 3/6

7¼ x 4¾; [1] [6] (signed * on recto of [1] $_3$; [1] $_1$ and [1] $_2$ are front endpapers, counted in pagination), 2-23 [8]; pp xii, 352, comprising: pastedown endpaper, with publisher's device on verso, pp [i-ii]; blank free endpaper pp [iii-iv]; half-title with THE ADELPHI LIBRARY in upper right corner, and with thirteen titles in the series (number 6 is *Sister Teresa*) listed in center compartment of three-compartment single-rule box on verso, pp [v-vi]; title-page as above, with "First Edition, 1901 | Second Edition (entirely rewritten), 1909" in center and "(All rights reserved.)" at bottom of verso, pp [vii-viii]; PREFACE pp ix-xii; text pp [1]-351; "The Gresham Press, | UNWIN BROTHERS, LIMITED, | WOKING AND LONDON" in center p [352]; white rear endpapers; all edges trimmed, top edges stained dark green; bound in red cloth, back cover plain, front cover gold lettered within

2. Now in the Duke University Library, Durham, North Carolina.

3. *The Library of Edmund Gosse* (B31).

4. Among the typographical changes are thirty-nine lines of text on pp 182, 184-87 and 189-91 instead of the forty lines found on these pages in the first edition, and on p 181 there are but two lines of chapter XXXI instead of the usual four.

single-rule blind stamped border SISTER | TERESA | GEORGE MOORE and spine gilt stamped [*decoration*] | SISTER | TERESA | [*decoration*] | GEORGE | MOORE | [*decoration*] | THE ADELPHI | LIBRARY [*the three words of series name within an elliptical border of dots*] | [*decoration*] | T. FISHER UNWIN [5]

Contents:

Text completely rewritten, "an entirely new book" according to GM's account in the "Preface," which is also new. This final revised text was used for two further editions:

2c — 6d edition, T. Fisher Unwin, London, August 1909, issued in paper wrappers and text printed in double columns.

3c — Benn's Essex Library, No. 13, Ernest Benn Ltd., London, August 1929. Although the revised text was used for this edition the original text of *Evelyn Innes*, of which *Sister Teresa* is a continuation, was used for its republication in this same series (A22-4a), so that the reader passing from one to the other finds a disconnected narrative.

See D:Ge-6 for a German translation.

A26

The Untilled Field

a First edition:

THE UNTILLED FIELD [*in red*] | BY | GEORGE MOORE. [*in red*] | LONDON | T. FISHER UNWIN [*red*] | PATERNOSTER SQUARE. | M·D·CCCC·III

Published 20 April 1903 at 6/-

7⅜ x 4⅞; [ ]⁴, [A]⁸, B-2C⁸, 2D⁴; pp [viii], 424, comprising: half-title, verso blank, pp [i-ii]; list of six NEW SIX SHILLING NOVELS. within single-rule box, with list of twelve books BY THE SAME AUTHOR. within single-rule box on verso, pp [iii-iv]; title-page as above, with "(All Rights Reserved.)" at foot of verso, pp [v-vi]; table of CONTENTS., verso blank, pp [vii-viii]; fly-titles for individual stories, versos blank, pp [1-2], [27-28], [117-18], [153-54], [175-76], [199-200], [221-22], [241-42], [259-60], [269-70], [279-80], [299-300], [395-96]; text pp 3-26, 29-115, 119-51, 155-73, 177-97, 201-20, 223-39, 243-57, 261-68, 271-77, 281-98, 301-93, 297-[420], with pp [116], [152], [174], [198], [240], [258], [278], [394] blank, and PRINTED BY SEALY, BRYERS AND WALKER, MID. AB-

5. The format of this edition matches The Adelphi Library edition of *Evelyn Innes* (A22-2e). In later states of the binding the front cover is plain and the spine is stamped in black.

BEY ST., DUBLIN. at foot of p [420]; publisher's advertisements pp [421-24]; white endpapers; top edges gilt, all edges trimmed; bound in bright red cloth, back cover plain, front cover blind stamped with decorative design of entwined leaves and publisher's monogram, gilt lettered THE | UNTILLED FIELD | BY GEORGE MOORE and spine gilt lettered THE | UNTILLED | FIELD | BY | GEORGE MOORE [*all within 2 x 1 5/16-inch single-rule gilt box*][1] | T. FISHER UNWIN [*within ½ x 1 5/16-inch single-rule gilt box*]

Contents: "In the Clay" previously unpublished. "Some Parishioners," an early version of section V, called "The Window" in later editions, originally published in a Gaelic version as "Naoim Aiteamail" (Local Saint) in *An T-Úr-Gort* (D:Ga-2). "The Exile" revised from Gaelic version published as "An Deoraide" in *An T-Úr-Gort*, and English version in HARPER'S WEEKLY, 20 September 1902, and PALL MALL MAGAZINE, October 1902. "Home Sickness" revised from Gaelic version published as "Galar Duitce" in *An T-Úr-Gort*, and English version in HARPER'S WEEKLY, 16 August 1902, and PALL MALL MAGAZINE, September 1902. "A Letter to Rome," previously unpublished. "Julia Cahill's Curse" revised from "The Golden Apples" in ENGLISH ILLUSTRATED MAGAZINE, April 1902. "A Play-house in the Waste" revised from Gaelic version published as " 'San n-Diotram Dub" (In the Dark Wilderness) in *An T-Úr-Gort*. "The Wedding Gown" revised from version published in ENGLISH ILLUSTRATED MAGAZINE, June 1902; a revision of the Gaelic version published as "An Guna-Posta" (D:Ga-1) in THE NEW IRELAND REVIEW, January 1902, and reprinted in *An T-Úr-Gort*; all a rewriting of "Grandmother's Wedding Gown" in LADY'S PICTORIAL, Christmas number, 1887. "The Clerk's Quest" revised from "Mr. Dumpty's Quest" published in both Gaelic (D:Ga-3) and English versions in THE NEW IRELAND REVIEW, November 1902; a revision of "Mr. Dumpty's Ideal" in ST. JAMES GAZETTE, 3 September 1890. "Alms-Giving" revised from version published in both Gaelic (D:Ga-4) and English in THE NEW IRELAND REVIEW, December 1902; a revision of "Charity" in THE SPEAKER, 6 July 1895; which was in turn a revision of the story as it appeared in THE SKETCH, 13 September 1893. "So On He Fares" previously unpublished. "The Wild Goose," an early version of final section originally published in Gaelic as "Tir-grad" (Patriotism) in *An T-Úr-Gort*. "The Way Back" previously unpublished.

Remainder sheets of the first edition were reissued in a variety of bindings, lettered in black on front cover and spine; and were also used, with a cancel title-leaf, for:

a2 — Bell's Indian and Colonial Library, No. 487, London, issued in both cloth and wrappers.

1. Thomas Warburton in NOTES AND QUERIES says there is a variant state of the spine lettering with the author's name on two lines instead of one, but no copy of this state has been located.

2a First American edition:

The [*red*] | Untilled Field [*red*] | [*double rule*] | BY | George Moore | AU-THOR OF "ESTHER WATERS," "EVELYN INNES," | "SISTER TERESA," ETC. | [*double rule*] | [*publisher's device in red*] | [*double rule*] | Philadelphia | J. B. Lippincott Company | 1903 | [*all within double-rule border, which with three double rules noted above form a four-compartment box*]

Published 13 June[2] at $1.50

7½ x 5⅛; [1]⁸, 2-24⁸; pp 384, comprising: half-title, with advertisement for *Sister Teresa* on verso, pp [1-2]; title-page as above, with: Copyright, 1903 | BY | J. B. LIPPINCOTT COMPANY | Published April, 1903 | in center and "Printed by | J. B. Lippincott Company, Philadelphia, U. S. A." at bottom of verso, pp [3-4]; table of CONTENTS, verso blank, pp 5-[6]; fly-titles for individual stories, versos blank, pp [7-8], [31-32], [111-12], [143-44], [163-64], [183-84], [203-4], [221-22], [237-38], [247-48], [255-56], [273-74], and [359-60], text pp 9-29, 33-109, 113-41, 145-61, 165-82, 185-202, 205-19, 223-35, 239-45, 249-54, 257-72, 275-358, and 361-81, with pp [30], [110], [142], [162], [220], [236,] and [246] blank; white endpapers; all edges trimmed; green head band; bound in medium green cloth, back cover plain, front cover stamped in white: The | Untilled | Field | [*entwined Celtic cross*] | George Moore [*all within double heavy-rule box, with initial H in lower left corner*] and spine stamped in white: The | Untilled | Field | by George | Moore | [*gilt harp of Erin*] | Lippincott [*double heavy rules at both top and bottom of spine*]

Contents:

Text varies from first edition (a above) and is very likely earlier, as it was probably set from proof pages of the Unwin edition before GM's customary last-minute revisions. Plates of this edition were used for:

2a2 — Brentano Uniform Edition, New York, 1917.

b Continental edition, revised:

THE | UNTILLED FIELD | BY | GEORGE MOORE | AUTHOR OF "CELIBATES," "SISTER TERESA," ETC. ETC. | COPYRIGHT EDI-TION | LEIPZIG | BERNHARD TAUCHNITZ | 1903

Published May

6½ x 4⅝; [1]⁸, 2-19⁸; pp 304, comprising: half-title, with list of three books "By the same Author" on verso, pp [1-2]; title-page as above, verso blank, pp [3-4]; dedicatory letter to MY DEAR JOHN EGLINTON pp [5]-6; table of CONTENTS., verso blank, pp [7-8]; text pp [9]-302; PRINT-ING OFFICE OF THE PUBLISHER. center p [303]; p [304] blank; followed by a 32-page inserted publisher's catalogue dated June 1, 1903.; no

2. According to copyright data in Library of Congress; the April date on verso of title-leaf may refer to publication of first edition (a above).

endpapers; all edges untrimmed; issued in cream paper wrappers, with publisher's lists pp [2-4]; front cover lettered in black including publisher's imprint, copyright notice, and VOL. 3656. | THE UNTILLED FIELD BY GEORGE MOORE. | IN ONE VOLUME. and spine stamped in black, with eight sets of double rules (heavy and light), two at top and two at bottom: BRITISH | AUTHORS | TAUCHNITZ | EDITION. | [*rules*] | VOL. 3656. | [*rules*] | G. MOORE | 6. | [*rules*] | THE | UNTILLED | FIELD. | [*rules*] | PRICE | M 1,60.

Contents:

In the dedicatory letter, dated "May, 1903," which is found in no other edition, GM says, "I have omitted two stories . . . and I have introduced many other little changes." The two omitted stories are "In the Clay" and "The Way Back", and among the changes, the section "Some Parishioners" is divided into four stories, with the first retaining the original title and the others retitled "Patchwork," "The Marriage Feast," and "The Window." Stories from this edition presumably were used for:

2b — *The Untilled Field: A Selection*, The Students Series, Leipzig, 1930. No copy located, but advertised in later Tauchnitz catalogues.

c Second English edition, revised:

THE | UNTILLED FIELD | BY | GEORGE MOORE | [*publisher's device of windmill, flanked by initials* W *and* H, *within single-rule border*] | LONDON | WILLIAM HEINEMANN

Published October 1914 at 6/-

7½ x 4¾ ; [ ]⁸, A-T⁸, U⁶; pp [2], xiv, 316, comprising: blank leaf, not paginated; half-title, with list of WORKS BY GEORGE MOORE on verso, pp [i-ii]; title-page as above, with "LONDON: WILLIAM HEINEMANN. 1914" at foot of verso, pp [iii-iv]; PREFACE pp v-xi (misnumbered x); p [xii] blank; table of CONTENTS, verso blank, pp xiii-[xiv]; text pp [1]-316, with BILLING AND SONS, LTD., PRINTERS, GUILFORD. at foot of p 316; followed by a 16-page inserted catalogue of publisher's advertisements; white endpapers; top and fore edges trimmed, bottom edges untrimmed; bound in dark blue cloth, publisher's monogram in blind in lower right corner of back cover, front cover blind stamped with large elongated parallel design enclosed within double-rule border, spine gilt lettered THE | UNTILLED | FIELD | GEORGE | MOORE [*all within long single-rule gilt border with scallop design at top and bottom*] | HEINEMANN

A second impression, published January 1915, is noted on verso of its title-leaf; the final gathering is U⁸, with the added leaves blank; there is no inserted catalogue; and the back cover is plain.

Contents:

The "Preface" is new, the text is revised from that used for Tauchnitz edition (b above), and the title of "The Marriage Feast" is changed to "The Wedding Feast." Sheets of this revised edition were used for:

c2 — Heinemann Colonial Library, No. 492, London, 1914. The text of this second revised English edition, including the "Preface," was used when *The Untilled Field* and *The Lake* were included in a single volume in:

2c — Carra Edition, Volume VIII, Boni and Liveright, New York, 1923. There is a tipped-in frontispiece of a reproduction of a painting of GM, protected by a tissue guard sheet.

d Third English edition, revised:

Published January 1926 at 7/6 in format similar to second English edition (c above)

7⅜ x 4¾; [ ]⁸, A-R⁸, S⁴; pp xvi, 280, comprising: half-title, with list of WORKS BY GEORGE MOORE on verso, pp [i-ii]; title-page same as second English edition, with "First Published 1903. | New Edition, October, 1914. | New Impression, January, 1915. | New Edition, January, 1926." in center and PRINTED IN GREAT BRITAIN BY | BILLING AND SONS, LTD., GUILDFORD AND ESHER at bottom of verso, pp [iii-iv]; PREFACE pp v-xi; p [xii] blank; table of CONTENTS, verso blank, pp xiii-[xiv]; author's note, verso blank, pp xv-[xvi]; text pp [1]-280; white endpapers; all edges trimmed; binding, like title-page, identical with previous Heinemann edition, the plates of which were used for the preface and text through p 216.

Contents:

In the author's note, new to this edition, GM says, "the new edition of *The Untilled Field* will allow me to seek an outline that eluded me in the first version of 'The Wild Goose'; and should I find the needed outline, the story will become, perhaps, dearer to me than the twelve [*sic*] that precede it and that need no correction." Actually there are fourteen stories in all, thirteen preceding "The Wild Goose," which was completely rewritten and much shortened for this final version.

e Fourth English edition, revised:

Published April 1931 at 7/6 in format similar to second and third English editions (c and d above)

7⅜ x 4¾; [ ]¹⁰, A-R⁸, S⁴, T-U⁸; pp [2], xviii, 312, comprising: blank leaf, not paginated; half-title, with list of WORKS BY GEORGE MOORE on verso, pp [i-ii]; title-page same as second and third English editions with addition of LTD. to publisher's imprint, with publication dates, plus "New Edition, April, 1931" and printer's imprint as in third edition, on verso, pp [iii-iv]; author's note, now dated "January 1926," verso blank, pp v-[vi]; PUBLISHER'S NOTE, verso blank, pp vii-[viii]; PREFACE pp ix-xv; p [xvi] blank; table of CONTENTS, verso blank, pp xvii-[xviii]; text pp [1]-310; pp [311-12] blank; white endpapers; top and fore edges trimmed, bottom edges untrimmed; binding identical with previous Heinemann editions; the plates of the 1926 edition having been used for the preface (repaginated) and text through p 280.

Contents:

The "Publisher's Note," possibly written by GM, states, "The first English edition of *The Untilled Field* (1903) contained two stories: 'In the Clay' and 'The Way Back,' which were removed from the second (1914) and subsequent editions. In the present edition the author has included a new tale, 'Fugitives,' based upon the subject matter of the other two, and here printed for the first time." This final text was used for:

2e — Uniform Edition, Heinemann, London, December 1932 (dated 1933 on title-page). Reissued in a different binding as:

2e2 — Ebury Edition, Heinemann, March 1937.

In addition to the previously noted Gaelic versions (D:Ga-1, D:Ga-2, D:Ga-3, and D:Ga-4), see D:Cz-1 for Czech translations of "A Letter to Rome," "A Play-house in the Waste," and "The Clerk's Quest"; D:Ge-1, D:Ge-2, D:Ge-4, and D:Ge-14 for German translations of "Home Sickness," "The Wedding Gown," "The Window," and "The Wild Goose." A French translation, *Champ Sterile*, Paris, Stock, 1923, "avec une preface d'Ed Jaloux," listed (p 217) by G. P. Collet in *George Moore et La France* (B58) and again by Jean C. Noël in *George Moore: L'Homme et L'Oeuvre* (B60), has proven to be a ghost.[3]

A27

The Lake

a First edition:

The Lake | By | George Moore | Author of 'Esther Waters,' 'Evelyn Innes,' etc. | [*publisher's device of windmill, flanked by initials* W *and* H, *within single-rule box*] | London | William Heinemann | 1905

Published 10 November at 6/-

7⅜ x 4⅞ ; [ ]⁴ (-[ ]₁), 1-21 ⁸; pp vi, 336, comprising: half-title, with list of eleven "New 6s. Novels" on verso, pp [i-ii]; title-page as above, with "Copyright. New York: D. Appleton & Co. 1905. | Copyright. London: William Heinemann. 1905. | This Edition enjoys copyright in | all countries signatory to the Berne | Treaty, and is not to be imported | into the United States of America." on verso, pp [iii-iv]; dedicatory letter A EDOUARD DUJAR-

3. I am indebted to Prof. Roger Lhombreaud for attempting to trace the title in France and for determining that it had "not been published by Stock or any other publisher." The listing of this title by M. Collet and M. Noël may possibly be accounted for by the fact that in 1923 Stock did publish *Le Lac* (D:Fr-21), with a preface by Jaloux, and that GM originally intended *The Lake* to be a part of *The Untilled Field*.

DIN. pp [v]-vi; text pp [1]-334, with BILLING AND SONS, LTD., PRINT-
ERS, GUILDFORD at foot of p 334; pp [335-36] blank; white endpapers;
top and fore edges trimmed, bottom edges untrimmed; bound in red cloth,
publisher's windmill device, with initials, within single-rule box, as on title-
page, on center of back cover in blind, front cover gilt lettered: The Lake |
George Moore | and spine gilt lettered: The | Lake | George | Moore | Heine-
mann

In at least one first-edition copy, in the collection of Sir Rupert Hart-
Davis, there is a leaf preceding the half-title leaf, not paginated, with publisher's lists on both sides headed NEW PUBLICATIONS.

Contents:

Previously unpublished. Intended as a part of *The Untilled Field* (A26),
the story "proved to be too long and perhaps too complex" to be included in
that volume (Hone, p 247). Sheets of this edition, but with preliminary
sheets of second edition (c below), were reissued later in both bright red and
a cheaper lighter red cloth.[1]

2a First American edition:

THE LAKE | BY | GEORGE MOORE | AUTHOR OF "EVELYN IN-
NESS," [*sic*] | "ESTHER WALTERS," [*sic*] ETC. | [*publisher's device*] |
NEW YORK | D. APPLETON AND COMPANY | 1906

Published 17 February at $1.50

7⅜ x 5; [1]⁸, 2-20⁸; pp [iv], 316, comprising: half-title, verso blank,
pp [i-ii]: title-page as above, with "COPYRIGHT, 1905, BY | D. APPLE-
TON AND COMPANY | Published February 1906" on verso, pp [iii-iv];
text pp 1-309 [2]; p [310] blank; publisher's advertisements pp [311-16]; white
endpapers; all edges trimmed; bound in light green ribbed cloth, back cover
plain, single-rule border in blind on front cover, which is stamped in white:
THE LAKE | by | George Moore [*all within single-rule border with rounded
corners*] and spine lettered in white: THE | LAKE | Moore | Appletons

Contents:

The text is the same as first edition (a above), but with dedicatory letter to
Edouard Dujardin omitted.

b Continental edition, revised:

THE LAKE | BY | GEORGE MOORE | AUTHOR OF "EVELYN IN-
NES," "SISTER TERESA," "CONFESSIONS | OF A YOUNG MAN,"
ETC. | REVISED FOR THE TAUCHNITZ EDITION | COPYRIGHT
EDITION | LEIPZIG | BERNHARD TAUCHNITZ | 1906

1. This issue was possibly used for Heinemann's Colonial Library, for *The Lake*
was advertised as being No. 317 in that series.
2. First impression is designated by a small numeral one in parentheses [(1)] at
the foot of last page of text. Later impressions are indicated by succeeding numbers,
agreeing with the number of the impression. Also the second misprint (WALTERS
for WATERS) on title-page is corrected in later impressions.

6½ x 4⅝; [1]⁸, 2-19⁸; pp 304, comprising: half-title, with list of five books "By the same author" on verso, pp [1-2]; title-page as above, verso blank, pp [3-4]; dedicatory letter A EDOUARD DUJARDIN, pp [5]-6; text pp [7]-303; PRINTING HOUSE OF THE PUBLISHER. in center of p [304]; followed by a 32-page inserted publisher's catalogue; no endpapers; all edges untrimmed; issued in cream paper wrappers with publisher's lists pp [2-4], front cover lettered in black including publisher's imprint, copyright notice and: VOL. 3863. | THE LAKE BY GEORGE MOORE. | IN ONE VOLUME. and spine lettered in black as in the Tauchnitz Edition of *The Untilled Field* (A26-b) except for volume number, the figure following author's name, 7., and title, THE | LAKE.

Contents:

As stated on title-page, this is a revised text with the minor revisions occurring chiefly in chapter XIV, and although this edition was issued later than the second English edition (c below) it precedes it textually.

c Second English edition:

Published late November[3] at 6/- in a format similar to first edition (a above)

7⅜ x 4⅞; [ ]⁴, 1-19⁸, 20⁴; pp [2], vi, 312, comprising: blank leaf, not paginated; half-title, with list of ten "New 6s. Novels." on verso, pp [i-ii]; title-page same as first edition (a above), with "First printed, November, 1905 | Second Impressions November, 1905" in center and copyright notices at foot of verso as in first edition, except first two lines are transposed, pp [iii-iv]; dedicatory letter as in first edition p [v]-vi; text pp [1]-311, with printer's imprint as in first edition (p 334) at foot of p 311; p [312] blank; endpapers, edges and binding identical with first edition.

Contents:

There are minor revisions throughout and from page 101 to page 186 the text is rewritten, with a new chapter VII replacing chapters VII-XI of first edition. In a letter to Edmund Gosse, accompanying a presentation copy of this edition, GM wrote regarding the revisions, "You advised me to revise the middle chapters, suggesting that the correspondence might be carried on between the two priests. That was all and that was enough." [4]

Sheets of this edition were later issued in blue cloth binding.

d Third English edition, revised:

THE LAKE | BY | GEORGE MOORE | 19 [*publisher's windmill device*] 21 | [*rule which is also base of device*] | LONDON: WILLIAM HEINEMANN

Published February 1921 at 7/6

3. This edition precedes the first American (2a) and Tauchnitz (b) editions chronologically, but is a later text.
4. *The Library of Edmund Gosse*, p 186 (B31).

7⅜ x 4¾ ; [ ]⁶, 1-17⁸, [18]² (tipped in); pp [2], x, 276, comprising: blank leaf, not paginated; half-title, with list of thirteen titles "By the Same Author" on verso, pp [i-ii]; title-page as above, with "First printed, November, 1905 | Second Impression, November, 1905 | New Edition, February, 1921" in center and "LONDON WILLIAM HEINEMANN 1921" in lower left corner of verso, pp [iii-iv]; ÉPÎTRE DEDICATOIRE pp v-vi; PREFACE pp vii-x; text pp [1]-273, with "Printed in Great Britain by Billing and Sons, Ltd., Guildford and Esher" at foot of p 273; pp [274-76] blank; white end-papers; top and fore edges trimmed, bottom edges untrimmed; bound in dark blue cloth, publisher's circular monogram device in blind in lower right corner of back cover, front cover blind stamped with large elongated paneled design enclosed within double-rule box, and spine gilt lettered THE | LAKE | GEORGE | MOORE [*all within long gilt single-rule border with scallop-shaped design at top and bottom*]⁵ | HEINEMANN

Contents:

"Épître Dedicatoire" is dedicatory letter, "A Edouard Dujardin," of previous editions; the "Preface" is new; and text is rewritten, with two of the principal characters, Rose Leicester and Ralph Ellis, renamed Nora Glynn and Walter Poole. This final revised text was used when *The Lake* was included with *The Untilled Field* in:

2d — Carra Edition, Volume VIII, Boni and Liveright, New York, 1923, previously noted above (A26-2c). The final text also was used for:

3d — Uniform Edition, Heinemann, London, December 1932. Reissued in a different binding as:

3d2 — Ebury Edition, Heinemann, London, September 1936.

See D:Fr-21 for a French translation; and D:It-2 for an Italian one.

A28
Reminiscences of the Impressionist Painters

a First edition:

THE TOWER PRESS BOOKLETS | NUMBER THREE [*two printer's ornaments*] | REMINISCENCES OF THE | IMPRESSIONIST PAINTERS | BY GEORGE MOORE. [*printer's ornament*] | DUBLIN: MAUNSEL & CO., LTD., | 60 DAWSON STREET. MCMVI.

5. The normal binding has three scallops at top and bottom of spine, but Florian J. Shasky has a copy in his collection which has only two, as on the binding of the 1918 and 1926 Heinemann editions of *Confessions of a Young Man* (A12-2d and A12-2d2).

Published May 1906 at 1/- in an edition of 500 copies

6½ x 4; [A]⁸, B-C⁸, D⁴; pp [xvi], 9-48, comprising: blank leaf, pp [i-ii]; half-title, verso blank, pp [iii-iv]; title-page as above, with PRINTED AT THE TOWER PRESS, THIRTY-EIGHT CORNMARKET, DUBLIN. at foot of verso, pp [v-vi]; prefatory letter pp [vii-xv]; p [xvi] blank; text pp 9-48; all edges untrimmed; no endpapers; heavy gray overlapping wrappers, back cover and spine plain, list of other titles in series on inside of rear wrapper, front cover stamped in black below a sketch of a crumbling stone tower (after a drawing by Mrs. Murray Robertson) within a single-rule border THE TOWER PRESS BOOKLETS | NUMBER THREE [*three printer's ornaments*] | REMINISCENCES OF THE | IMPRESSIONIST PAINTERS. | BY GEORGE MOORE.

Contents:

Prefatory letter to "My Dear Steer," previously unpublished. *Reminiscences of the Impressionist Painters* is text of lecture delivered at the request of Sir Hugh Lane on the occasion of an exhibition of Impressionist painting in Dublin, and as printed here it is revised from earlier publication in SCRIBNER'S MAGAZINE, February 1906.

The lecture, revised, included in section VI of *Hail and Farewell: Vale* (A31:III-a).

See D:Ge-13 for German translation of prefatory letter and lecture.

A29

Memoirs of My Dead Life

a First edition:

MEMOIRS OF | MY DEAD LIFE | BY | GEORGE MOORE | [*publisher's device of windmill, flanked by letters* W *and* H, *within single-rule box*] | LONDON | WILLIAM HEINEMANN | 1906

Published June at 6/- in an edition of 2,000 copies

7⅜ x 4⅞ ; [ ]⁴, A-X⁸; pp viii, 336, comprising: blank leaf pp [i-ii]; half-title, with list of twelve WORKS BY GEORGE MOORE on verso, pp [iii-iv]; title-page as above, with "Copyright 1906 by William Heinemann" in center of verso, pp [v-vi]; table of CONTENTS, verso blank, pp vii-[viii]; text, with shoulder section-titles throughout, pp [1]-335; "Printed by T. and A. CONSTABLE, Printers to His Majesty | at the Edinburgh University Press" at foot of p [336]; white endpapers; top and fore edges trimmed, bottom edges untrimmed; bound in dark, nearly black cloth, publisher's monogram in blind in lower right corner of back cover, front cover blind stamped with a large elongated paneled design enclosed within double-rule border;[1] spine gilt lettered MEMOIRS | OF MY | DEAD LIFE | GEORGE | MOORE [*all within long gilt single-rule box with scallop-shaped design at top and bottom*] | HEINEMANN

Contents:

"Spring in London" revised from "Moods and Memories I" in DANA, May 1904, and in LIPPINCOTT'S MAGAZINE, June 1904; a revision of "London in April" in THE HAWK, 3 June 1890, and "Spring in London" in PALL MALL BUDGET, 5 April 1894. "Flowering Normandy" revised from "Moods and Memories II" in DANA, May 1904, and LIPPINCOTT'S MAGAZINE, June 1904; a revision of "To Paris and Back" in THE HAWK, 3 June 1890, and "Flowering Normandy" in THE SPEAKER, 25 May 1895. "A Waitress," revised from "Moods and Memories III" in DANA, June 1904, and LIPPINCOTT'S MAGAZINE, July 1904; a revision of "Notes and Sensations" in THE HAWK, 11 February 1890. The untitled poem in "The Waitress" was originally published as "À une Poitrinaire" in *Pagan Poems* (A3), and also was used in *Mike Fletcher* (A14), and in the 1904 and subsequent editions of *Confessions of a Young Man* (A12-c et seq.). "The End of Marie Pellegrin"[2] revised from "Moods and Memories VI" in DANA, September and October 1904, and LIPPINCOTT'S MAGAZINE, August 1904 and January 1905; a revision of "Notes and Sensations" in THE HAWK, 11 March 1890. "La Butte" revised from "Moods and Memories IV" in DANA, July 1904, and LIPPINCOTT'S MAGAZINE, July 1904; a revision of "Notes and Sensations" in THE HAWK, 16 September 1890. The first third of "Spent Love" revised from "Moods and Memories V" in LIPPINCOTT'S MAGAZINE, July 1904, and DANA, August 1904; a revision of "Notes and Sensations" in THE HAWK, 9 September 1890. "Ninon's Table d'Hôte" revised from "Notes and Sensations" in THE HAWK, 29 July 1890. "The Lovers of Orelay" previously unpublished but Malcolm Brown in *George Moore: A Reconsideration* suggests that "A Parisian Idyl" in *Pagan Poems* (A3) may be the genesis of this sketch. "In the Luxembourg Gardens," previously unpublished. "A Remembrance" revised from original appearance in THE NEW REVIEW, August

1. This is the first volume issued in the Heinemann standard binding, which reproduces in blind the front cover design by Arthur Moore for *The Strike at Arlingford* (A18). Other titles issued in this binding include the three volumes of *Hail and Farewell: Ave* (A31:I-a), *Salve* (A31:II-a), and *Vale* (A31:III-a); *Muslin* (A34-a); *Lewis Seymour and Some Women* (A36-2a); the 1918 and 1926 editions of *Confessions of a Young Man* (A12-2d and A12-2d2); the 1914, 1926 and 1931 editions of *The Untilled Field* (A26-c, A26-d and A26-e); the 1918 edition of *A Mummer's Wife* (A6-2c); the 1920 edition of *Esther Waters* (A19-c); and the 1921 edition of *The Lake* (A27-d).

2. The story is about a Parisian *cocotte* of the 1870s, and another story about the same subject, "Mort de Lucie Pellegrin," published in 1880 by GM's friend, Paul Alexis, is contrasted with GM's version in "George Moore and Paul Alexis: The Death of La Pellegrin," by Robert J. Niess, in THE ROMANIC REVIEW, February 1947.

1891, and LIVING AGE, 10 October 1891. "Bring in the Lamp" revised from "Notes and Sensations" in THE HAWK, 18 February 1890. "Sunday Evening in London" revised from "Impressions in St. James's Park" in THE SPEAKER, 30 February 1893. "Resurgam" revised from "My Own Funeral" in LIPPINCOTT'S MAGAZINE, November 1901.

A second impression of 1,500 copies, with minor textual revisions, issued August 1906; a third impression, with further minor revisions, issued March 1908; and other impressions issued February 1911 and May 1913.

2a First American edition:

Memoirs of | MY DEAD LIFE | BY | GEORGE MOORE | Author of "Evelyn Inness," [sic] "Esther Waters," | "The Lake," etc. | [publisher's device] | D. APPLETON AND COMPANY | NEW YORK | 1907

Published 10 November 1906 at $1.50

7⅜ x 4⅞; [ ]⁸, A-B⁸, 1⁴, 2-20⁸; pp xlvi, 314, comprising: half-title, verso blank, pp [i-ii]; title-page as above, with COPYRIGHT, 1906, BY | D. APPLETON AND COMPANY in center and "Published November, 1906" below and to left on verso, pp [iii-iv]; table of CONTENTS, verso blank, pp v-[vi]; APOLOGIA PRO SCRIPTIS MEIS, preceded by publisher's note, pp vii-xlvi; text pp 1-310;[3] publisher's advertisements pp [311-14]; white endpapers; all edges trimmed; bound in light blue-gray ribbed cloth, back cover plain, front cover stamped in white MEMOIRS OF | MY DEAD LIFE | GEORGE MOORE [all within single-rule box] and spine lettered in white MEMOIRS | OF | MY DEAD | LIFE | [rule] | MOORE | APPLETONS

Contents:

"Apologia pro Scriptis Meis,"[4] found in no other edition, is new and is GM's commentary on the expurgations made in this edition by Appleton in "The Lovers of Orelay" and "In the Luxembourg Gardens."[5] In addition to these bowdlerizations, the text differs somewhat from that of the first edition

---

3. The first impression is designated by a small numeral one in parentheses [(1)] at right and below final line of text; later impressions are indicated by successive numbers, agreeing with number of the impression, and these impressions have a different imposition: [1]⁸, 2-22⁸, 23⁴.

4. GM used the same title for the completely different preface to the Carra Edition, where it is found in Volume I, Lewis Seymour and Some Women (A36-4a).

5. When the manuscript of Memoirs of My Dead Life was submitted to Appleton the two episodes were not included, "But the copy supplied for the press consisted of proof-sheets of the English edition containing the questionable episodes . . . The upshot of an amusing exchange of letters was that Moore consented to the suppression of a few short passages in both chapters on condition that the American edition should include as a special foreword an 'Apologia pro Scriptis Meis'," according to Samuel Chew in the section on "The House of Appleton," which is a part of the "Historical Introduction" to Fruit Among the Leaves: An Anniversary Anthology (B55).

(a above) and is an earlier state, having been set from proof pages of the Heinemann edition before GM made last-minute alterations.[6]

b Continental edition, revised:

MEMOIRS OF MY DEAD LIFE | BY | GEORGE MOORE | AUTHOR OF | "EVELYN INNES," "SISTER TERESA," "CONFESSIONS OF A YOUNG MAN," | "THE LAKE," ETC. | COPYRIGHT EDITION | LEIP-ZIG | BERNHARD TAUCHNITZ | 1906

6½ x 4⅝; [1]⁸, 2-17⁸, 18⁴; pp 280, comprising: half-title with list of six books "By the same Author" on verso, pp [1-2]; title-page as above, verso blank, pp [3-4]; table of CONTENTS, verso blank, pp [5-6]; text pp [7]-278 (with fly-titles, versos blank, pp [7-8], [37-38], [47-48], [63-64], [91-92], [105-6], [139-40], [167-68], [187-88], [211-12], [229-30], and pp [46], [90], [104], [138], [166], [210], [228] blank); PRINTING OFFICE OF THE PUBLISHER. center p [279]: p [280] blank; followed by a 32-page inserted publisher's catalogue; no endpapers; all edges untrimmed; issued in cream paper wrappers, with publisher's lists pp [2-4]; front cover lettered in black same as Tauchnitz editions of *Sister Teresa* (A25-2b), *The Untilled Field* (A26-b), and *The Lake* (A27-b) except for: VOL. 3921. | MEMOIRS OF MY DEAD LIFE BY GEORGE MOORE. | IN ONE VOLUME. and spine lettered in black the same as other volumes in the series except for volume number, number following author's name, 9., and the title, MEMOIRS | OF MY | DEAD LIFE.

Contents:

The text is the same as the second impression of the first edition (a above), except "The Lovers of Orelay" and "In the Luxembourg Gardens" are omitted and "Spring in London" is retitled "Theme and Variations" and includes additional material [7] (pp 16-35) found in no other edition in English until the Author's Edition (d below) and the Moore Hall Edition (2d below).

c Second English edition, expanded:

Published November 1915 at 6/- in a format similar to first edition (a above)

7⅜ x 4⅞; [ ]⁴, A-Y⁸, Z⁴, Z2² (inserted between Z_2 and Z_3); pp viii, 364, comprising: blank leaf pp [i-ii]; half-title with list of sixteen WORKS BY GEORGE MOORE on verso, pp [iii-iv]; title-page same as first edition (a above) except date changed to 1915, with "First printed, June 1906. | New Editions, August 1906, March 1908. | Reprinted, February 1911,

---

6. A set of page proofs of the Heinemann edition, "Moore's own copy, with about 35 of his autograph corrections on about 30 pages, in all about 160 words; also a number of deletions in the same hand," was item 804 in the A. Edward Newton sale, 14 May 1941, at Park-Bernet Galleries, Inc., New York. Page 112 of these proofs is used as an illustration in Newton's *The Amenities of Book-Collecting*, Boston, 1918.

7. See A45 for a separate printing of an earlier version of this additional material.

May 1913. | New Edition, November 1915." in center and "Copyright 1906 by William Heinemann." at foot of verso, pp [v-vi]; table of CONTENTS, verso blank, pp vii-[viii]; text, with shoulder section-titles throughout, pp [1]-361; printer's imprint as in first edition (p [336]) at foot of p [362]; pp [363-64] blank,[8] white endpapers; top and fore edges trimmed, bottom edges untrimmed; binding similar to previous Heinemann impressions.

Contents:

Same as third (1908) impression of first edition with a new section, "Euphorion in Texas," [9] originally published in THE ENGLISH REVIEW, July 1914, added between "Bring in the Lamp" and "Sunday Evening in London," the plates of the third impression being used for the balance of the text, with page numbers altered on final two sections.

Further impressions issued February 1919, June 1921, July 1923, and December 1925, each indicated by a notation on verso of its title-leaf.

d Second American (Author's) edition, revised and expanded:

MEMOIRS OF MY DEAD LIFE | BY | GEORGE MOORE | Author's Edition | [*cameo ornament*] | New York | Privately printed for subscribers only by | BONI AND LIVERIGHT | 1920

Published 15 December [10] in an edition of 1,500 copies

9½ x 6⅛; [1-20][8]; pp [6], viii, 9-314, comprising: two blank leaves, not paginated; half-title, with list of twenty WORKS BY GEORGE MOORE on verso, not paginated; title-page as above, with COPYRIGHT, 1906, BY | D. APPLETON & COMPANY | COPYRIGHT, 1920, BY | GEORGE MOORE at top, "All Rights Reserved" in center, and notice of limitation as below at bottom of verso, pp [i-ii]; EPISTLE DEDICATORY, verso blank, pp [iii-iv]; PREFATORY LETTER pp v-vi; table of CONTENTS, verso blank, pp [vi-viii]; text, with shoulder section-titles throughout, pp 9-308; pp [309-14] blank; royal blue endpapers; all edges untrimmed; cream head and tail bands; white parchment spine, with blue paper-covered board sides, matching endpapers; black leather label on spine, gilt stamped MEMOIRS | [*ornament*] OF [*ornament*] | MY DEAD | [*ornament*] LIFE [*ornament*] | [*three dots, two above one*] | GEORGE | [*small solid triangle*] MOORE [*small solid triangle*] | [*all within decorative border*]

Notice of limitation:

A limited Edition issued for private circulation only and consisting of fifteen | hundred numbered copies. The type was distributed | after printing. Published November, 1920. | No. _____ [*numbered in ink*]

8. In some copies this blank leaf is omitted and in its place is an inserted 16-page catalogue of publisher's announcements.

9. In the periodical printing the first word of the title is misspelled "Euphorian," and this spelling was retained when the story was printed separately (A43).

10. According to copyright data in Library of Congress.

Contents:

The "Epistle Dedicatory, To T. R. Smith" (Boni and Liveright editor) and the "Prefatory Letter" to Horace Liveright are both new; the former is used in no other edition and the latter only in the reprint (d2) below; a new section, "Lui et Elles," incorporating in a revised form much of the material added to the first section of the Tauchnitz edition (c above), is inserted between "Spring in London" and "Flowering Normandy," and the complete text is revised. This edition was used for a reprint without the shoulder section-titles reproduced by photo-offset lithography:

d2 — A Boar's Head Book, Walker-deBerry, Inc., Cambridge, Mass., 1960; issued in heavy paper wrappers with a reproduction of the sketch of GM by Manet and a quotation from the book on back cover, and a Brassaï photograph of a street in Montmartre on front cover.

2d Third English (Moore Hall) edition:

Memoirs | of My Dead Life | OF | Galanteries, Meditations | and Re-membrances | Soliloquies or Advice to Lovers, | — with many miscellaneous Reflections | on Virtue & Merit | By | George Moore of Moore Hall Co Mayo | [*woodcut of Moore Hall*] | LONDON | Published by Heinemann. [*all reproduction of hand lettering in imitation of an 18th-century engraved title-page*]

Published June 1921 at 42/- in an edition of 1,030 copies

8⅞ x 5⅝; [A]⁸, [a]² (tipped in), B-Y⁸, U² (tipped in); pp xx, 292, comprising: half-title, with list of WORKS BY GEORGE MOORE on verso, pp [i-ii]; inserted leaf with colored reproduction of a daguerreotype of GM at the age of nine on verso, not paginated, protected by tissue guard sheet, also not paginated; title-page as above, with "London: William Heinemann, 1921." at foot of verso, pp [iii-iv]; notice of limitation as below, verso blank, pp [v-vi]; EPISTLE DEDICATORY pp vii-ix; p [x] blank; PRELUDE pp xi-xviii; table of CONTENTS, verso blank, pp [xix-xx]; text, with shoulder section-titles throughout, pp [1]-290, with PRINTED IN GREAT BRITAIN BY RICHARD CLAY & SONS, LIMITED | BUNGAY, SUFFOLK. at foot of page 290; pp [291-92] blank; pale blue endpapers; all edges untrimmed; pale blue silk head band; white parchment spine, with pale blue paper-covered board sides, matching endpapers; white label on spine, lettered in brown: Memoirs | of My | Dead Life | GEORGE | MOORE | Heinemann

Notice of limitation:

MEMOIRS OF MY DEAD LIFE | [*rule*] | This edition, printed from hand-set | type on English hand-made paper, | is limited to one thousand and thirty | copies, of which one thousand are for | sale. This is No. . . . . . [*numbered in ink*] | George Moore [*signed in ink*]

Contents:

The "Epistle Dedicatory" to "My Dear Gosse," dated May 5, 1921, and the "Prelude," which was published in THE OBSERVER, 26 June 1921, are both new, but the text, with a few minor revisions, is the same as the Author's Edition (d above). The text of this edition was used for:

3d — Carra Edition, Volume X, Boni and Liveright, New York, 1923, but in place of the daguerreotype of GM as a child, which is referred to in the "Prelude," there is a tipped-in frontispiece of a reproduction of a painting, protected by a tissue guard sheet lettered in red at foot of verso: "HOMAGE TO MANET" | From a painting by Sir William Orpen, R. A., in the Manchester | Art Gallery. | Under the famous picture of Mlle. Gonzales by Manet are | seated (left to right) George Moore, P. Wilson Steer, Sir | Hugh Lane and Professor Tonks. Standing at the right are | D. S. MacColl and Walter Sickert.

e Fourth English (Uniform) edition, revised:

MEMOIRS OF | MY DEAD LIFE | BY | GEORGE MOORE | [*vignette*] | London | William Heinemann Ltd. | 1928

Published April at 10/6

8⅞ x 5½; [a]⁸, b² (tipped in), A-R⁸; pp xx, 272, comprising: blank leaf, pp [i-ii]; half-title, with list of WORKS BY GEORGE MOORE on verso, pp [iii-iv]; title-page as above, with list of eleven printings (called "Editions") in center and "Printed in Great Britain by T. and A. CONSTABLE LTD. | at the University Press, Edinburgh" at foot of verso, pp [v-vi]; EPISTLE DEDICATORY pp vii-ix; p [x] blank; PRELUDE pp xi-xvii; p [xviii] blank; table of CONTENTS, verso blank, pp [xix-xx]; text, with shoulder section-titles throughout, pp [1]-270; pp 271-72 blank; extra spine label tipped in between page [272] and free rear endpaper; white endpapers; all edges untrimmed; brown cloth spine, with marbled paper-covered board sides, white paper label on spine, lettered in brown: Memoirs | of My | Dead | Life | George | Moore | Heinemann

Contents:

The text is revised, with "Lui et Elles" of the Author's Edition (d above) and Moore Hall Edition (2d above) omitted, but with "Elizabeth" of that sketch and of *Vale* (A31:III-a) introduced into "Spring in London"; the preliminary matter of the Moore Hall Edition is retained, with the exception of the frontispiece, although the daguerreotype reproduced for it continues to be referred to in the "Prelude." Reissued in a different binding as:

e2—Ebury Edition, Heinemann, London, September 1936.

See D:Ch-1 for Chinese; D:Cz-4 and D:Cz-5 (?) for Czech; D:Fr-13, D:Fr-17, D:Fr-19, D:Fr-20 for French; D:Ge-7, D:Ge-8, D:Ge-9, D:Ge-10, D:Ge-11, D:Ge-15, D:Ge-16 for German; D:It-4 for Italian; and D:Sw-2 for Swedish translations, of all or portions of *Memoirs of My Dead Life*.

A30

The Apostle

a First edition:

THE APOSTLE | A DRAMA IN THREE ACTS | BY GEORGE MOORE | DUBLIN: MAUNSEL AND CO. LTD. | 96 MIDDLE ABBEY STREET | 1911

Published 30 May at 3/6

7⅞ x 5¼; [A]⁴, B-G⁸, H² (tipped in), [ ]² (tipped in); pp [viii]; 104, comprising: half-title, verso blank, pp [i-ii]; title-page as above, with "All rights reserved." in center and "Printed by Maunsel & Co., Ltd., Dublin." at foot of verso, pp [iii-iv]; dedicatory letter to "My dear Mary Hunter," verso blank, pp [v-vi]; table of CONTENTS, verso blank, pp [vii-viii]; A PREFA-TORY LETTER p 1-35; p [36] blank; fly-title, with PERSONS IN THE PLAY on verso, pp [37-38]; text pp 39-100; p [101] blank; publisher's advertisements pp [102-4]; white endpapers; top edges trimmed, fore and bottom edges untrimmed; bound in mauve cloth, back cover plain except for single-rule border in blind at outer edges, this is repeated on front cover, which is gilt lettered THE APOSTLE | A DRAMA IN THREE ACTS | BY | GEORGE MOORE | and spine gilt stamped [*rule*] | THE | APOSTLE | A DRAMA | IN THREE | ACTS | GEORGE | MOORE | MAUNSEL | [*rule*]

Contents:

"A Prefatory Letter on Reading the Bible for the First Time," addressed to Max Meyerfeld, translator of GM's works into German originally pub-lished in THE ENGLISH REVIEW, February 1911. *The Apostle* although sub-titled "A Drama in Three Acts" is really a scenario, published to protect the idea later developed in *The Brook Kerith* (A35) and is here expanded from its original publication in THE ENGLISH REVIEW, June 1910, where more of the story is in narrative form.

a2 First edition, American issue:

There is an American issue, using sheets (without final gathering), end-papers, and binding of the first edition, but with publisher's imprint on title-page reset, BOSTON: JOHN W. LUCE AND CO. replacing Maunsel's address and the date; "Copyright. 1911. George Moore." added above "All rights reserved." on verso of title-page; publisher's advertisements at end omitted; and LUCE & CO. substituted for MAUNSEL at foot of spine.

b Second edition, rewritten:

The APOSTLE | A DRAMA | IN | A PRELUDE AND THREE ACTS | By | GEORGE MOORE | London | William Heinemann Ltd. | 1923

Published June at 21/- in an edition of 1,030 copies

9 x 5⅜; [ ]⁴, A-Q⁴; pp [viii], 128, comprising: blank leaf, pp [i-ii];

half-title, with notice of limitation as below on verso, pp [iii-iv]; title-page as above, with "Printed in Great Britain by T. and A. CONSTABLE Ltd. | at the University Press, Edinburgh" at foot of verso, pp [v-vi]; EPISTLE DEDICATORY, with list of "CHARACTERS in the PLAY" on verso, pp [vii-viii]; text pp 1-57; p [58] blank; text pp 59-125; pp [126-28] blank; extra spine label tipped in between p [128] and free rear endpaper; pale blue endpapers; all edges untrimmed; white parchment spine, with pale blue paper-covered board sides, matching endpapers, and with white paper label on spine, lettered in brown: The | Apostle | A Drama | [*asterisk*] | GEORGE | MOORE | Heinemann

Notice of limitation:

This edition of THE APOSTLE by George | Moore is limited to one thousand and thirty | copies printed from hand-set type on Van | Gelder paper. One thousand copies are | for sale and thirty are for presentation. | No. . . . . . [*numbered in ink*] | George Moore [*signed in ink*]

Contents:

"Epistle Dedicatory," addressed to "My dear Granville Barker" and dated "22nd February 1923" is found in no other edition. *The Apostle*, published in THE DIAL, June and July 1923, is not so much a revision of the 1911 version (a above) as it is a dramatization of a portion of *The Brook Kerith* (A35), and is based to a large extent on the scenario "THE BROOK KERITH | a Spiritual drama | in Four Acts and Seven Scenes | by | George Moore and John Lloyd Balderston" which exists in typescript.[1]

A further revision of *The Apostle* was published in September 1930 as *The Passing of the Essenes* (A55).

See D:Ge-13 for German translations of the scenario and "Prefatory Letter" made from the ENGLISH REVIEW printings.

A31
Hail and Farewell
I Ave — II Salve — III Vale

I-a First edition:

'HAIL AND FAREWELL!' | [*rule*] | AVE [*red*] | BY | GEORGE MOORE | LONDON | WILLIAM HEINEMANN | 1911

Published 19 October at 6/-

7½ x 4¾ ; [ ]² (tipped in), A-Z⁸; pp [iv], 368, comprising: half-title, with 'HAIL AND FAREWELL!' | A TRILOGY | I. AVE | II. SALVE [In preparation] | III. VALE [In preparation] | on verso, pp [i-ii]; title-

---

1. Hone (p 280) mentions one in the possession of Dr. Max Meyerfeld, and I have one in my collection.

page as above, with "Copyright, London, 1911, by William Heinemann, | and Washington, U.S.A., by D. Appleton and Co." at foot of verso, pp [iii-iv]; text pp [1]-367, with BILLING AND SONS, LTD., PRINTERS, GUILDFORD at foot of p 367; p [368] blank; white endpapers; top and fore edges trimmed, bottom edges untrimmed; bound in dark blue cloth, publisher's circular monogram in blind in lower right corner of back cover, large elongated paneled design enclosed within double-rule border in blind on front cover, spine gilt stamped HAIL AND | FAREWELL | [*rule*] | AVE | GEORGE | MOORE [*all enclosed within gilt rule border with scallop-shaped design at top and bottom*] | HEINEMANN

There are two issues of the first edition: (1) As above. (2) As above, with an additional leaf tipped in between free front endpaper and [ ]₁, recto blank, with advertisement for two books BY THE SAME AUTHOR on verso.[1]

Contents:

"Overture" originally published in the ENGLISH REVIEW, March 1910; sections I-XV previously unpublished.

A second impression, with minor textual revisions, issued May 1914. Further impressions published 1919,[2] 1921, and 1927. Sheets of the second impression were used for:

I-a2 — Heinemann's Colonial Library, No. 432, London, n.d.

I-2a First American edition:

HAIL AND FAREWELL | [*rule*] | AVE | BY | GEORGE MOORE | [*publisher's device*] | NEW YORK | D. APPLETON AND COMPANY | 1911

Published 24 November at $1.75

7½ x 5⅛; [1]⁸, 2-24⁸, 25⁴; pp vi, 386, comprising: half-title, with HAIL AND FAREWELL | A TRILOGY | I. AVE | II. SALVE [In preparation] | III. VALE [In preparation] | on verso, pp [i-ii]; title-page as above, with "COPYRIGHT, 1911, BY | D. APPLETON AND COMPANY | Published November, 1911" on verso, pp [iii-iv]; PREFATORY NOTE signed "[THE PUBLISHER]" pp v-vi; text pp [1-384][3]; pp [385-86] blank; white endpapers; top edges gilt; fore and bottom edges un-

1. Listed by Danielson as being the first issue, but none of the presentation copies seen have this additional leaf, and in a letter, dated "December 18, 1926," inserted in the Fayant copy of *Ave*, Danielson wrote "I have stated in my 'Bibliography of George Moore' that the first issue of this book is the one with the leaf of advertisements, but this is an error, as all review copies sent out are without the leaf of advertisements."

2. This impression, issued in February, is listed on the verso of the title-leaves of the Uniform and Ebury editions as being revised. This is not correct as the impression was printed from the type of 1914 impression, noted above as the "second impression."

3. See A29-n3.

trimmed; bound in dark green ribbed cloth, back cover plain, front cover plain except for single-rule border in blind, spine gilt stamped [*rule*] | HAIL | AND | FAREWELL | [*short rule*] | GEORGE | MOORE | [*rule*] | AVE | APPLETONS

Contents:

The publisher's "Prefatory Note," quoting GM's intentions regarding the writing of the book may have been written by him. The text is the same as the first edition, and was used, along with the publisher's note, for:

I-3a — Collection of British Authors, No. 4314, Bernhard Tauchnitz, Leipzig, 1912. The text of the second impression of the first edition was used for:

I-4a — Carra Edition, Volume XI, Boni and Liveright, New York, 1923. There is a tipped-in frontispiece, protected by a tissue guard sheet lettered in red at bottom of verso "GEORGE MOORE | When a boy." It is a sepia reproduction of the daguerreotype picture used as the frontispiece of the Moore Hall Edition of *Memoirs of My Dead Life* (A29-2d).

II-a First edition:

'HAIL AND FAREWELL!' | [*rule*] | SALVE [*red*] | BY | GEORGE MOORE | LONDON | WILLIAM HEINEMANN | 1912

Published 10 October at 6/-

7½ x 4¾; [ ]² (tipped in), A-Z⁸, A2⁶; pp [iv], 380, comprising: half-title, with 'HAIL AND FAREWELL!' | A TRILOGY | I. AVE | II. SALVE | III. VALE [in preparation] | on verso, pp [i-ii]; title page as above, with "Copyright, London, 1912" at foot of verso, pp [iii-iv]; text pp [1]-379, with BILLING AND SONS, LTD., PRINTERS, GUILDFORD at foot of p 379; p [380] blank; white endpapers; top and fore edges trimmed, bottom edges untrimmed; bound in dark blue cloth, publisher's circular monogram in blind in lower right corner of back cover, large elongated paneled design enclosed within double-rule border in blind on front cover, spine gilt stamped HAIL AND | FAREWELL | [*rule*] | SALVE | GEORGE | MOORE [*all enclosed within a gilt-rule border with scallop-shaped design at top and bottom*] | HEINEMANN

There are two issues of the first edition: (1) As above, with an ERRATA slip (1¾ x 3⅞) tipped in between [ ]₂ and A₁ (title-leaf and first leaf of text), noting errors "Bernaise" for "Béarnaise" on p 170 and "la vapeur et la tumulte" for "vapeur et tumulte" on p 203.[4] (2) As above, without errata slip and with errors on pp 170 and 203 corrected.

4. There are some copies with the errors on pp 170 and 203 but without the errata slip. These are not listed as a separate issue as the removal of the slip would change the status of the copies, and in any case the presence or absence of the slip would create a state and not a separate issue. Also, the "early issue" listed by Danielson "with the border design on back [spine] in light green" is not in fact an issue,

Contents:

Sections I-IV originally published as "In Search of Divinity" in the ENGLISH REVIEW, December 1911, January, and February 1912; sections V-X previously unpublished; section XI originally published as "Jubilation in the Garden" in the ENGLISH RVIEW, August 1912; sections XII-XXI previously unpublished.

The withdrawn sheets of the first issue were used for:

II-a2 — Heinemann's Colonial Library, No. 442, London, 1914.

II-2a First American edition:

HAIL AND FAREWELL | [*rule*] | SALVE | BY | GEORGE MOORE | [*publisher's device*] | NEW YORK | D. APPLETON AND COMPANY | 1912

Published 15 November at $1.75

7½ x 5⅛; [1]⁸, 2-25⁸; pp [iv], 396; comprising: half-title, with HAIL AND FAREWELL | A TRILOGY | I. AVE | II. SALVE | III. VALE [In preparation] | on verso, pp [i-ii]; title-page as above, with COPY-RIGHT, 1912, BY | D. APPLETON AND COMPANY on verso, pp [iii-iv]; text pp 1-[396]⁸; white endpapers; top edges gilt, fore and bottom edges untrimmed; bound in dark green ribbed cloth, back cover plain, front cover plain except for single-rule border in blind, spine gilt stamped [*rule*] | HAIL | AND | FAREWELL | [*short rule*] | GEORGE | MOORE | [*rule*] | SALVE | APPLETONS

Contents:

Same as first issue of first edition (II-a above). Text of the second issue of the first edition was used for:

II-3a — Collection of British Authors, No. 4376, Bernhard Tauchnitz, Leipzig, 1912. The first edition text, with slight revisions, was used for:

II-4a — Carra Edition, Volume XII, Boni and Liveright, New York, 1923. There is a tipped-in frontispiece, protected by a tissue guard sheet lettered in red along inner edge of verso MOORE HALL | "The house was burnt by the rebel army in Ireland and now stands among the many | ruins that overlook Lough Carra and decorate its islands." | G.M.

III-a First edition:

'HAIL AND FAREWELL!' | [*rule*] | VALE [*red*] | BY | GEORGE MOORE | LONDON | WILLIAM HEINEMANN

Published 4 March 1914 at 6/-

7⅜ x 4¾; [ ]² (tipped in), A-Y⁸, Z⁶; pp [iv], 364, comprising: half-title (second E in FAREWELL from different font of type), with 'HAIL AND FAREWELL!' | A TRILOGY | III. [*sic*] AVE | II. SALVE | III. VALE | on verso, pp [i-ii]; title-page as above, with "Copyright, 1914." at

---

as the "light green" stamping, when found, is the result of oxidation of the normal gilt stamping.

foot of verso, pp [iii-iv]; text pp [1]-363; with BILLING AND SONS, LTD., PRINTERS, GUILDFORD at foot of p 363; p [364] blank; white end-papers; top and fore edges trimmed, bottom edges untrimmed; bound in dark blue cloth, publisher's circular monogram in blind in lower right corner of back cover, large elongated paneled design enclosed within a double-rule border in blind on front cover, spine gilt stamped HAIL AND | FARE-WELL | [rule] | VALE | GEORGE | MOORE [all enclosed within a gilt-rule border with scallop-shaped design at top and bottom] | HEINEMANN

There are two states of the first edition: (1) As above, with errors on verso of half-title leaf. (2) As above, with errors on verso of half-title leaf corrected, and the leaf, a cancel, pasted on the stub of the cancelled leaf.[5]

Contents:

Sections I-V previously unpublished; section VI rewritten from *Reminiscences of the Impressionist Painters* (A28), which was also published in a slightly different form in SCRIBNER'S MAGAZINE, February 1906; section VII originally published as "Yeats, Lady Gregory and Synge" in the ENGLISH REVIEW, January, and February 1914; sections VIII-XIV previously unpublished.

A second impression, with the errors on verso of the half-title leaf corrected as in the second issue, was published identical in format and pagination with the previous impression, except the half-title leaf is a part of the gathering; the notation on verso of title-page leaf is "LONDON: WLLIAM HEINE-MANN. 1914. | Copyright."; and gathering H (pp 113-28) is reset with each page having 32 lines of text instead of 33, thus effecting the deletion of 171 words in 19 lines of text (last 15 on p 127 and first 4 on p 128 of first impression) regarding the picture dealing of Sir Hugh Lane. Sheets of the first and second impressions were combined for:

III-a2 — Heinemann's Colonial Library, No. 479, London, 1914.

III-2a First American edition:

HAIL AND FAREWELL | [rule] | VALE | BY | GEORGE MOORE | [publisher's device] | NEW YORK | D. APPLETON AND COMPANY | 1914

Published 17 April at $1.75

7½ x 5⅛; [1]² (tipped in), [2-25]⁸; pp [iv], 384, comprising: half-title, with HAIL AND FAREWELL | A TRILOGY | I. AVE | II. SALVE | III. VALE on verso, pp i-ii; title-page as above, with COPYRIGHT, 1914, BY | D. APPLETON AND COMPANY on verso, pp iii-iv; text pp 1-[384]³; white endpapers, top edges gilt, fore and bottom edges untrimmed; bound in dark green ribbed cloth, single-rule border in blind on front and back covers, spine gilt stamped [rule] | HAIL | AND | FAREWELL | [short rule] | GEORGE | MOORE | [rule] | VALE | APPLETONS

5. Some copies have a blank leaf inserted before the cancel.

Contents:

Text same as first edition (III-a above), including passage about Sir Hugh Lane deleted from later impressions of the English edition. This same text also was used for:

III-3a — Carra Edition, Volume XIII, Boni and Liveright, New York, 1923. There is a tipped-in frontispiece, protected by a tissue guard sheet, of a reproduction of a line drawing[6] of GM (by Henry Tonks) with a facsimile inscription: Always yours | George Moore

III-b Continental edition, revised:

HAIL AND FAREWELL | VALE | BY | GEORGE MOORE | AUTHOR OF | "CELIBATES," "EVELYN INNES," "SISTER TERESA," | "SPRING DAYS," ETC. | COPYRIGHT EDITION | LEIPZIG | BERNHARD TAUCHNITZ | 1914

6½ x 4⅜; [1]⁸, 2-21⁸, 22⁴; pp 344, comprising: half-title, with list of ten titles "By the same Author" on verso, pp [1-2]; title-page as above, verso blank, pp [3-4]; text pp [5]-342; PRINTING OFFICE OF THE PUBLISHER. center of p [343]; p [344] blank; followed by 32-page inserted publisher's catalogue; no endpapers; all edges untrimmed; issued in cream wrappers, with publisher's lists on pp [2-4], lettered in black on front cover and spine similar to other titles in Tauchnitz edition, including Vol. 4490.

Contents:

A short portion of section V is omitted and new material added from middle of p 105 to near bottom on p 109, but the passage about Sir Hugh Lane, omitted from later impressions of the first edition (III-a above), is included.

III-2b Second English edition:

Published February 1915 at 6/- in a format similar to first edition (III-a above)

7½ x 4¾; [ ]² (tipped in), A-Z⁸; pp [iv], 368, comprising: half-title, with 'HAIL AND FAREWELL!' | A TRILOGY | I. AVE | II. SALVE-III. VALE | on verso, pp [i-ii]; title-page as in first edition, with "First Published, March, 1914. | New Impression, February, 1915." in center and LONDON: WILLIAM HEINEMANN. 1914. at foot of verso, pp [iii-iv]; text pp [1]-367, other particulars as in first edition.

Contents:

Same as second impression of first edition, with passage about Sir Hugh Lane omitted, but with added material of Tauchnitz edition (III-b above) included on pp 110-15. Further impressions issued February 1920 and May 1926.

c First English two-volume edition, revised:

6. Same as frontispieces of first and first American editions of *Sister Teresa* (A25-a and A25-2a).

HAIL AND FAREWELL! | BY | GEORGE MOORE | VOL. I [II] | London | William Heinemann Ltd. | 1925

Published February at 84/- in an edition of 780 sets

9 x 5½; Vol. I: [ ]⁸, A-2G⁸; pp xvi, 480, comprising: blank page, with list of twenty-five WORKS BY GEORGE MOORE on verso, pp [i-ii]; half-title, with notice of limitation as below on verso, pp [iii-iv]; title-page as above, with "Printed in Great Britain by T. and A. CONSTABLE LTD. | at the University Press, Edinburgh" on verso, pp [v-vi]; ART WITHOUT THE ARTIST pp vii-xvi; fly-title AVE, verso blank, pp [1-2]; text pp 3-317; p [318] blank; fly-title SALVE, verso blank, pp [319-20]; text pp 321-478; pp [479-80] blank;

Vol. II: [ ]⁴, A-2D⁸, 3E² (tipped in); pp [viii], 436, comprising: blank leaf, pp [i-ii]; blank page, with list of twenty-five WORKS BY GEORGE MOORE on verso, pp [iii-iv]; half-title, with notice of limitation as below except for number and signature on verso, pp [v-vi]; title-page as above, with printer's imprint as in Vol. I on verso, pp [vii-viii]; fly-title SALVE, verso blank, pp [1-2]; text continued, pp 3-147; p [148] blank; fly-title VALE, verso blank, pp [149-50]; text pp 151-[435]; p [436] blank; light blue endpapers in both volumes; all edges untrimmed; white parchment spines, with light blue paper-covered board sides matching endpapers; white paper labels on spines lettered in brown: Hail and | Farewell | I [II] | GEORGE | MOORE | Heinemann

Notice of limitation:

This edition, in two volumes, printed from hand-set | type on Van Gelder hand-made paper, is limited to | seven hundred and eighty sets, of which seven | hundred and fifty are for sale. | This is No. . . . . . [*numbered in ink*] | George Moore [*signed in ink*]

Contents:

"Art Without the Artist" also published in THE FORTNIGHTLY REVIEW, March 1925. *Ave* revised from its original appearance in one volume (I-a above). *Salve* revised from its original appearance in one volume (II-a above). *Vale* revised from its its original appearance in one volume (III-a above), with added material of Tauchnitz edition (III-b above) and 1915 and subsequent Heinemann impressions (III-2b above) omitted, but restoring the passage about Sir Hugh Lane deleted from the second Heinemann impression.

2c First American two-volume edition:

HAIL AND FAREWELL! | BY | GEORGE MOORE | VOLUME I [II] | [*publisher's device*] | D. APPLETON AND COMPANY | NEW YORK [*two fleurets*] MCMXXV [*all within border of printer's ornaments*]

Published 23 October 1925 at $7.50

8½ x 5⅝; Vol. I: [1-31]⁸, [32]⁴; pp xvi, 488, comprising: half-title, with list of four titles "By GEORGE MOORE" on verso, pp [i-ii]; inserted frontispiece, facing title-page, of reproduction of portrait of GM by Mark Fisher, with facsimile signature "George Moore" at foot of page, not paginated nor noted in collation: title page as above, with COPYRIGHT, 1911, 1912, 1925, BY | D. APPLETON AND COMPANY in center and PRINTED IN THE UNITED STATES OF AMERICA at foot of verso, pp [iii-iv]; ART WITHOUT THE ARTIST pp v-xv; p [xvi] blank; fly-title AVE, verso blank, pp [1-2]; text pp 3-[324]; fly-title SALVE, verso blank, pp [325-26]; text pp 327-[488]⁹;

Vol. II: 1-[28]⁸, [29]⁴; pp [iv], 452, comprising; half-title, with list of four titles "By GEORGE MOORE" on verso, pp [i-ii]; title-page as above, with COPYRIGHT, 1912, 1914, 1925, BY | D. APPLETON AND COMPANY and printing notice as in Vol. I on verso, pp [iii-iv]; fly-title SALVE, verso blank, pp [1-2]; text continued pp 3-[152]; fly-title VALE, verso blank, pp [153-54]; text pp 155-[445]³; p 446 blank; publisher's advertisements pp [447-49]; pp [450-52] blank; white endpapers in both volumes; cream and green head and foot bands; all edges trimmed; bound in purple cloth, back covers plain, single-rule border blind stamped on outer edges of front covers which are gilt stamped HAIL and | FAREWELL! | [*rule*] | GEORGE MOORE and spine gilt stamped HAIL | and | FAREWELL! | * [**] | GEORGE | MOORE | APPLETON

Contents:

Text same as two-volume English edition (c above). This revised text, with the addition of a six-line footnote on p 10 of *Vale* regarding a statement made by Dennis Gwynn in his biography of Edward Martyn about GM's Catholic ancestry, also was used for:

3c — Uniform Edition, three volumes, Heinemann, London, April 1933. Reissued in a different binding as:

3c2 — Ebury Edition, three volumes, Heinemann, London, June 1937.

A32

Esther Waters: A Play

a First edition:

ESTHER WATERS | BY GEORGE MOORE | A PLAY IN FIVE ACTS | LONDON: WILLIAM HEINEMANN | 1913

Published January at 2/6 in an edition of about 970 copies (see note 1 below)

8⅝ x 5⅜; [ ]⁸, A-1⁸, D⁴, L² (tipped in); pp xvi, 156 comprising: half-title, with list of three titles of "Works by George Moore" within single-rule box on verso; pp [i-ii]; title-page as above, with "Copyright 1913" in lower left corner of verso, pp [iii-iv]; list of acts and settings of the play, verso blank, pp [v-vi]; playbill of first performance, verso blank, pp [vii-viii]; PREFACE pp [ix-xv]; p [xvi] blank; text pp 1-[153] with pp [36] and [94] blank and PRINTED BY | BALLANTYNE & COMPANY LTD | AT THE BALLANTYNE PRESS | TAVISTOCK STREET COVENT GARDEN | LONDON at foot of p [153]; pp [154-56] blank; white endpapers; all edges trimmed; bound in gray-green paper-covered boards, back and front covers plain, with a white paper label on spine lettered in green ESTHER | WATERS | [*ornament*] | GEORGE | MOORE | [*ornament*] | LONDON: | HEINEMANN | 1913 [*all within a hairline-rule box*]

There are three states of the spine label and two binding variants, resulting in four separate issues of the first English edition: (1) As above, with rounded spine. (2) As above, with rounded spine, and with lettering on spine label expanded by the insertion of A PLAY IN | FIVE ACTS following title and above first ornament. (3) As above, with flat spine, and with the revised label. (4) As above, with flat spine and new spine label reset from slightly different type and type ornaments, and with date omitted.[1]

Contents:

The text is a dramatization[2] of a portion of *Esther Waters* (A19). The play was recommended to the Stage Society by Bernard Shaw and was produced for two performances at the Apollo Theatre, London, opening 10 December 1911. A copy of the playbill of this production is given on p [vii].

a2 First edition, American issue:

In April 1913 an American edition of the play, *Esther Waters*, was published at $1.25, using sheets and binding of the first edition (a above) with the first two preliminary leaves and spine label reset: p [ii] blank; publisher's imprint on title-page changed to "BOSTON: JOHN W. LUCE AND COMPANY | 1913" in smaller type; "Printed in England" added to center of title-leaf verso, and copyright notice in lower left corner omitted; rounded spine, and publisher's imprint on label changed to JOHN W. | LUCE & CO. | 1913

1. In a letter dated 2 July 1925 (now in the Frank Fayant collection), answering a query from A. J. A. Symons regarding the omission of the date, E. Brett of Heinemann's explained, "The binders tell me that it was in the last binding order that they discovered that they had lost the labels. This being so, 800 copies would have the date on and about 170 would be without it." From this it appears that the publishers, and presumably Mr. Symons, were unaware of the earliest state of the label without the explanatory subtitle.

2. For an account of another and later unpublished dramatization, see "George Moore at Work," by Barrett H. Clark, in THE AMERICAN MERCURY, February 1925, and reprinted in *Intimate Portraits*, New York, 1951. A film adaptation of *Esther Waters* made by Michael Gordon and William Rose was produced in 1949 by Wessex Film Productions and distributed by the Rank organization. It was produced and directed by Ian Dalrymple and Peter Proud, with Kathleen Ryan, Dirk Bogarde, Fay Compton, Cyril Cusack, Margaret Diamond, Morland Graham, and George Hager among those in the large cast.

A33

Elizabeth Cooper

a First edition:

ELIZABETH COOPER | A COMEDY IN THREE ACTS | BY GEORGE MOORE | MAUNSEL AND CO. LTD. | DUBLIN AND LONDON | 1913
   Published July 1913[1] at 2/-

7⅜ x 4⅞ ; [A]⁸, B-E⁸; pp 80, comprising: half-title, verso blank, pp [1-2]; title-page as above, with "Copyright 1913, George Moore" in center and PRINTED BY | BALLANTYNE & COMPANY LTD | LONDON at foot of verso, pp [3-4]; PERSONS IN THE PLAY, verso blank, pp [5-6]; text pp 7-80; white endpapers; all edges trimmed; bound in olive green cloth, single-rule border in blind on back and front covers, the latter gilt lettered ELIZABETH COOPER | A COMEDY BY | GEORGE MOORE | and spine gilt lettered ELIZABETH | COOPER | A | COMEDY | BY | GEORGE | MOORE | MAUNSEL
   Contents:
Previous to publication the play was produced 22 June 1913 by the Incorporated Stage Society at the Haymarket Theatre in London, and a copy of the playbill of this production is on p [5]. Each of the three acts was published in an issue of INTERNATIONAL MAGAZINE (New York), July, August, and September 1913.

a2 First American edition:

Sheets of the first edition (a above) cut down [7¼ x 4⅞] were used for the American edition published 8 July 1913 at 75¢, with the publisher's imprint on title-page reset BOSTON: JOHN W. LUCE & CO | DUBLIN:

---

1. Late in 1904 an earlier version of *Elizabeth Cooper* was set in type by The Ballantyne Press (which also printed this edition), and three sets of sheets were printed. According to William K. Magee (John Eglinton), who had one of the sets which was given him by GM, it is "unbound, in eight sheets, and without title-page. The text runs to 117 pp., [which is] slightly longer than the 1913 edition." This earlier printing was arranged by Dr. James Starkey (Seumas O'Sullivan) of Dublin at GM's request for copyrght purposes. GM had worked on the play for a number of years, sometimes with Mrs. Pearl Craigie (John Oliver Hobbes) with whom he previously had collaborated on *The Fool's Hour* (B6) and *Journeys End in Lovers Meeting* (B11), and during their joint work on the present play it also had been called *The Three Lovers* and *The Peacock's Feathers*. GM wished to protect his interest in the play when he came to a parting of the way with Mrs. Craigie, but he must have reached an understanding with her, as the three sets of sheets were not used for copyright purposes. In addition to the set given Mr. Magee, which is now in the library of the Humanities Research Center of the University of Texas, a set was given to Dr. Starkey, and it was this set that was later in the possession of Ernest Boyd, and is possibly the same set catalogued circa 1929 by Brentano's Bookstore in New York. The present location of this set and of the third set, presumably kept by GM, are unknown.

MAUNSEL & CO. LTD | 1913, and book bound in tan paper-covered boards, back cover plain, front cover lettered in brown ELIZABETH | COOPER | A COMEDY | By GEORGE | MOORE [*within a full-page Aubrey Beardsley design depicting the stage of a theater with four harlequinade figures in orchestra pit*], flat spine lettered in brown E | L | I | Z | A | B | E | T | H | C | O | O | P | E | R | LUCE | & CO.

Elizabeth Cooper was rewritten and published in 1920 as *The Coming of Gabrielle* (A39).

See D:Fr-18 for a French translation and production. No trace has been found of a German translation mentioned by Hone (p 284), who, however, does not state that it was ever produced or published.

A34
Muslin

a First edition with new title:

MUSLIN | BY | GEORGE MOORE | [*publisher's windmill device, flanked by letters* W *and* H, *within a single-rule box*] | LONDON | WILLIAM HEINEMANN

Published 16 September 1915 at 6/- in an edition of 2,000 copies

7⅜ x 4¾ ; [ ]¹⁰ (±[ ]₂), A-X⁸, Y⁴; pp xx, 344, comprising: half-title, with list of sixteen WORKS BY GEORGE MOORE on verso, pp [i-ii]; title-page as above, with "Originally published under the title of | 'A Drama in Muslin,' 1886. | New Edition, September, 1915." in center and "LONDON: WILLIAM HEINEMANN. 1915." at foot of verso, pp [iii-iv]¹; PREFACE

1. All copies of the first impression, including those blind stamped PRESENTATION COPY on title-page, seem to have the title-leaf tipped in on a stub, and apparently there is no explanation other than the possibility of a misprint on either the recto or verso of the original leaf serious enough to cause it to be cancelled. The publisher's records show, according to Miss Grace Cranston of William Heinemann Ltd., that 2,000 sets of sheets were printed for them in July 1915 and at the same time 1,000 sets were printed for Brentano's (see a2 below). The records also show that 2,030 cancel title-leaves were printed in August, but without an explanation of why they were printed. One hypothesis is that all 3,000 sets were inadvertently printed with the Brentano imprint on the title-page. According to Miss Cranston "ten copies . . . were specially bound up in demy 8vo format for the author in September 1915." Untrimmed Brentano sheets (8¾ x 5½) were used for these author's copies but they were placed in a special Heinemann binding similar to the regular edition with the addition of a double-rule border in blind at outer edges of front cover, on the spine the gilt panel is elongated, the side rules are heavier, and there is a short rule between the title and the author's name. GM presented one of these special copies to Maud Cunard dated "October 1st 1915" and it is now in the collection of Sir Rupert Hart-Davis.

pp v-xx; text pp [1]-343, with BILLING AND SONS, LTD., PRINTERS, GUILDFORD, ENGLAND. at foot of p [343]; p [344] blank; followed by an inserted 16-page publisher's catalogue; white endpapers; top and fore edges trimmed, bottom edges untrimmed; bound in dark blue cloth with publisher's monogram device in blind in lower right corner of back cover, front cover blind stamped with large elongated paneled design enclosed within double-rule border, spine gilt lettered MUSLIN | GEORGE | MOORE [*all within a long gilt single-rule box with scallop-shaped design at top and bottom*] | HEINEMANN

Further impressions were issued with title-leaf an integral part of the first gathering. Some copies do not have the inserted publisher's catalogue at end, and others have a catalogue which lists (p [15]) *Muslin* among the NEW NOVELS OF 1915.

Contents:

The "Preface" is new and, as stated on verso of the title-leaf, the text is a rewritten version of *A Drama in Muslin* (A9).

a2 First American, Brentano Uniform edition:

MUSLIN | BY | GEORGE MOORE | NEW YORK | BRENTANO'S | 1915

$7\frac{7}{8}$ x $5\frac{1}{4}$; [ ]^{10}, A-X^8, Y^4; pp xx, 344, comprising: sheets printed from plates of English edition (a above), but with title-page reset as above and PRINTED IN GREAT BRITAIN. at foot of verso in place of LONDON: WILLIAM HEINEMANN. 1915.; white endpapers; all edges trimmed; bound in green ribbed cloth, back and front covers plain, gilt decorations at top and bottom of spine which is gilt lettered MUSLIN | GEORGE | MOORE | BRENTANO'S

Contents:

Same as first edition (a above). Other editions using the rewritten, retitled text include:

a3 — Heinemann's Colonial Library, London, circa 1915; issued in both wrappers and red cloth, using sheets of the later impressions of the first edition, with title-leaf an integral part of first gathering.

2a — Collection of British Authors, in two volumes, Nos. 4541 and 4542, Bernhard Tauchnitz, Leipzig, 1920.

3a — Carra Edition, Volume III, Boni and Liveright, New York, 1922, with a tipped-in frontispiece, protected by a tissue guard sheet lettered in red at foot of verso GEORGE MOORE | From a painting by J. B. Yeats — 1905 | In the Collection of John Quinn, Esq.

4a — Uniform Edition, Heinemann, London, October 1932. Reissued in a different binding as:

4a2 — Ebury Edition, Heinemann, London, September 1936.

A35

The Brook Kerith[1]

a First edition:

THE BROOK KERITH | A SYRIAN STORY | BY GEORGE MOORE | PRINTED FOR T. WERNER LAURIE LTD. | BY THE RIVERSIDE PRESS LTD., EDINBURGH | 1916

Published 23 August at 7/6 in an edition of 2,000 copies[2]

8¾ x 5⅜; [a]⁴, A-2F⁸, 2G⁴; pp [viii], 472, comprising blank page, with list of three books "By GEORGE MOORE" in a three-compartment box on verso, pp [i-ii]; half-title, verso blank, pp [iii-iv]; title-page as above, verso blank, pp [v-vi]; A DEDICATION (fifteen lines in two paragraphs),[3] verso blank, pp [vii-viii]; text pp 1-471; "THE RIVERSIDE PRESS LIMITED, EDINBURGH" in center p [472]; white endpapers; top edges trimmed, fore and bottom edges untrimmed; bound with smooth brown cloth[4] spine and corners, with marbled paper-covered board sides, spine simulating a leather binding with five raised horizontal bands and three medallions in blind, and with white paper label, lettered in black: The | Brook | Kerith | [*ornament*] | GEORGE | MOORE | T. Werner Laurie, Ltd. | LONDON

There are two issues of the first edition: (1) As above. (2) An issue of 200 copies[5] for use in circulating libraries, the sheets slightly cut down (8½ x 5½), all edges trimmed, bound in gray cloth, publisher's monogram within a circle in center of back cover, front cover plain, spine lettered in black: The | Brook | Kerith | [*rule*] | George | Moore | T. Werner | Laurie Ltd.

1. *The Brook Kerith*, perhaps to a greater extent than any other work by GM, shows his painstaking effort to perfect his writing. Practically every new printing has minor revisions, and while none can be considered a major rewriting the cumulative effect is of a new text. I have, therefore, assigned a single textual letter to all editions until the final text was achieved, but have noted each edition that contains revisions.

2. In a letter to John Eglinton, dated September 25, 1916, GM wrote "Werner Laurie is now selling the third edition, which is certainly the fourth thousand and may be the fifth. The first edition was two thousand and the second may have been the same."

3. In all impressions after the first the dedication is set in fourteen lines in one paragraph as in signed, limited edition (a2 below).

4. Danielson lists the cloth as being "imitation leather" and further notes "Owing to the orders coming in so rapidly, the publishers had to increase the size of the edition, and as the binders had saved only a certain amount of tan imitation leather, they were instructed to use the nearest material they could to bind the balance; these remaining copies were bound in half brown pegamoid." All copies seen of the first impression are bound in smooth cloth, and all copies seen of the second, third, and fourth impressions (called "editions" in publication notices) are bound in the darker pebbly "pegamoid." The smooth cloth was again used for the fifth impression (see a3 below).

5. According to Danielson.

A second impression, with minor revisions, published 11 September; a third impression, 17 September; and a fourth, 9 October.

Contents:

Previously unpublished, but based on *The Apostle* (A30-a). Both are dedicated to Mary Hunter, whose gift of a Bible in 1898 started GM's thoughts toward the present story.

a2 Limited edition:

Published 23 August at 35/- in an edition of 250 copies

9 x 5⅝; printed from plates of first edition (a above) with all particulars, including title-page, as in that edition, except dedication (p [v]) is set in fourteen lines in one paragraph; a single leaf ([b]^1) is tipped in following dedication leaf ([a]$_4$) with notice of limitation as below on recto, verso blank, pp [ix-x]; gray endpapers; all edges untrimmed; white parchment spine, with gray paper-covered board sides, matching the endpapers; white paper label on spine, lettered in blue: Edition de Luxe | The | Brook | Kerith | [*ornament*] | GEORGE | MOORE | T. Werner Laurie, Ltd. | LONDON [*all within single-rule box*]

Notice of limitation:

This edition de luxe consists of | 250 copies, numbered and signed. | This is No. . . . . . [*numbered in ink*] | George Moore [*signed in ink*]

Contents:

Same as first edition (a above).

a3 Fifth impression, with preface:

Published December 1921 at 21/- in an edition of 500 copies[6]

8⅞ x 5⅞; printed from corrected plates of first edition (a above), with all particulars as in that edition, except first gathering is [a]^8; printer's imprint on title-page changed to THE DUNEDIN PRESS LTD., EDINBURGH and date changed to 1921; PREFACE pp [ix]-xiv; p [472] blank; gray endpapers; all edges untrimmed; binding as in first edition.

Contents:

The "Preface," originally published as " 'The Brook Kerith.' Mr. George Moore's New Preface. How St. Paul Died." in THE SUNDAY TIMES, 6 November 1921, is new and found in no other edition. In it GM relates "that the text has been slightly amended here and there."

2a First American edition:

THE | BROOK KERITH | A Syrian Story | BY | GEORGE MOORE | [*double rule*] | So he went and did according unto the word of the Lord: for he | went and dwelt by the brook Kerith, that is before Jordan. And the | ravens brought him bread and flesh in the morning, and bread and | flesh in the evening; and he drank of the brook — I Kings xvii. 5,6. | [*double rule*] |

6. According to *Books of the "Nineties"* (see A22-n2).

New York | THE MACMILLAN COMPANY | 1916 | All rights reserved
Published 23 August[7] at $1.50

7½ x 5⅛; [A] [1] (tipped in between B_2 and B_3), B-2I [8] (signed on recto of third leaves), [2K][2] (tipped in); pp [vi], 496, comprising: half-title, with publisher's monogram and world-wide addresses on verso, pp [i-ii]; title-page as above, with "COPYRIGHT, 1916, | BY GEORGE MOORE. | [*rule*] | Set up and electrotyped. Published May, 1916." in center and "Norwood Press | J. S. Cushing Co.–Berwick & Smith Co. | Norwood, Mass., U.S.A." at bottom of verso, pp [iii-iv]; A DEDICATION (fourteen lines in one paragraph), verso blank, pp [v-vi]; text pp 1-486, with "Printed in the United States of America." at foot of p 486; publisher's notice within single-rule box in center of p [487]; p [488] blank; publisher's advertisements pp [489-95]; p [496] blank; white endpapers; top and bottom edges trimmed, fore edges untrimmed; bound in dark green cloth, back cover plain, ornamental border in blind on front cover, which is gilt lettered THE | BROOK KERITH | GEORGE MOORE | [*ornament*], and spine gilt stamped THE | BROOK | KERITH | MOORE | [*ornament*] | MACMILLAN [*with ornamental border at top and bottom of spine*]

Contents:

Same as first edition (a above).

Second and third impressions issued September 1916, reimposed B-2I [8] (signed on recto of fourth leaves), [2K][4], and with notation of reprintings added on verso of title-leaf.

2a2 New American edition, with preface:

Published 10 October[8] 1916 at $1.50

7½ x 5⅛; B-2I [8] (signed on recto of seventh leaves), 2K [8]; pp xii, 500; printed from reimposed plates of first American edition (2a above) with all particulars the same except NEW EDITION WITH A PREFACE added on title-page before publisher's imprint, and notation "New edition with a preface, October, 1916." added on verso, pp [iii-iv]; PREFACE pp vii-x; fly-title, verso blank, pp [xi-xii]; and pp [496-500] blank.

7. Actual date of publication according to copyright data in Library of Congress, and this is confirmed by R. L. DeWilton, assistant editor-in-chief of Macmillan Company, New York, who informs me regarding the statement "Published May, 1916" on verso of title-leaf, "We did plan to publish our first edition in May of 1916, but we postponed it to coincide with the publication of the English edition, and consequently our date was August 23, 1916."

8. Mr. DeWilton further informs me, "So far as I can gather from our rather faulty records of that early time, this edition was probably published either October 10 or October 30." The earlier date has been assigned as subsequent Macmillan printings have the publication notice on the verso of the title-leaf "New Edition with Preface, October, 1916 | Reprinted October, 1916." The reprinting date seems to account for the second date listed by Mr. DeWilton.

Contents:

The "Preface," which is new and found in no other edition, is based on a letter, "Mr. George Moore on Christ's Divinity," in the PALL MALL GAZETTE, 4 September 1916; the text has minor revisions and is basically the same as that of the second impression of the first edition (a above) published 11 September 1916.

New impressions October 1916, March 1917, and November 1926. Sheets of the March 1917 impression were used for:

2a3 — Brentano Uniform Edition, New York, 1917, with cancel tipped in title-leaf which has recto as in new American edition (2a2 above) including Macmillan imprint, but with verso as in first American edition (2a above), except THIS EDITION SPECIALLY PRINTED FOR BRENTANO'S is added after the publication date. This revised text also was used for:

3a — Collection of British Authors, two volumes, Nos. 4536 and 4537, Bernhard Tauchnitz, Leipzig, 1920.

4a — Carra Edition, Boni and Liveright, New York, 24 November 1923. There is a tipped-in frontispiece protected by a tissue guard sheet lettered in red at foot of verso "GEORGE MOORE | From a Pencil Sketch by "Jack" Yeats | on an Abbey Theatre Programme." The author's "Note" (pp [ix-x]) is principally quoted from "Apologia pro scriptis meis," the introductory essay to the Carra Edition, printed in Volume I, *Lewis Seymour and Some Women* (A36–4a). In it GM says, "for a thorough revision of the text I had to wait for the Carra edition," although most of the revisions first appeared in the fifth impression of the first English edition (a3 above).

b Second English (Uniform) edition, revised:

THE | BROOK KERITH | A SYRIAN STORY | BY | GEORGE MOORE | [*vignette*] | London | William Heinemann Ltd. | 1927

Published November at 10/6

9 x 5½; a⁴, A-2F⁸, 2G² (tipped in); pp [viii], 468, comprising: blank leaf, except for signature letter on recto, pp [i-ii]; half-title, with two titles PREVIOUSLY PUBLISHED IN | THE SAME FORMAT listed on verso, pp [iii-iv]; title-page as above, with list of previous impressions (called "editions") concluding with "Seventh ″ [Edition] (revised) 1927" in center and "Printed in Great Britain by the Riverside Press Limited | Edinburgh" at foot of verso, pp [v-vi]; A DEDICATION, verso blank, pp [vii-viii]; text pp 1-468; extra spine label tipped in on lower left corner of recto of free endpaper; white endpapers; all edges untrimmed; brown cloth spine, with marbled paper-covered board sides, white paper label on spine lettered in brown: The | Brook | Kerith | George | Moore | Heinemann

Contents:

This final text was again revised and incorporates most of the revisions made in previous printings. Reissued in a different binding as:

b2 — Ebury Edition, Heinemann, London, November 1937.

2b First illustrated edition:

GEORGE MOORE | THE BROOK KERITH [*in blue*] | A SYRIAN STORY | WITH TWELVE ENGRAVINGS | BY | STEPHEN GOODEN | [*engraving of seated shepherd and dog*] | LONDON | WILLIAM HEINE-MANN LTD. | 1929

Published 28 March in an edition of 375 copies

10¼ x 9⅜; [ ]⁴, A-Y⁸, Z⁶, plus nine inserted engravings and ten tissue guard sheets (see below); pp [viii], 364, comprising: half-title, with notice of limitation as below on verso, pp [i-ii]; tissue guard sheet, not paginated; title-page as above, verso blank, pp [iii-iv]; A DEDICATION, verso blank, pp [v-vi]; LIST OF ILLUSTRATIONS,⁹ verso blank, pp [vii-viii]; text pp 1-[362], with engravings at top of p 1 and bottom of p [362], and nine inserted engravings, each protected by tissue guard sheet, facing pp 18, 72, 88, 110, 184, 226, 240, 264, and 286, not paginated; pp [363-64] blank; white endpapers; all edges untrimmed; green and gold headband; bound in full parchment over beveled boards; back and front covers plain, spine gilt stamped GEORGE MOORE | THE | BROOK KERITH | [*small diamond*] | ENGRAVINGS BY | STEPHEN GOODEN | HEINEMANN

Notice of limitation:

This edition of *The Brook Kerith*, printed | on hand-made paper from hand-set type, | is limited to 375 copies. This is number . . . . . [*numbered in ink*] | George Moore [*signed in ink*] | Stephen Gooden [*signed in ink*]

Contents:

Text same as second English edition (b above).

3b First American illustrated edition:

GEORGE MOORE | THE BROOK KERITH [*in blue*] | A SYRIAN STORY | WITH TWELVE ENGRAVINGS | BY | STEPHEN GOODEN | [*engraving of seated shepherd and dog*] | NEW YORK | THE MACMIL-LAN COMPANY | 1929

Published 18 June at $35 in an edition of 500 copies

10 x 6⅛; [1]¹ (tipped in), [2]¹², [3-25]⁸, [26]⁴, plus nine inserted engravings and ten tissue guard sheets (see below); pp [x], 392, comprising: notice of limitation as below, verso blank, pp [i-ii]; half-title, verso blank, pp [iii-iv]; tissue guard leaf, not paginated; title-page as above, with "COPY-RIGHT, 1916 AND 1929, | BY GEORGE MOORE. | [*rule*] | Set up and electrotyped. Published May, 1916. | [*rule*] | Reprinted twice, September, 1916. | New Edition with Preface, October, 1916. | Reprinted October,

9. See nos. 55-66 in *An Iconography of the Engravings of Stephen Gooden*, by Campbell Dodgson, London, 1944.

1916; March, 1917. | Reissued November, 1926. | Special limited and illustrated Edition completely revised | and reset. Published June, 1929." on verso, pp [v-vi]; A DEDICATION, verso blank, pp [vii-viii]; LIST OF IL- LUSTRATIONS, verso blank, pp [ix-x]; text pp 1-391, with engravings at top of p 1 and bottom of p 391, and inserted engravings, each protected by a tissue guard sheet, facing pp 18, 76, 96, 118, 198, 246, 262, 288, and 310, not paginated; p [392] blank; black endpapers; top edges gilt, fore and bottom edges untrimmed; cream head and tail bands; white vellum spine, with black paper-covered board sides, matching endpapers, front and back covers stamped with gilt rule at juncture of black paper sides and vellum spine, back cover otherwise plain, front cover gilt stamped with facsimile "George Moore" signature, spine gilt lettered GEORGE MOORE | THE | BROOK KERITH | ENGRAVINGS BY | STEPHEN GOODEN | [*dot*] MACMILLAN [*dot*][10]

Notice of limitation:

Of this revised and reset edition of | *THE BROOK KERITH* 500 copies | have been printed for American sale, | of which this is number . . . . . [*numbered in ink*] | George Moore [*signed in ink*] | Stephen Gooden [*signed in ink*]

Contents:

Same as English illustrated edition (2e above). Plates of this edition, without the Gooden engravings, were used for:

2b2 — Popular edition, Macmillan, New York, 1936; reprinted July 1956. This final revised text also was used for:

4b — Penguin Books, No. 844, Harmondsworth, Middlesex, 14 November 1952.

A dramatization of a portion of *The Brook Kerith* was published in 1923 as *The Apostle* (A30-b) and revised in 1930 as *The Passing of the Essenes* (A55).

See D:Fr-24 for a French translation.

A36

Lewis Seymour and Some Women

a First edition with new title:

LEWIS SEYMOUR | AND SOME WOMEN | BY | GEORGE MOORE |

10. Selected in 1930 as one of the "Fifty Books of the Year" by the American Institute of Graphic Arts.

96

[publisher's diamond-shaped device] | NEW YORK | BRENTANO'S | 1917
Published 26 January at $1.50

7⅞ x 5⅜; [1]⁸, [2-11]¹⁶ ([11]₁₅ and [11]₁₆ are free and pastedown end-papers, not counted in pagination); pp xxi, 320, comprising: half-title, with list of ten WORKS OF GEORGE MOORE | NEW AND REVISED EDI-TION in single-rule box on verso, pp [i-ii]; title-page as above, with "Copy-right, 1917, by Brentano's" in center of verso, pp [iii-v]; PREFACE pp v-xi; p [xii] blank; text pp 1-320; front endpapers white, rear endpapers part of final gathering; top edges trimmed and stained dark green, fore and bottom edges untrimmed; bound in green ribbed cloth, back and front covers plain, gilt decorations at top and bottom of flat spine, which is gilt lettered LEWIS | SEYMOUR | AND SOME | WOMEN | GEORGE | MOORE | BREN-TANO'S

Contents:

Text is a further rewriting of *A Modern Lover* (A5), and although most characters, many incidents, and much of the dialogue of the earlier book is retained, it is described by GM in the new "Preface" as being a "new book from end to end." Five chapters are added, eight chapters of the original story are omitted, and the latter half of the book is largely rewritten. One new portion in chapter XXI is based on "Souvenir sur Mallarmé" in THE BUTTERFLY, Summer 1909.

Later impressions have a different imposition: [1-20]⁸, [21]⁴, [22]² (tipped in); with list of nine titles on verso of half-title leaf in NEW AND UNIFORM [*in place of* REVISED] EDITION; publisher's device on title-page in orange, rear endpapers separate and not a part of the final gathering, and bound in a darker green cloth with rounded spine.

2a First English edition:

LEWIS SEYMOUR | AND SOME WOMEN | BY | GEORGE MOORE | *[publisher's windmill device, flanked by letters* W *and* H, *within a single-rule box]* | LONDON | WILLIAM HEINEMANN
Published March 1917¹ at 6/-

1. At least six copies were printed, of what might be called an "advance unpub-lished state," dated 1916 on verso of title-leaf, some bound in white paper wrappers lettered in black on front cover LEWIS SEYMOUR | AND | SOME WOMEN, and others bound in same binding used for regular edition. These copies have two un-signed gatherings, [ ]⁴ and [ ]¹ (tipped in), in place of the unsigned gathering [ ]⁶; the PREFACE is on pp v-x; and there are textual differences on pp vi-viii, 26, 59, 73-74, 90, 95-96, 104-5, 108, 114-15, 126-28, 199, 200, 220, 248-49, 257, 260-63, 265, 268, 270, 274-77, 279-85, and 310; plus differences in paragraphing, capitaliza-tion, and setting throughout. One of these copies, listed in Volume III (p 158) of *The Ashley Library: A Catalogue of Printed Books, Manuscripts and Autograph Letters*, privately printed, London, 1923, is inscribed, "This is one of six copies of *Lewis Seymour and Some Women* printed without alterations from the author's Manuscript. The book was, however, never issued in this form; certain passages were

7½ x 4⅝; [ ]^6, A-T^8, U^2 (tipped in), [u]^1 (tipped in between U$_1$ and U$_2$); pp xii, 310, comprising: half-title, with list of WORKS OF GEORGE MOORE on verso, pp [i-ii]; title-page as above, with LONDON: WILLIAM HEINEMANN. 1917. | at foot of verso, pp [iii-iv]; PREFACE pp v-xi; p [xii] blank; text pp [1]-310; with BILLING AND SONS, LTD., PRINTERS, GUILDFORD, ENGLAND at foot p 310; followed by an inserted, separately numbered 16-page undated catalogue of publisher's advertisements; white endpapers; top and fore edges trimmed, bottom edges untrimmed; bound in dark blue cloth, publisher's monogram device in blind in lower right corner of back cover, front cover blind stamped with large elongated paneled design enclosed within double-rule border, spine gilt stamped LEWIS | SEYMOUR | AND | SOME | WOMEN | GEORGE | MOORE [*all enclosed within gilt rule border with scallop-shaped design at top and bottom*] | HEINEMANN

Contents:

Same as first edition (a above), except for last-minute revisions made by GM on the page proofs, including three additional lines in French on final page of text which are found in no other printing, including the "advance unpublished state" (described in note 1) and subsequent impressions of this edition issued April 1917 and October 1928 with further slight revisions and with new imposition: [1]^8, 2-19^8, 20^{10}; pp xii, 312. The first edition text also was used for:

3a — Standard Collection, No. 80, Conrad, Paris, 1918.

4a Second American (Carra) edition:

LEWIS SEYMOUR | AND SOME WOMEN | BY | GEORGE MOORE | [*rule*] | Carra Edition | [*rule*] | PRINTED FOR SUBSCRIBERS ONLY BY | BONI AND LIVERIGHT, INC., NEW YORK | 1922

Published 18 December at $8.50 in an edition of 1,000 copies

8¾ x 5½; [1]^{10}, [2-19]^8; pp xl, 268, comprising: blank leaf, pp [i-ii]; half-title, with reproduction of an Alvin Langdon Coburn photograph of GM tipped on verso; pp [iii-iv]; followed by a protective tissue guard sheet, not paginated; title-page as above, with "LEWIS SEYMOUR AND SOME | WOMEN | (Carra Edition) | [*rule*] | Copyright 1917, by Brentano's. | Copyright 1922 by | Boni & Liveright, Inc. | [*rule*] | Printed in the United States of America" in center of verso, pp [v-vi]; EPISTLE DEDICATORY, verso blank, pp [vii-viii]; notice of limitation as below, verso blank, pp [ix-x]; APOLOGIA PRO SCRIPTIS MEIS pp xi-xxxiii; p [xxxiv] blank; PREFACE pp xxxv-xxxix; p [xl] blank; text pp 1-265; pp [266-68] blank; grayish-blue paper-covered board sides, matching endpapers; white paper label on spine, printed in black, except as noted: Lewis | Seymour | and Some |

excised, and others rewritten in the version finally published. C. S. Evans, General Manager to William Heinemann."

Women | [*decorative rule*] | George Moore [*in red*] | [*decorative rule*] | Carra Edition | Volume I [*two plain rules, with decorative rule between, all in red, at both top and bottom*]

Notice of limitation:

This edition consists of 1000 numbered sets | of twenty-one volumes each. The first vol- | ume is numbered, and signed by the author. | This set is No. . . . . . [*number stamped in blue*] | George Moore [*signed in ink*]

Contents:

"Epistle Dedicatory to Thomas Ruttledge," dedicating the Carra Edition[2] to GM's "oldest and dearest friend," who also served as agent for his Irish properties. "Apologia pro scriptis meis,"[3] the general introduction to the Carra Edition, was previously published in FORTNIGHTLY REVIEW, October 1922. "Preface" same as first edition (a above) except for omission of final nine words of second paragraph. *Lewis Seymour and Some Women* same as first edition.

A37
A Story-Teller's Holiday

a First edition:

A STORY-TELLER'S | HOLIDAY | BY | GEORGE MOORE | LONDON | PRIVATELY PRINTED FOR SUBSCRIBERS ONLY BY | Cumann Sean-eolais na h-Eireann [*in Gaelic characters*] | 1918

Issued[1] July by T. Werner Laurie in an edition of 1,000 copies

2. Twenty-one volumes, plus two supplementary volumes in a matching format, were printed on paper watermarked with a facsimile of GM's signature. Eighteen of the volumes have tipped-in frontispieces, sixteen being reproductions of photographs, paintings or sketches of GM. In addition to *Lewis Seymour and Some Women*, the Carra Edition includes *A Mummer's Wife* (A6-3c); *Muslin* (A34-3a); *Spring Days* (A13-3b); *Esther Waters* (A19-2c); *Evelyn Inness* [sic] (A22-3a); *Sister Teresa* (A25-3a); *The Untilled Field* (A26-2c) and *The Lake* (A27-2d) in one volume; *Confessions of a Young Man* (A12-e) and *Avowals* (A38-3a) in one volume; *Memoirs of My Dead Life* (A29-3d); *Hail and Farewell*, three volumes (A31:I-4a, A31:II-4a, and A31:3a); *A Story-Teller's Holiday* (A37-3a); *Héloïse and Abélard* (A40-2b) in two volumes; *The Brook Kerith* (A35-4a); *In Single Strictness* (A44-b); *Modern Painting* (A17-b4); *Conversations in Ebury Street* (A46-2a); *Daphnis and Chloe* (A49-2a) and *Perronik* [sic] *the Fool* (A50-a) in one volume. *Pure Poetry* (A47-2a) and *Ulick and Soracha* (A51-2a) were issued as supplementary volumes in a format and on paper matching the Carra Edition, although not actually a part of it, but unnumbered copies of the two were included with remaindered sets.

3. Completely different from the preface to the first American edition of *Memoirs of My Dead Life* (A29-2a), which has the same title.

1. Owing to the attempted legal suppression of *The Brook Kerith* and the libel suit instituted on the publication of *Lewis Seymour and Some Women*, GM decided that

8⅞ x 5¼; [a]⁴, [b]¹ (tipped in), A-Y⁸, Z² (tipped in); pp [x], 356, comprising: blank leaf pp [i-ii]; half-title, verso blank, pp [iii-iv]; title-page as above, verso blank, pp [v-vi]; A LEAVE-TAKING (misnumbered v), verso blank, pp [vii-viii]; fly-title with notice of limitation as below, verso blank, pp [ix-x]; text pp 1-355; with THE RIVERSIDE PRESS LIMITED, EDINBURGH at foot of p 355; p [356] blank; greenish-blue endpapers; all edges untrimmed; parchment spine, with greenish-blue paper-covered board sides matching the endpapers, white paper label on spine, lettered in brown: A | Story-Teller's | Holiday | [ornament] | GEORGE | MOORE | Privately | Printed

Notice of limitation:

This edition consists of 1000 copies, | numbered and signed. | This is No. . . . . . [stamped number] | George Moore [signed in ink]

Contents:

"A Leave-Taking" previously published in THE TIMES LITERARY SUPPLE-MENT, 21 March 1918. Chapter III, partially (portion on the ruins of Dublin) previously published in THE EVENING NEWS, 5 June 1916. Chapter V partially previously published as "A June Trip Through Ireland" in THE EVENING NEWS, 29 June 1916. Final two sentences of chapter XVI, all of chapter XVII, and first twenty-three pages of chapter XVIII (pp 72-95) previously translated into French by G. Jean-Aubry and published as "Curithir et Laidine" (D:Fr-16) in MERCURE DE FRANCE, 18 April 1918. Other sections previously unpublished. In chapter XII on p 48 the second and third words in line 14 ("Nouvelle Athènes") are blacked out.

2a First American edition:

A STORY-TELLER'S | HOLIDAY | BY | GEORGE MOORE | NEW YORK | PRIVATELY PRINTED FOR SUBSCRIBERS ONLY BY | Cumann Sean-eolais na h-Eireann [in Gaelic characters] | 1918

Issued[2] 25 September at $6.75 by Boni & Liveright in an edition of 1,250 copies

9½ x 6¼; [1-23]⁸; pp [viii], 360, comprising: blank leaf, pp [i-ii]; half-title, with notice of limitation as below on verso, pp [iii-iv]; title-page as above, with "COPYRIGHT, 1918, BY | GEORGE MOORE | [rule] | All Rights Reserved" in center of verso, pp [v-vi]; fly-title, verso blank, pp [vii-viii]; A LEAVE-TAKING, verso blank, pp [1-2]; text pp 3-358; pp [359-60] blank; white endpapers; all edges untrimmed; black head and foot bands; bound in black buckram, back and front covers plain, spine blind stamped to simulate a leather binding with seven raised horizontal bands, with red

---

in the future his books would be issued privately in limited editions. As Hone (p 343) relates it, "A Story-Teller's Holiday was the first of these limited editions, which it pleased Moore to issue under the sign of Cumann Sean-eolais na h-Eireann (Society for Irish Folklore), but no such society has ever existed."

2. See note 1.

leather label between second and third bands from top, gilt stamped [*rule*] |
A [*swag letter*] | STORY- | TELLER'S | HOLIDAY | [*three ornaments*] |
George | Moore | [*rule*]

Notice of limitation:

1250 copies of this work have been printed | of which this is number
. . . . . [*number stamped in red*]

Contents:

Same as first edition (a above), except that the two words blacked out in
chapter XII are here omitted. The original text also was used for:

3a — Carra Edition, Volume XIV, Boni and Liveright, New York, 1923;
with a tipped-in frontispiece, protected by a tissue guard sheet lettered in
red at foot of verso GEORGE MOORE | From an Etching by William
Strang[3]

b Third American edition, revised and expanded:

A | STORY-TELLER'S | HOLIDAY | BY | GEORGE MOORE | VOL. I
[II] | Issued for Subscribers only by | HORACE LIVERIGHT | NEW
YORK | 1928

Published July at $20 in an edition of 1,250 sets

8¾ x 5⅜; Vol. I: [1]² (tipped in), [2-17]⁸, [18]⁴; pp x, 258, comprising:
half-title, with notice of limitation as below on verso, pp [i-ii]; title-page,
with "A Story-Teller's Holiday | Copyright, 1918, by Boni & Liveright, Inc. |
[*rule*] | Ulick and Soracha | Copyright, 1926, by Boni & Liveright, Inc. |
[*rule*] | Copyright, 1928, by | Horace Liveright, Inc." in center and "Printed
in the United States of America" at foot of verso, pp [iii-iv]; dedication, verso
blank, pp [v-vi]; PREFACE pp vii-ix; p [x] blank; text pp 1-257; p [258]
blank;

Vol. II: [1-17]⁸, pp [vi], 266, comprising: half-title, verso blank, pp [i-ii];
title-page as above, with copyright and printing notices as in Vol. I on verso,
pp [iii-iv]; fly-title, verso blank, pp [v-vi]; text pp 1-263; pp [264-66] blank;
both volumes printed on laid paper watermarked with facsimile signature
"George Moore";[4] white endpapers; green head bands; all edges untrimmed;
bound in dark green buckram, blind stamped on back and front covers with
an all-over design of stylized flowers and vines within a single-rule border,
spine gilt stamped [*rule*] | A [*four swirl ornament*] | STORY- [*single-swirl
ornament*] | TELLER'S | HOLIDAY | [*rule*] | GEORGE | MOORE | [*single
(double) ornament(s)*] [*ornamental design, matching blind stamping on
covers, within single-rule border*] | 1928 | [*rule*]

Notice of limitation:

This edition of A STORY-TELLER'S | HOLIDAY in two volumes is
strictly | limited to Twelve Hundred and Fifty | Sets Numbered and Signed. |

---

3. Reproduction of etching previously used as the frontispiece of the first edition
of *Confessions of a Young Man* (A12-a).

4. Same as paper used for Carra Edition (see A36-n2).

George Moore [*signed in ink*] | This Copy is Number | [*stamped number*]
Contents:

Vol. I: "Dear Lady of my thoughts, dear Lady Cunard," dedication reprinted from *Ulick and Soracha* (A51). "Preface," by Ernest Longworth, written at GM's request for this revised edition. Chapters I-XLIII revised from same chapters in first edition (a above), with the two words blacked out in chapter XII restored.

Vol. II: Chapter XLIV revised from same chapter in first edition. Chapters XLV-LVII are a revision of *Ulick and Soracha* (A51). Chapter LVIII is a revision of "The Hermit's Love Story," originally published in COSMO-POLITAN MAGAZINE, June 1927, and in NASH'S MAGAZINE, August 1927, called "Dinoll and Crede" in the "Preface" to this edition. Chapters LIX-LXVI are a revision of chapters LIV-LXI of first edition.

Plates of this edition, without repagination, were used for a one-volume edition:

b2 — Black and Gold Library, Horace Liveright, New York, 1929.

2b Second English (Uniform) edition:

A | STORY-TELLER'S | HOLIDAY | BY | GEORGE MOORE | VOL. I [II] | [*vignette*] | London | William Heinemann Ltd. | 1928

Published November at 21/-

8⅞ x 5½; Vol. I: * ⁶, A-Q ⁸, R ² (tipped in); pp [2], x, 260, comprising: blank leaf, except for signature in lower left corner of recto, not paginated; half-title, with list of WORKS BY GEORGE MOORE on verso, pp [i-ii]; title-page as above, with "Printed in Great Britain by T. and A. CON-STABLE LTD. | at the University Press, Edinburgh" at foot of verso, pp [iii-iv]; dedication, verso blank, pp [v-vi]; PREFACE pp vii-ix; p [x] blank; text pp [1]-258; pp [259-60] blank;

Vol II: [ ] ² (tipped in), A-Q ⁸, R ⁴; pp [iv], 264, comprising: half-title, with list on verso as in Vol. I, pp [i-ii]; title-page as above, with printer's imprint as in Vol. I at foot of verso, pp [iii-iv]; text pp [1]-263; p [264] blank; white endpapers in both volumes; all edges untrimmed; brown cloth spines, with marbled paper-covered board sides; white paper labels on spine, lettered in brown: A | Story- | Teller's | Holiday | I [II] | George | Moore | Heinemann

Contents:

Same as expanded and revised third American edition (b above). Reissued in a different binding as:

2b2 — Ebury Edition, two volumes, Heinemann, London, February 1938.

See D:Ge-17 for a German translation of chapters XLV-LIII of the first edition text, but which were omitted from the revised text and included as "Alfred Nobbs" in *Celibate Lives* (A52).

A38

Avowals

a First edition:

AVOWALS | BY | GEORGE MOORE | LONDON | PRIVATELY PRINTED FOR SUBSCRIBERS ONLY BY | Cumann Sean-eolais na h-Eireann [*in Gaelic characters*] | 1919

Issued[1] September at 42/- in an edition of 1,000 copies

8⅞ x 5½; [a]⁴, [b]¹ (thinner paper, tipped in), A-T⁸, U⁴; pp [x], 312, comprising: two blank leaves, pp [i-iv]; half-title, with list of three books "By GEORGE MOORE | (Privately printed)" and dates of publication on verso, pp [v-vi]; title-page as above, verso blank, pp [vii-viii]; notice of limitation as below, verso blank, pp [ix-x]; text pp 1-310; THE RIVER-SIDE PRESS LIMITED, EDINBURGH in center p [311]; p [312] blank; bluish-gray endpapers; all edges untrimmed; parchment spine with bluish-gray paper-covered board sides matching the endpapers, front and back covers plain, white label on spine, lettered in brown: Avowals | [*ornament*] | GEORGE | MOORE | Privately | Printed

Notice of limitation:

This edition consists of 1000 copies | numbered and signed. | This is No. . . . . . [*stamped number*] | George Moore [*signed in ink*]

Contents:

Chapter I originally appeared as "Imaginary Conversations: Gosse and Moore" in THE FORTNIGHTLY REVIEW, October and November 1918, and in THE DIAL, 5 and 19 October, and 2 November 1918. Chapter II originally appeared as "Imaginary Conversations: Gosse and Moore, Second Conversation," in THE FORTNIGHTLY REVIEW, January and February 1919, and in THE DIAL, 22 March, 5 and 19 April 1919. Chapter III rewritten from "Literature and Morals" in CENTURY MAGAZINE, May 1919, a revision of "Freedom of the Pen: A Conversation with George Moore," by John Lloyd Balderston, in THE FORTNIGHTLY REVIEW, October 1917, the genesis of both being *Literature at Nurse* (A7). Chapters IV-XI based on "Avowals: Being a New Series of the Confessions of a Young Man" in LIPPINCOTT'S MAGAZINE, September 1903 through February 1904, and without the subtitle in PALL MALL MAGAZINE, March through August 1904; the letter from Walter Pater in chapter XI was originally published in the "Preface" of the 1904 and subsequent editions of *Confessions of a Young Man* (A12-c et seq.). Chapter XII rewritten from "Une Promenade Sentimentale" in THE ENGLISH REVIEW, October 1910. Chapter XIII is the French lecture, "Shakespeare et Balzac," delivered by GM 18 February 1910 at the Salle de l'Agri-

1. See A37-n1.
2. Sizes approximate due to extreme deckle edges.

culture, Paris, and originally published in REVUE BLEUE, 26 February, and 5 March 1910, with an English translation, "Shakespeare and Balzac," published in CENTURY MAGAZINE, May 1914. Chapters XIV-XV previously unpublished except for portion in the latter chapter about GM's visit to Mallarmé which is based on "Souvenir sur Mallarmé" in THE BUTTERFLY, Summer 1909, and also used as the basis of a portion of chapter XXI in *Lewis Seymour and Some Women* (A36), and final four pages which had originally appeared as "La Réponse de Georges Moore à sa Cousine Germaine une Carmelite Depuis 23 ans qui lui a demandé de Brûler ses Livres" in THE IRISH REVIEW, April 1911. Chapter XVI rewritten from "The Dusk of the Gods: A Conversation on Art with George Moore," by John Lloyd Balderston, in THE ATLANTIC MONTHLY, August 1916.

2a First American edition:

AVOWALS | BY | GEORGE MOORE | NEW YORK | PRIVATELY PRINTED FOR SUBSCRIBERS ONLY BY | BONI AND LIVERIGHT | 1919

Issued 10 September at $8.00 in an edition of 1,250 copies

9½ x 6⅛; [1-20]⁸; pp [iv], 316, comprising: half-title, with notice of limitation as below on verso, pp [i-ii], title-page as above, with "COPYRIGHT, 1919, BY | GEORGE MOORE | [*rule*] | All rights reserved" in center and "Printed in the United States of America" at foot of verso, pp [iii-iv]; fly-title, verso blank, pp [i-2]; text pp 3-313; pp [314-16] blank; white endpapers; all edges untrimmed; blue head and foot bands; bound in blue buckram, back and front covers plain, spine blind stamped to simulate a leather binding with seven raised bands, with black leather label on spine between second and third bands from top, gilt stamped [*rule*] | AVOWALS | [*three ornaments*] | George | Moore | [*rule*]

Notice of limitation:

1250 copies of this book have been printed | of which this is number . . . . . [*number stamped in red*]

Contents:

Same as first edition (a above). This text, with the exception of chapter XIII, the French lecture "Shakespeare et Balzac,"[3] was used for:

3a — Carra Edition, Volume IX, Boni and Liveright, New York, 20 June 1923, with *Confessions of a Young Man* also included in the volume and which was previously noted (A12-e). The type for this edition of *Avowals* was reimposed, with fewer lines per page, for a trade edition:[4]

3a2 — Boni and Liveright, New York, 1926.

b Second English (Uniform) edition:

3. In Carra Edition transferred to *Conversations in Ebury Street*, Volume XX (A46-2a).

4. Matching other Boni and Liveright trade editions; see A52-2a for description.

AVOWALS | BY | GEORGE MOORE | [*vignette*] | London | William Heinemann Ltd. | 1924

Published November at 10/6

$8\frac{1}{2}$ x $5\frac{1}{4}$; [ ]⁴, A-S⁸, T⁴, T2² (inserted between T_2 and T_3); pp [viii], 300, comprising: blank leaf, pp [i-ii]; half-title, verso blank, pp [iii-iv]; title-page as above, with "First published, in a Limited | Edition only, in 1919" in center and "Printed in Great Britain by T. and A. CONSTABLE LTD. | at the University Press, Edinburgh" at foot of verso, pp [v-vi]; ON THE VANITY OF PREFACES, verso blank, pp [vii-viii]; text pp [1]-297; pp [298-300] blank; extra spine label tipped in on lower right corner of p [300]; white endpapers; all edges untrimmed; brown cloth spine, with marbled paper-covered board sides, white paper label on spine, lettered in brown: Avowals | George | Moore | Heinemann

Contents:

The short preface, "On the Vanity of Prefaces," is new, and the text, including the French lecture, "Shakespeare et Balzac," has minor revisions throughout. Reissued in a different binding as:

b2 — Ebury Edition, Heinemann, London, September 1936. This revised text, but again without the French lecture, was used for an edition identical in format with the earlier Boni and Liveright trade edition (3a2 above):

2b — Horace Liveright, New York, 1928.

A39
The Coming of Gabrielle

a First edition with new title:

The COMING of | GABRIELLE | A COMEDY | By | GEORGE MOORE | LONDON | PRIVATELY PRINTED FOR SUBSCRIBERS ONLY BY | Cumann Sean-eolais na h-Eireann [*in Gaelic characters*] | 1920

Issued[1] in December at 21/- in an edition of 1,000 copies

$8\frac{7}{8}$ x $5\frac{1}{4}$; [a]⁸, [ ]¹ (tipped in between [a]₂ and [a]₃), b⁸, A-I⁸, K² (tipped in); pp [i-iv], [2], v-xxxii, 148, comprising: half-title, verso blank, pp [i-ii]; title-page as above, with list of five books "BY GEORGE MOORE |

---

1. See A37-n1.

2. Which may have been the same as the extensive autograph corrections made by GM in a presentation copy of this edition now in the Special Collections Department of the University of Kansas Library, which is inscribed on the title-page, "To Alfred Sutro from George Moore with many apologies for the disorder of the text. But there is no other."

(Privately Printed)" and dates of publication on verso, pp [iii-iv]; notice of limitation as below, verso blank, not paginated; PREFACE pp v-xxx; blank page, with list of "PEOPLE in the PLAY" and AUTHOR'S NOTE on verso, pp [xxxi-xxxii]; text pp 1-146, with p [50] blank; THE RIVERSIDE PRESS LIMITED, EDINBURGH in center p [147]; p [148] blank; bluish-gray endpapers; all edges untrimmed; blue and white head band; white parchment spine with bluish-gray paper-covered board sides, matching end-papers, white paper label on spine, lettered in black: The | Coming | of | Gabrielle | [ornament] | GEORGE | MOORE | Privately | Printed

Notice of limitation:

This edition consists of 1000 copies | numbered and signed. | This is No. . . . . . [stamped number] | George Moore [signed in ink]

Contents:

"Preface" also published in THE FORTNIGHTLY REVIEW, December 1920, and reprinted, with omission of first five and last two paragraphs, as "The Decline of the Drama" in THE DIAL, January 1921. *The Coming of Gabrielle* is a revision of *Elizabeth Cooper* (A33), and in its present form previously was published in THE ENGLISH REVIEW, March, April and May 1920, an act in each number.

2a First American edition:

The | Coming of Gabrielle | A COMEDY | BY | GEORGE MOORE | BONI AND LIVERIGHT | PUBLISHERS [space] NEW YORK | 1921

Published 4 May at $4.00 in an edition of 895 copies

$8\frac{1}{8}$ x $6\frac{1}{4}$; [1-8]^8, [9]^4; pp 136, comprising: half-title, with list of twenty-one WORKS BY GEORGE MOORE on verso, pp [1-2]; title-page as above, with "COPYRIGHT, 1921, | BY BONI AND LIVERIGHT, INC. | [rule] | All rights reserved" at top and nine-line production CAUTION note | [rule] | "Printed in the United States of America" at foot of verso, pp [3-4]; notice of limitation as below, verso blank, pp [5-6]; PREFACE pp 7-26; fly-title, verso blank, pp [27-28]; author's NOTE, with list of PEOPLE IN THE PLAY on verso, pp [29-30]; text pp 31-[133]; pp [134-36] blank; royal blue endpapers; all edges trimmed; top edges stained blue; white parchment spine with blue paper-covered board sides, back cover plain, black leather label on upper left corner of front cover, gilt stamped [ornament] GEORGE [ornament] | [ornament] MOORE'S [ornament] | THE COMING | OF GABRIELLE [all within decorative gilt border], and black leather label on spine, gilt lettered THE | COMING | OF | GABRIELLE | [three ornaments] | GEORGE | MOORE

Notice of limitation:

This edition is limited to 895 numbered copies | of which this is No. . . . . . [numbered in ink]

Contents:

Text differs slightly from that of first edition (a above) and may well be earlier.

b Continental edition, revised:

THE COMING OF | GABRIELLE | A COMEDY | BY | GEORGE MOORE | AUTHOR OF | "CELIBATES," "EVELYN INNES," "SISTER TERESA," | "THE UNTILLED FIELD," ETC. | COPYRIGHT EDITION | LEIPZIG | BERNHARD TAUCHNITZ | 1922

Published September

6½ x 4⅝; [1]⁸, 2-16⁸; pp 256, comprising: half-title, with list of thirteen titles in "TAUCHNITZ EDITION | By the same Author" on verso, pp [1-2]; title-page as above, verso blank, pp [3-4]; PREFACE pp [5]-39; p [40] blank; fly-title, verso blank, pp [41-42]; list of PEOPLE IN THE PLAY and AUTHOR'S NOTE pp [43-44]; text pp [45]-253, with p [116] blank; p [254] blank; PRINTED BY BERNHARD TAUCHNITZ, LEIPZIG in center p [255]; p [256] blank;³ no endpapers; all edges untrimmed; white paper wrappers, inner faces blank, back cover lists "Latest Volumes | September 1922," front cover lettered in black TAUCHNITZ EDITION | COLLECTION OF BRITISH AND AMERICAN AUTHORS | VOL. 4587 | [*double rule*] | THE | COMING OF GABRIELLE | BY | GEORGE MOORE | IN ONE VOLUME | LEIPZIG: BERNHARD TAUCHNITZ | PARIS: LIBRAIRIE HENRI GAULON, 39, RUE MADAME | [*double rule*] | [*three-line copyright notice*] | [*all within heavy and light double-rule border, which with double-rule borders noted above form a three-compartment box*] EACH SOLD SEPARATELY and spine stamped in black [*two double rules as in border on front cover*] | TAUCHNITZ | EDITION | BRITISH | AND | AMERICAN | AUTHORS | [*double rule*] | VOL. 4587 | [*double rule*] | GEORGE | MOORE | 18 | [*double rule*] | THE COMING | OF | GABRIELLE | [*double rule*] | [*asterisk*] | [*double rule*]

Contents:

Text revised. Further unpublished revisions² were made when the play was presented for three performances in July 1923 at St. James's Theatre, London, with Athene Seyler in the title role.

A40

Héloïse and Abélard

a First edition:

HÉLOÏSE AND ABÉLARD | BY | GEORGE MOORE | IN TWO VOLUMES | VOLUME I [II] | LONDON | PRIVATELY PRINTED

3. In some copies there is a 32-page inserted catalogue of publisher's advertisements following p [256].

FOR SUBSCRIBERS ONLY BY | Cumann Sean-eolais na h-Eireann [*in Gaelic characters*] | 1921

Issued[1] 17 February at 63/- in an edition of 1,500 sets

9 x 5½; Vol. I: a⁴, [b]¹ (tipped in), A-Q⁸, R⁴; pp [x], 264, comprising: two blank (except for signature in lower left corner of p [i]) leaves pp [i-iv]; half-title, with list of six books "BY GEORGE MOORE | (Limited Editions)" on verso, pp [v-vi]; title-page as above, with dedication A MADAME X on verso, pp [vii-viii]; notice of limitation as below, verso blank, pp [ix-x]; text pp 1-262; THE RIVERSIDE PRESS LIMITED, EDINBURGH center of p [263]; p [264] blank[2];

Vol. II: A-Q⁸, pp 256, comprising: half-title, verso blank, pp [1-2]; title-page as above, verso blank, pp [3-4]; text pp 5-252; printer's imprint as in Vol. I, center of p [253]; pp [254-56] blank; bluish-gray endpapers; all edges untrimmed; gray and cream head bands; parchment spines, with paper-covered board sides matching endpapers, front and back covers plain, white labels on spines, lettered in brown: Héloïse | and | Abélard | * [**] | GEORGE | MOORE | Privately | Printed

Notice of limitation:

This edition consists of one thousand | five hundred copies, numbered and | signed. | This is No. . . . . . [*stamped number*] | George Moore [*signed in ink*]

Contents:

Volume I: Chapters I-IV, and first section of chapter V, previously unpublished; end of chapter V and beginning of chapter VI previously published as "How Héloïse passed the winter of 1117" in THE DIAL, November 1920; end of chapter VI, chapter VII, and part of chapter VIII previously published as "Héloïse first meets Abélard" in THE CENTURY MAGAZINE, October 1920; chapters VII, VIII, and IX previously published as "Héloïse and Abélard" in THE FORTNIGHTLY REVIEW, September, and October 1920; chapters X-XX previously unpublished.

Volume II: Chapters XXI-XLII previously unpublished.

b First American edition:

HÉLOÏSE AND ABÉLARD | BY | GEORGE MOORE | IN TWO VOLUMES | VOLUME I [II] | PRIVATELY PRINTED FOR SUBSCRIBERS ONLY BY | BONI AND LIVERIGHT : : NEW YORK | 1921

1. See A37-n1.

2. Some sets have an inserted slip (5⅜ x 3⅞) lettered in red: HÉLOÏSE AND ABÉLARD | CAUTION | BONI and LIVERIGHT of New York, who are | manufacturing and publishing a limited, unsigned edition of this book in the U.S.A., | have instructed the Customs officials at all U.S.A. ports to regard as contraband and to | confiscate all copies of this English edition | that are sent or introduced in any form into | the U.S.A. | T. WERNER LAURIE LTD.

Issued 12 May at $15 in an edition of 1,250 sets

9⅝ x 6¼ ; Vol. I: [1-15]⁸; pp [x], 230, comprising: two blank leaves, pp [i-iv]; half-title, with list of twenty-one WORKS BY GEORGE MOORE on verso, pp [v-vi]; title-page as above, with "COPYRIGHT, 1921, BY | BONI AND LIVERIGHT, INC. | [rule] | All Rights Reserved" at top, publisher's note[3] on tipped-in slip (2½ x 5½) in center, and notice of limitation as below at foot of verso, pp [vii-viii]; dedication A MADAME X, verso blank, pp [ix-x]; text pp 1-[224]; pp [225-30] blank;

Vol. II: [1-2]⁸, [3]⁴ (tipped in between [2]₄ and [2]₅), [4-15]⁸; pp [vi], 18, *1-8*, 19-218, comprising: two blank leaves, pp [i-iv]; half-title, verso blank, pp [v-vi]; title-page as above, with copyright notice and notice of limitation as in Vol. I on verso, pp [1-2]; publisher's note[4] on tipped in slip (2½ x 5½); fly-title, verso blank, pp [3-4]; text pp 5-18, text of additional material pp *1-8*; text continued pp 19-217; p [218] blank; royal blue endpapers in both volumes; cream head and foot bands; all edges untrimmed; parchment spine, with paper-covered board sides matching endpapers, front and back covers plain, black leather labels on spines gilt stamped HÉLOÏSE | [ornament] & [ornament] | ABÉLARD | [three dots, two above one] | GEORGE | MOORE | [dot] | VOLUME ONE [TWO] [all within ornamental border]

Notice of limitation:

This edition is strictly limited to Twelve | Hundred and Fifty sets, of which Twelve | Hundred numbered sets are for sale. | No. . . . . . [numbered in ink]

Contents:

The text is same as first edition (a above), with the addition of eight pages of new material inserted in Volume II. This is substantially the same as the long alternative passage to a section of chapter XXII printed in *Fragments from Héloïse & Abélard* (A41), but differs somewhat in wording and apparently is an earlier text. This text, slightly revised and including the new material, was used for:

2b — Carra Edition, Volumes XV and XVI, Boni and Liveright, New York, 1923; with reproduction of an etching tipped in as a frontispiece in first volume, protected by tissue guard sheet lettered in red at foot of verso "Peter Abélard installs his wife, Héloïse, | as abbess of the convent of Paraclete." The type of the Carra Edition, reimposed with fewer lines per page, was used for:

3. This edition of "Héloïse & Abélard" contains some | supplementary pages written too late to be printed with | the rest of the text. They will be found inserted in | page nineteen of volume two. This matter appears only | in the American edition.

4. TO THE READER. | [rule] | Immediately following page 18 of volume 2 will | be found some supplementary pages written too late to | be printed in their proper place in the text. These | pages are numbered 1 to 8 and this matter appears | only in the American edition.

2b2 — Boni and Liveright, two volumes,[5] New York, November 1925. The plates of this edition were used for a one-volume edition:

2b3 — Black and Gold Library, Horace Liveright, New York, July 1932.

3b Second English (Uniform) edition:

HÉLOÏSE AND | ABÉLARD | BY | GEORGE MOORE | [*vignette*] | London | William Heinemann Ltd. | 1925

Published November at 10/6

8½ x 5¼ ; [ ]² (tipped in), A-2F⁸, 2G⁶; pp [iv], 476, comprising: half-title, with title PREVIOUSLY PUBLISHED IN | THE SAME FORMAT on verso, pp [i-ii]; title-page as above, with "First published in a Limited | Edition only, in 1921" in center and "Printed in Great Britain by T. and A. CONSTABLE LTD. | at the University Press, Edinburgh" at foot of verso, pp [iii-iv]; text pp [1]-475; p [476] blank; extra spine label tipped in before free rear endpaper; white endpapers; all edges untrimmed; brown cloth spine, with marbled paper-covered board sides, white paper label on spine, lettered in brown: Héloïse | and | Abélard | George | Moore | Heinemann

Contents:

Text same as Carra Edition (2b above), but omitting the dedication A MADAME X which is included in all other editions.[6] Reprinted 1926 (twice), 1928, 1930, 1933 (twice), and 1935. Reissued in a different binding as:

3b2 — Ebury Edition, Heinemann, London, September 1936.

A41

Fragments from Héloïse & Abélard

a First separate edition:

FRAGMENTS FROM | HÉLOÏSE & ABÉLARD | BY GEORGE MOORE | LONDON | PRIVATELY PRINTED FOR SUBSCRIBERS BY | Cumann Sean-eolais na h-Eireann [*in Gaelic characters*] | 1921

Issued[1] July at 2/6 in an edition of 2,000 copies[2]

9 x 5½ ; [a]⁴, A*⁸ (inserted between [a]₂ and [a]₃); pp 24, comprising: title-page as above, verso blank, pp [1-2]; sonnet in French, verso blank,

---

5. In format matching other Boni and Liveright trade editions of GM's works (see A52-2a for description).

6. Also included in later impressions of this edition, which are reimposed [A]⁸, B-EE⁸, FF¹⁰ (FF₂ signed FF* on recto) to accommodate the dedication leaf and conjugate blank leaf preceding half-title.

1. See A37-n1.

2. According to Danielson.

pp 3-[4]; PREFACE pp 5-7; p [8] blank; text pp 9-18; ERRATA pp 19-23; PRINTED BY | THE RIVERSIDE PRESS LIMITED, EDINBURGH in center of p [24]; no endpapers; all edges untrimmed; stitched with blue silk cord; bluish-gray overlapping wrappers, back plain, lettered in brown on front: FRAGMENTS FROM | HÉLOÏSE & ABÉLARD | BY GEORGE MOORE from same setting of type as title-page.

Contents:

"La Réponse de Georges Moore en forme de sonnet à son ami Edouard Dujardin (l'auteur de 'La Source de Fleuve Chrétien') qui l'avait invité à Fontainebleau pour manger de l'alose" is slightly revised from original publication in THE FORTNIGHTLY REVIEW, September 1920; "Preface" previously unpublished; an alternative passage ("These pages to replace page 25, vol. ii") is slightly revised from its earlier publication as an insert in volume two of the first American edition of *Héloïse and Abélard* (A40-b); and the "Errata" includes corrections and additions to volume two, chiefly to correct the boy Astrolabe's speech from an eleven-year-old to a nine-year-old.

"La Réponse . . . de l'alose" is reprinted in *Letters . . . to Ed. Dujardin* (A54).

The alternative passage along with the additions and corrections of the "Errata" are included in the Carra and subsequent editions of *Héloïse and Abélard* (A40-2b et seq.).

A42
Moore Versus Harris

a First edition:

MOORE VERSUS HARRIS | An intimate correspondence be- | tween George Moore and Frank | Harris relating to the Brook Kerith, | Heloise and Abelard, astonishing | criticism of George Bernard Shaw, | Moore's rejection of Oscar Wilde as | an artist, important and amazing | statements about other contem- | porary men of letters, disclosing the | true valuation George Moore | places on his own personality and books. | INCLUDING | fac-simile reproductions of letters and auction | records of some of the letters printed herein, | also caricatures by Max Beerbohm and by | the late Claude [*sic*] Lovat Fraser. | PRIVATELY PRINTED FOR SUB-SCRIBERS | DETROIT, MICHIGAN. | 1921

Issued in an edition of 1,000 copies

9½ x 6¼; [ ]⁸; pp 16, comprising: blank leaf pp [1-2]; half-title, verso blank, pp [3-4]; title-page as above, with notice of limitation as below on verso, pp [5-6]; introduction by Guido Bruno p 7; caricature of Harris and Beerbohm by Beerbohm p 8; letter from GM to Harris, with caricature of "G.B.S. by Claude [sic] Lovat Fraser" at end, pp 9-10; letter from GM to Harris p 11; letter from Harris to GM p 12; facsimile of letter from Harris to Bruno p 13; letter from GM to Harris pp 14-15; facsimile of part of a page of Anderson Catalogue listing two letters from GM to Harris; white endpapers, wrapped around and sewn with text; all edges untrimmed; bound in black cloth, back and spine[1] plain, front cover gilt lettered in upper left corner MOORE | VERSUS | HARRIS

Notice of limitation:

1,000 copies of this book | have been printed of which | this is No. . . . . . [numbered in ink]

Contents:

Includes three letters (circa 1915, late 1916, and 27 September 1920) from GM to Harris, the second of which was previously included by Harris in the article, "George Moore and Jesus," in Contemporary Portraits: Second Series (B27), a revision of the same article in PEARSON'S MAGAZINE, December 1916 and January 1917.

2a Second edition:

[title-page reset, but first 13 lines same as first edition (a above)] | caricatures by Max Beerbohm, the late | Claude [sic] Lovat Fraser, and Grace Plunkett; | also a remarkable character sketch of Harris | by G. Bernard Shaw. | PRIVATELY PRINTED IN CHICAGO, ILLINOIS | 1925

Issued in an edition of 1,000 copies

6¼ x 4⅞; [ ]¹²; pp 24, comprising: blank leaf pp [1-2]; title-page as above, with notice of limitation as below on verso, pp [3-4]; fly-title, verso blank, pp [5-6]; caricature of Harris and Beerbohm by Beerbohm, verso blank, pp [7-8]; introduction by Guido Bruno p 9; letter from GM to Harris pp 10-11; letter from GM to Harris p 12; caricature of GM by Grace Plunkett p [13]; letter from Harris to GM p 14; facsimile of letter from Harris to Bruno p [15]; letter from GM to Harris pp 16, 18-19; caricature of "G. Bernard Shaw by C. L. Fraser" p [17]; letter from Shaw to Bruno p 20; reproduction of a drawing of Shaw by J. H. Dowd on right side p [21]; p [22] blank; reproduction of a drawing of Harris p [23]; p [24] blank; all edges trimmed; wire stapled; issued in various colored bristol board covers, back cover plain, front cover lettered in black in upper right corner MOORE | VERSUS | HARRIS [same setting of type as that used on fly-title]

Notice of limitation:

One thousand copies of this book | have been printed and the type | distributed. This is No. . . . . . [numbered in ink]

1. Flat in some copies, rounded in others.

Contents:

The letters from and to GM are the same as in first edition (a above), as are the Beerbohm and Fraser caricatures and the facsimile of the letter to Bruno, which are reduced in size to fit the smaller page size of this edition.

A43
Euphorian in Texas

a First separate edition:

TEN CENT POCKET SERIES NO. 285 | Edited by E. Haldeman-Julius | Euphorian [*sic*] in | Texas | George Moore | HALDEMAN-JULIUS COM-PANY | GIRARD, KANSAS

Published 23 February 1922

4⅞ x 3⅜; [ ]³²; pp 64, comprising: title-page as above, verso blank, pp [1-2]; "Euphorian in Texas" pp [3]-28; "The Marquise | By Geo. Sand" pp 29-63; p [64] blank; no endpapers; all edges trimmed; wire stapled in center fold; issued in light blue wrappers, lettered on front cover in black as on title-page.[1]

A later impression, circa 1924, has first line of title-page reset LITTLE BLUE BOOK NO. with figure 285 larger and occupying two lines, title printed in one line, and PRINTED IN THE UNITED STATES OF AMER-ICA added at foot of verso.

In impressions still current the text of *Euphorian in Texas* is printed alone and the booklet has a different imposition: [ ]¹⁶; pp 32, comprising: title-page and verso as in later impression (noted above) with the title in a single line, but with the addition of a subtitle "An Unconventional Amour,"[2] pp [1-2]; half-title, verso blank, pp [3-4]; text pp [5]-29; list of OTHER LITTLE BLUE BOOKS pp [30]-32; no endpapers, all edges trimmed; wire

1. This seems to be the earliest impression, despite the fact that Henry E. Halde-man, present head of the Haldeman-Julius Company, informs me that "Five Cent Pocket Series" was the original title of the series and that "The Marquise" previously had been issued in the series 16 June 1921. Earlier and conflicting evidence, however, is offered by E. Haldeman-Julius, the originator of the Little Blue Books, who in telling of their beginnings in *The First Hundred Million* (New York, 1928), states that the price of the booklets was first 25¢, then dropped to 10¢, and finally after a number of experimental sales starting in 1922 was standardized for a time at 5¢ each. Contemporary advertisements of the firm confirm these statements. Further de-tails about dating the various issues of the titles in this series can be found in "The Haldeman-Julius 'Little Blue Books' as a Bibliographical Problem" by Richard Colles Johnson and G. Thomas Tanselle in THE PAPERS OF THE BIBLIOGRAPHICAL SOCIETY OF AMERICA, Vol. 64, First Quarter, 1970.

2. In later advertisements the subtitle is listed as the title of the booklet, which according to *The First Hundred Million* sold very poorly until the subtitle was added.

stapled in center fold; issued in light blue wrappers,[3] lettered on front in black as on title-page.

Contents:

Euphorian in Texas reprinted from THE ENGLISH REVIEW, July 1914, where the first word of title is also spelled "Euphorian."

The story is included, with "Euphorion"[4] correctly spelled, in the 1915 Heinemann and subsequent editions of *Memoirs of My Dead Life* (A29-c et seq.).

A44

In Single Strictness

a First edition:

IN SINGLE | STRICTNESS | BY | GEORGE MOORE | [*vignette*][1] | London | William Heinemann | 1922

Published July at 42/- in an edition of 1,030 copies

9 x 5⅜; [ ]⁶, A-T⁸, U⁴; pp [2], x, 312, comprising: blank leaf, not paginated; half-title, with list of sixteen WORKS BY GEORGE MOORE on verso, pp [i-ii]; title-page as above, with "London: William Heinemann 1922" at foot of verso, pp [iii-iv]; notice of limitation as below, verso blank, pp [v-vi]; ADVERTISEMENT pp vii-[viii], with vignette in space at end of text on p [viii]; table of CONTENTS, verso blank, pp [ix-x]; text, with shoulder sectional titles throughout, pp 1-[312], with "Printed in Great Britain by T. and A. CONSTABLE LTD. | at the Edinburgh University Press" at foot of p [312]; bluish-gray endpapers; all edges untrimmed; cream and gray headband; parchment spine, with paper-covered board sides, matching endpapers; white paper label on spine, lettered in brown: In Single | Strictness | GEORGE | MOORE | Heinemann

Notice of limitation:

This edition, printed from hand-set type on Dutch | hand-made paper, is limited to one thousand and | thirty copies, of which one thousand are for sale. | This is No . . . . . [*numbered in ink*] | George Moore [*signed in ink*]

3. Sometimes issued in flexible brown paper wrappers, with series device and printer's union label in black on back cover.

4. In classical mythology Euphorion is the son of Helen and Achilles.

1. Drawing of Romanesque colonnades, arches and statues, giving the effect of an engraving by Piranesi. This vignette was later used on the title-pages of a number of books by GM, including all of the titles in the Uniform and Ebury editions.

Contents:

"Wilfred Holmes" previously published in LONDON MERCURY, February 1922; "Priscilla and Emily Lofft" rewritten from "Emma Bovary" in LIP-PINCOTT'S MAGAZINE, May 1902; "Hugh Monfret" is a further development[2] of the theme of "John Norton" in *Celibates* (A21), a revision of *A Mere Accident* (A10); "Henrietta Marr" is a revision of "Mildred Lawson" in *Celibates*; "Sarah Gwynn" previously unpublished.

Shortly after the publication of *In Single Strictness*, GM rewrote the ending of "Hugh Monfret" and had it printed on six pages, numbered 191-96, to replace pp 191-200 of the first edition. A few presentation copies have these pages loosely inserted, and accompanying the Edmund Gosse copy (listed in Maggs Bros. Catalogue 531, 1930) are two letters from GM to Gosse regarding them. In one GM says, "I think you will approve of the new end to the story entitled 'Hugh Monfret.' I enclose the new pages thinking that you might like to paste them into your copy of 'In Single Strictness.' The printer sent me twelve pulls." In the other letter he said, "I hope you will let me know on a postcard how the new end of Hugh Monfret strikes you. Let me confess, I either ran away from the subject or my inspiration died in the last pages. In the actual text the man melted into nothingness, an unpermissable nothingness, a nothingness that his catholicism cannot condone."

2a First American edition:

IN SINGLE STRICTNESS | BY | GEORGE MOORE | [*circular floral ornament, in red*] | New York | Printed Privately for Subscribers only by | BONI AND LIVERIGHT | 1922

Published 10 September at $10 in an edition of 1,050 copies

9½ x 6¼; [1]^8, [2]^2 (tipped in between [1]$_1$ and [1]$_2$), [3-21]^8; pp [2], viii, 314, comprising: blank leaf, not paginated; half-title, with list of twenty-

---

2. "Hugh Monfret" may also be a development of the plot outlined by GM to William Heinemann, who in turn (circa 1915) related it to George H. Doran, who retells it in his autobiography, *Chronicles of Barabbas 1884–1935*, New York, 1935, (pp 269-70), "One day in great elation Moore came to Heinemann and outlined the plot of what he termed to be a great novel. In brief, a young man of family and distinction and title falls in love with a daughter of an equally distinguished house. The marriage is arranged. The wedding takes place at St. Margaret's, Westminister. On the bridal night the bridegroom discovers his totally unthought-of and unsuspected impotency. The following day in humiliation and despondency he arranges for the dissolution of the marriage — the complete release of the woman he loves. He makes handsome settlement and departs immediately for a protracted voyage around the world on a sailing-ship. On board he meets a plump little sailor-boy and lives happily ever afterwards. 'There,' exclaimed Moore, 'is a plot for you!' Heinemann protested that no such book could be printed and published in England. But Moore contended: 'Why not! it is simply a modernizing of the Greek practice which pleased and thrilled the male and in addition gave protection to the innocence of Grecian women.'"

one WORKS BY GEORGE MOORE on verso, pp [i-ii]; title-page as above, with "IN SINGLE STRICTNESS | Copyright, 1922, by | Boni & Liveright, Inc. | [*rule*] | Printed in the United States of America" at top and notice of limitation as below at foot of verso, pp [iii-iv]; ADVERTISEMENT pp v-vi; table of CONTENTS, with AN ACKNOWLEDGEMENT[3] on verso, pp [vii-viii]; text, with sectional shoulder titles throughout, pp 1-[314]; royal blue endpapers; all edges untrimmed; white head and tail bands; parchment spine, with paper-covered board sides, matching the endpapers, back and front covers plain, black leather label on spine, gilt stamped [*ornament*] IN [*ornament*] | SINGLE | STRICT- | [*ornament*] NESS [*ornament*] | [*three dots in form of an inverted triangle*] GEORGE | [*dot*] MOORE [*dot*] | [*all within ornamental border*] [4]

Notice of limitation:

This edition is limited to one thousand | and fifty numbered and signed copies | of which one thousand only are for sale | This is No. . . . . . [*numbered in ink*] | George Moore [*signed in ink*]

Contents:

Same as first edition (a above).

b Second American (Carra) edition, revised:

IN | SINGLE STRICTNESS | BY | GEORGE MOORE | [*rule*] | Carra Edition | [*rule*] | PRINTED FOR SUBSCRIBERS ONLY BY | BONI AND LIVERIGHT, INC., NEW YORK | 1923

Published at $8.50 in an edition of 1,000 copies

8¾ x 5½; [1]⁴, [2-20]⁸, [21]⁶; pp [4], viii, 312, comprising: two blank leaves, not paginated; half-title, with reproduction of painting tipped on verso, pp [i-ii]; tissue guard sheet, lettered in red at foot of verso "GEORGE MOORE | From a painting by Walter Sickert | In the National Gallery– Dublin" not paginated; title-page as above, with "IN | SINGLE STRICT- NESS | (Carra Edition) | [*rule*] | Copyright, 1922, by | Boni & Liveright, Inc. | [*rule*] | Printed in the United States of America" in center and notice of limitation[5] at foot of verso, p [iii-iv]; ADVERTISEMENT pp v-vi; table of CONTENTS, verso blank, pp [vii-viii]; text[6] pp 1-310; pp [311-12]

---

3. The best thanks of the Author and the Publishers | are due to Mr. Arthur Brentano for his per- | mission to use in this volume some pages from a book entitled *Celibates*, which he publishes.

4. GM wrote, in a presentation copy to Henry Tonks, "My dear Tonks, here is a book for you. The inside is delightful, the outside hideous. The inside is by me, the outside by Liveright. Your old friend, George Moore."

5. Same as in other volumes of Carra Edition (see A36-4a).

6. Plates of first American edition (2a above), except for pp 192-201, were used for this printing, with page numbers at top instead of bottom of pages, and shoulder titles omitted. Pages 192-97 reset to replace pp 192-201, with pp 198-310 renumbered, but in the table of contents the page numbers of the last two stories were not corrected to correspond with the proper pages, now 198 and 285.

blank; bluish-gray endpapers; all edges trimmed; white parchment spine, with paper-covered board sides, match-endpapers, white paper label on spine, lettered in black, except as noted: In | Single | Strictness | [*decorative rule*] | George Moore [*in red*] | [*decorative rule*] | Carra Edition | Volume XVIII | [*with two plain rules above and below decorative rule, all in red, at top and bottom of label*]

Contents:

Same as first American edition (2a above), but with the new and shortened ending of "Hugh Monfret" noted following the description of contents of the first edition (a above).

In Single Strictness, omitting "Hugh Monfret," republished as *Celibate Lives* (A52).

See D:Sp-1 for Spanish translations of "Henrietta Marr" and "Wilfred Holmes." In a letter to John Eglinton, dated "8-13-23," GM wrote, "Hugh Monfret pleases me no longer and I have asked the French translator to omit it . . . ," however, no French translation has been located of either *In Single Strictness* or *Celibate Lives*.

A45
Insert for Memoirs of My Dead Life

To be inserted on page 6, "Memoirs of My Dead | Life," after the words "characteristic of Park | Lane," line 11, from the bottom of the page.

Printed circa 1923-24[1]

7⅝ x 4⅝; [ ]⁸; pp [16], comprising: text with heading as above on p [1], pp [1-15], with "[The MS. abruptly breaks off.]" at end of text, top of p [15]; p [16] blank; issued as printed on a single sheet, folded, but uncut, unsewn, and unopened; printed on paper similar to that used in the first edition and other early Heinemann printings of *Memoirs of My Dead Life* (A29-a), with the type, general typographical features and running head of those impressions duplicated pp [2-15], but with shoulder titles omitted.

Contents:

This is an unauthorized printing of a discarded draft of material added to the Tauchnitz edition of *Memoirs of My Dead Life* (A29-b), beginning as

1. For Max Harzof, a New York book dealer, who had this fragment set and printed to be used as an interesting gift to his collector customers. I am indebted to Edward Lazare, a former associate of Mr. Harzof, for information regarding the approximate date of the printing.

that does, but developing quite differently.[2] GM was unaware of this printing and first learned of it about 1930 when he was shown a copy by Frank Fayant. Previously A. J. A. Symons had requested permission to have the fragment printed, but in a letter dated "3rd March, 1926" GM refused, saying "These pages were stolen by one of my secretaries and sold, I think in America . . . I should be very sorry indeed to see these pages published." The original manuscript was listed in the 1913 Christmas Catalogue of C. W. Beaumont, London; was later sold at auction in the United States; and is now in the collection of Arthur A. Houghton, Jr., of New York.

A46
Conversations in Ebury Street

a First edition:

CONVERSATIONS IN | EBURY STREET | BY | GEORGE MOORE | [*vignette*] | London | William Heinemann Ltd. | 1924

Published January at 42/- in an edition of 1,030 copies

9 x 5⅜; [ ]⁴, A-R⁸, S⁴; pp [viii], 280, comprising: blank leaf pp [i-ii]; half-title, with list of seventeen WORKS BY GEORGE MOORE on verso, pp [iii-iv]; title-page as above, with "Printed in Great Britain by T. and A. CONSTABLE LTD. | at the University Press, Edinburgh" at foot of verso, pp [v-vi]; notice of limitation as below, verso blank, pp [vii-viii]; text pp 1-277; pp [278-80] blank; extra spine label tipped on lower right corner p [280]; bluish-gray endpapers; all edges untrimmed; parchment spine with paper-covered board sides matching endpapers; back and front covers plain; white label on spine, lettered in brown: Conversations | in | Ebury Street | GEORGE | MOORE | Heinemann

Notice of limitation:

This edition, printed from hand-set type on Van | Gelder hand-made paper, is limited to one thousand | and thirty copies, of which one thousand are for sale. | This is No. . . . . . [*numbered in ink*] | George Moore [*signed in ink*]

Contents:

Chapter I originally published as "Conversation in Ebury Street" in LONDON MERCURY, August 1922, and in ATLANTIC MONTHLY, September 1922. Chapter II, previously unpublished.[1] Chapter III is a reworking of "Balzac"

---

2. The two versions are both quoted by Rupert Hart-Davis, in tracing GM's relationship to Lady Cunard, in the "Introduction" to *Letters to Lady Cunard* (A65).

1. Most of the chapters stated as being "previously unpublished" have distinct echoes of GM's earlier critical articles.

in *Impressions and Opinions* (A15). Chapters IV-V were originally published as "George Moore and John Freeman" in THE DIAL, October 1923; chapters VI-XI previously unpublished. Chapter XII is a rewriting of the article on Verlaine, "A Great Poet," in *Impressions and Opinions.* Chapter XIII is a rewriting of the article on Rimbaud and Laforgue, "Two Unknown Poets," in *Impressions and Opinions.* Chapter XIV previously unpublished. Chapter XV also published as section II of "The Thesis" in *Pure Poetry* (A47). Chapter XVI originally published as "The Cinderella of Literature" in THE FORTNIGHTLY REVIEW, April 1923, and as "Mr. Moore Talks to Mr. Gosse" in THE ATLANTIC MONTHLY, April 1923. Chapter XVII originally published as "George Moore and Granville Barker" in THE FORTNIGHTLY REVIEW, July 1923, and in THE DIAL, August 1923. Chapter XVIII previously unpublished. Chapter XIX originally published as "Sunt lacrimae rerum" in THE FORTNIGHTLY REVIEW, December 1923.

2a First American (Carra) edition:

CONVERSATIONS | IN EBURY STREET | BY | GEORGE MOORE | [*rule*] | Carra Edition | [*rule*] | PRINTED FOR SUBSCRIBERS ONLY BY | BONI AND LIVERIGHT, INC., NEW YORK | 1924

Published February at $8.50 in an edition of 1,000 copies

8¾ x 5½; [1-19]⁸, [20]¹ (tipped in); pp [vi], 300, comprising: blank leaf, pp [i-ii]; half-title, verso blank, pp [iii-iv]; publisher's note[2] on slip [3 x 4⅜] tipped in, not paginated; title-page as above, with "CONVERSATIONS IN EBURY STREET | (Carra Edition) | [*rule*] | Copyright, 1924, by | Boni & Liveright, Inc. | [*rule*] | Printed in the United States of America" in center and notice of limitation[3] at foot of verso, pp [v-vi]; fly-title, verso blank, pp [1-2]; text pp 3-298; pp [299-300] blank; bluish-gray endpapers; all edges untrimmed; white parchment spine, with bluish-gray paper-covered sides, matching endpapers, white label on spine, lettered in black, except as noted: Conver- | sations | in Ebury | Street | [*decorative rule*] | George Moore [*in red*] | [*decorative rule*] | Carra Edition | Volume XX | [*two plain rules, with decorative rule between them, all in red, at top and bottom of label*]

Contents:

Text same as first edition (a above), with the addition of the French lecture, "Shakespeare et Balzac," transferred from *Avowals* (A38-3a) and

2. TO SUBSCRIBERS | The CARRA Edition of the works of | GEORGE MOORE originally planned for | twenty-one volumes has been completed in | twenty volumes. The present volume (*Con- | versations in Ebury Street*) is the last. | Any new books by GEORGE MOORE will be | added to this set and subscribers are ur- | gently requested to leave their name and | address with their bookseller or direct with | Boni & Liveright, so that they may be noti- | fied when a new volume is ready.

3. Same as other volumes of Carra Edition (see A36-4a), except "twenty" and not "twenty-one" volumes are specified.

included as chapter IV, making twenty chapters in this edition instead of the nineteen in previous editions. The type of this edition, reimposed with fewer lines per page, was used for:

2a2 — Boni and Liveright, New York, September 1924;[4] reprinted January 1925.

b Second English (Uniform) edition, revised:

CONVERSATIONS IN | EBURY STREET | BY | GEORGE MOORE | [*vignette*] | London | William Heinemann Ltd. | 1930

Published February at 10/6

9 x 5⅜; [A]⁸, B-R⁸, S⁴ (—S₄); pp [xviii], 270, comprising blank leaf, pp [i-ii]; half-title, with list of six titles PREVIOUSLY PUBLISHED IN | THE SAME FORMAT on verso, pp [iii-iv]; title-page as above, with "First published, in a Limited Edition, 1924 | New and Revised Edition, February, 1930" in center and "Printed in Great Britain at | The Windmill Press, Kingswood, Surrey" at foot of verso, pp [v-vi]; ADVERTISEMENT, verso blank, pp [vii-viii]; text pp 1-270; extra spine label tipped on recto of free rear endpaper; white endpapers; all edges untrimmed; brown cloth spine, with marbled paper-covered board sides, white paper label on spine, lettered in brown: Conver- | sations | in | Ebury | Street | George | Moore | Heinemann

Contents:

"Advertisement" previously unpublished; text same as first edition (a above) with addition of a new conversation between Mrs. Harley-Caton and GM inserted as chapter XII. Reissued in a different binding as:

b2 — Ebury Edition, Heinemann, London, September 1936. An offset impression, reproduced slightly reduced from sheets of this edition, issued in:

b3 — The Landmark Library, No. 12, Chatto & Windus, London, 24 July 1969.

A47

Pure Poetry

a First edition:

PURE POETRY | an anthology edited by | George Moore | [*publisher's device*] | 1924 | The Nonesuch Press | 30 Gerrard Street Soho W [*all within a quadruple-rule border, with decorative ornaments at top and bottom*]

Published 4 September at 17/6 in an edition of 1,250 copies

9½ x 5½; [ ]⁴ (endpapers and binder's leaves), [a]⁶, A-K⁶, L⁴, [ ]⁴,

---

4. In format matching other Boni and Liveright trade editions; see A52-2a for description.

(binder's leaves and endpapers); pp [4], xii, 128, [4], comprising: two blank binder's leaves conjugate with endpapers, not paginated; blank leaf pp [i-ii]; half-title, verso blank, pp [iii-iv]; title-page as above, with notice of limitation as below on verso, pp [v-vi]; table of THE | CONTENTS pp vii-ix; p [x] blank; sectional title, verso blank, pp [xi-xiii]; THE THESIS pp 1-43; p [44] blank; sectional title, verso blank, pp [45-46]; the poems pp 47-128; two blank binder's leaves conjugate with endpapers, not paginated; all edges untrimmed; parchment spine with gray Ingres paper-covered board sides, back and front covers plain, spine gilt lettered down PURE POETRY: GEORGE MOORE

Notice of limitation:

This edition, printed & made in Great | Britain by the University Press, | Edinburgh, is limited to 1250 copies, of which this is number [*numbered in ink*]

Contents:

Section II of "Part I: The Thesis" was previously published as chapter XV of *Conversations in Ebury Street* (A46); "Part II: The Poems" includes poems from Skelton and Nashe to Morris and Swinburne, illustrating GM's "Thesis."

2a First American edition:

AN ANTHOLOGY | of | PURE POETRY [*in red*] | EDITED WITH AN INTRODUCTION | BY | GEORGE MOORE | [*publisher's device, in red*] | NEW YORK | BONI AND LIVERIGHT [*in red*] | 1924

Published 21 November at $5.00 in an edition of 1,000 copies

8¾ x 6⅛; [1]² (tipped in), [2-11]⁸, [12]¹⁰; pp 184, comprising: half-title, with list of CARRA EDITION titles on verso, pp [i-ii]; title-page as above, with "Copyright, 1924, by | BONI & LIVERIGHT, INC. | [*rule*] | All rights reserved | Printed in the United States of America" and notice of limitation as below on verso, pp [iii-iv]; table of CONTENTS pp v-vi; fly-title, verso blank, pp [7-8]; INTRODUCTION pp 9-59; p [60] blank; text of poems pp 61-182; pp [183-84] blank; bluish-gray endpapers, with extra spine label tipped on paste-down endpaper; top and fore edges untrimmed, bottom edges trimmed; parchment spine, with bluish-gray paper-covered board sides, matching the endpapers, white label on spine, lettered in black, except as noted: An | Anthology | of | Pure | Poetry | [*decorative rule*] | George Moore [*in red*] | [*decorative rule*] | Boni & | Liveright | [*two plain rules, with decorative rule between, all in red, at top and bottom of label*]¹

Notice of limitation:

THIS FIRST EDITION OF ONE THOU- | SAND NUMBERED AND SIGNED COPIES | IS SPECIALLY PRINTED AND BOUND, | AND

---

1. Format of this edition matches volumes of Carra Edition, and unnumbered and unsigned copies were issued with remainder sets.

WILL NOT BE RE-ISSUED IN THIS | FORMAT. | NO. [*numbered in ink*] | George Moore [*signed in ink*]

Contents:

Same as first edition (a above), except "The Thesis" is called simply "Introduction," and the order of "The Poems" is slightly rearranged. Plates of this edition were used for:

2a2 — Boni and Liveright, New York, 1925.[2]

A48

A Letter to the Editor of THE TIMES

a First edition:

A LETTER | to the Editor of | The Times | BY GEORGE MOORE | [*short rule*] | Reprinted from | The Times Literary Supplement, | 10th December, 1925.

Printed[1] for private distribution in an edition of 50 copies

9 x 5¾; [ ]⁶; pp ii, 10, comprising: title-page as above, verso blank, pp [i-ii]; text pp 1-[8], with notice of limitation as below and "Printed and Published by THE TIMES PUBLISHING COM- | PANY, Limited, Printing House-square, London, E.C.4 | R8844" at foot of p [8]; pp [9-10] blank; no endpapers; no wrappers; center stitched.

Notice of limitation:

Of this pamphlet | FIFTY COPIES | only have been | reprinted. | 10th December, 1925.

Contents:

A letter dealing with a criticism in the TIMES LITERARY SUPPLEMENT, 26 November, of the C. K. Scott Moncrieff translation of *The Letters of Abélard and Héloïse* (B21) and of certain of GM's statements in its prefatory matter.

2. Issued in a format matching other Boni and Liveright trade editions (see A52-2a for description).

1. For Norman Gullick then on the staff of the TIMES LITERARY SUPPLEMENT. In a letter to me dated "18th August 1951" he wrote, "There are no particulars about my Moore offprint not detailed in the pamphlet itself. It was, by the way, a genuine 'private' issue, since I gave the copies away, not sold them."

A49

Daphnis and Chloe

a First edition:

THE | PASTORAL LOVES | OF | DAPHNIS | AND | CHLOE | DONE INTO ENGLISH | By GEORGE MOORE | [*decorative engraving*] | London | William Heinemann Ltd. | 1924

Published 15 December at 42/- in an edition of 1,280 copies

9⅛ x 5⅜; [ ]² (tipped in), A-K⁸, L² (tipped in); pp [iv], 164, comprising: half-title, with notice of limitation as below on verso, pp [i-ii]; title-page as above, with "Printed in Great Britain by T. and A. CONSTABLE LTD. | at the University Press, Edinburgh" at foot of verso, pp [iii-iv]; INTRODUCTION pp 1-[26]; PROEMIAL pp 27-[28]; BOOK THE FIRST pp 29-54, with engraving¹ top p 29; engraving, verso blank, pp [55-56]; text continued pp 57-[59], with engraving on lower half p [59]; p [60] blank; BOOK THE SECOND pp 61-84, with engraving top p 61; engraving, verso blank, pp [85-86]; text continued pp 87-[95], with engraving center p [95]; p [96] blank; BOOK THE THIRD pp 97-110, with engraving top p 97; engraving, verso blank, pp [111-12]; tipped in ERRATUM slip (1¹⁵⁄₁₆ x 5); text continued pp 113-[128], with engraving top p 129; engraving, verso blank, pp [155-56]; text continued pp 157-[164]; white endpapers; all edges untrimmed; cream cloth spine, gray paper-covered board sides, spine gilt lettered THE | PASTORAL | LOVES | OF | DAPHNIS | AND | CHLOE | GEORGE | MOORE | HEINEMANN

Notice of limitation:

This Edition is limited to 1280 copies, signed | by the author, of which 1250 are for | sale and 30 for presentation. | No. . . . . . [*numbered in ink*] | George Moore [*signed in ink*]

Contents:

"Introduction" previously unpublished; "Proemial" and *The Pastoral Loves of Daphnis and Chloe* are the previously unpublished translation of the story by Longus, based on the French translation by Jacques Amyot first published in 1559.

2a First American edition:

Daphnis and Chloe, with minor textual differences probably due to its having been set from proof pages of the first edition (a above) prior to GM's usual last-minute corrections, was issued with *Peronnik the Fool* as Volume XXI of the Carra Edition, and a collation of the volume is given under the latter title (A50-a). The first edition text of *Daphnis and Chloe* was printed separately for:

1. Engraved head and tail pieces and four illustrations reproduced from originals by the Regent, Philip of Orleans, in the 1718 French edition.

3a — The Windmill Library, William Heinemann Ltd., London, 1927. It was again published in the same volume with *Peronnik the Fool* for:

4a — Uniform Edition, Heinemann, June 1933. (For collation see A50-2b). Reissued in different binding as:

4a2 — Ebury Edition, Heinemann, March 1937.

5a — Second American edition, illustrated:

THE PASTORAL LOVES OF | DAPHNIS AND CHLOE | By LONGUS | Done into English, with an Introduction, by | GEORGE | MOORE | Illustrated with Etchings by | RUTH REEVES | [*circular etching of heads of Chloe and Daphnis with their names in Greek at rim*] | New York | The Limited Editions Club | 1934

Published 25 January at $10 in an edition of 1,500 copies for members of the club

11¼ x 7⅞; [1]⁶, [2-9]⁸, [10]¹⁰; pp [2], xxvi, 132, comprising: blank page, with etching on verso, not paginated; title-page[2] as above, with "The contents of this book are copyrighted, 1934, by | The Limited Editions Club, Inc." at top and "Printed in the United States of America" at foot of verso, pp [i-ii]; INTRODUCTION pp iii-xxiii; p [xxiv] blank; PROEMIAL, verso blank, pp xxv-[xxvi]; text pp 1-130 (with etched headpieces pp 1, 31, 65, 97; etched tail-pieces pp 30, 63, 95; full-page etchings pp [9], [23], [42], [51], [61], [71], [78], [84], [104], [116], [127]; and pp [10], [24], [41], [52], [62], [64], [72], [77], [83], [96], [103], [115], [128] blank); notice of limitation as below, verso blank, pp [131-32]; white endpapers; top edges gilt, fore and bottom edges untrimmed; tan head and foot bands; bound in tan stained lambskin, decorative border in blind on back and front covers, with circular border in blind on center of front cover enclosing circular gilt bas-relief of two heads lettered around top edge "Daphnis and Chloe" in Greek characters, border in blind at top and bottom of spine, which is gilt lettered up DAPHNIS AND CHLOE

Notice of limitation:

This edition of DAPHNIS AND CHLOE consists of | fifteen hundred copies made for the members of | The Limited Editions Club. Designed by | Porter Garnett and printed[3] under his | direction on the hand-press at | Pittsburg, Pennsylvania. | This is Copy No. [*numbered in ink within decorative box*] | [*circular etching*] | Illustrated with etchings by | Ruth Reeves & here | signed by her: | Ruth Reeves [*signed in ink*]

Contents:

Same as first edition (a above).

2. It is interesting to note that this is the only edition of GM's translation that has the name of Longus on its title-page.

3. An advance notice sent out to members says, "The type is Mr. Garnett's special revision of Lutetia, set by hand and used here for the first time; it is printed by hand on hand-made Bishopstoke all-rag paper."

6a — Fourth English edition, illustrated:

The Pastoral Loves of | Daphnis & Chloe | Done into English by George Moore | With Etchings By Marcel Vertès | Folio Society [*asterisk*] London [*asterisk*] 1954 | [*reproduction of etching*]

Published June at 21/-; issued 1 November in U.S. by Philip C. Duschnes at $5.00

9¾ x 7¼; [A]⁴, B-M⁴ (with plate foldings around C, F, I); pp 96 (plus six unpaginated leaves, blank on one side and with reproduction of etchings facing pp 17, 24, 41, 48, 65, 72) comprising: half-title, verso blank, pp [1-2]; blank page, with reproduction of etching on verso, pp [3-4]; title-page as above, with "George Moore's translation | is here used by kind permission of C. D. Medley | [*ornamental rule*] | Set in Centaur type and printed | in Great Britain by | Charles Batey at the University Press, Oxford | who also reproduced the etchings by collotype | Bound by James Burn" on verso, pp [5-6]; "Foreword," verso blank, pp 7-[8]; "Proemial" pp 9-10; text pp 11-95 (with six inserted illustrations as noted above); p [96] blank; white endpapers; all edges trimmed; pale blue and white headband; light blue covered-board sides, with white parchment spine, gilt stamped up DAPHNIS AND CHLOE and with monogram FS at foot.

Contents:

The "Foreword" is an editorial comment by the publishers and replaces GM's "Introduction" found in previous editions; "Proemial" and *Daphnis and Chloe* same as in previous editions.

A50

Peronnik the Fool

a First (Carra) edition:

DAPHNIS AND CHLOE | PERRONIK [*sic*] THE FOOL | BY | GEORGE MOORE | [*rule*] | Carra Edition | [*rule*] | PRINTED FOR SUBSCRIBERS ONLY BY | BONI AND LIVERIGHT, INC., NEW YORK | 1924

Published 22 December at $8.50 in an edition of 1,000 copies

8⅞ x 5⅜; [1-12]⁸; pp [x], 182, comprising: blank leaf, pp [i-ii]; half-title, verso blank, pp [iii-iv]; title-page as above, with "DAPHNIS AND CHLOE | (Carra Edition) | [*rule*] | Copyright, 1924, by | Boni & Liveright, Inc. | PERRONIK [*sic*] THE FOOL | Copyright, 1921, by | The Dial Publishing Co. | [*rule*] | Copyright, 1924, by | Boni & Liveright, Inc. | [*rule*] | Printed in the United States of America" in center and notice of limitation[1]

---

1. Same as in other volumes of Carra Edition (see A36-4a).

at bottom of verso, pp [v-vi]; table of CONTENTS, verso blank, pp [vii-viii]; sectional title, verso blank, pp [ix-x]; INTRODUCTION pp 1-20; PROEMIAL pp 21-22; sectional title, verso blank, pp [23-24]; text of DAPHNIS AND CHLOE pp 25-123, with pp [72] and [96] blank; p [124] blank; sectional title, with author's note[2] on verso, pp [125-26]; PERON-NIK THE FOOL pp 127-81; pp [182] blank; bluish-gray endpapers; all edges untrimmed; parchment spine, with bluish-gray paper-covered board sides, match endpapers, white paper label on spine, lettered in black, except as noted: Daphnis | & Chloe | [*rule*] | Perronik [*sic*] | the Fool | [*decorative rule*] | George Moore [*in red*] | [*decorative rule*] | Carra Edition | Volume XXI [*two plain rules, with decorative rule between, all in red, at both top and bottom*]

Contents:

"Introduction," "Proemial," and *The Pastoral Loves of Daphnis and Chloe* are the same as A49-a, with minor textual differences, having been set from page proofs of that edition, prior to last-minute corrections; "Peron-nik the Fool," previously published in THE DIAL, November 1921. The story is an old Breton legend and can be found in Sonvestre's *Foyer Breton*.[3] Although "Peronnik" is misspelled on spine label, title-page, and copyright notice, it is correctly spelled in text.

2a First separate, second American, edition:

GEORGE MOORE | [*decorative rule, in red*] | P [*large swag initial, in red*] eronnik | the fool | [*decorative rule, in red*] | 1926

Published 13 August at $12.50 in an edition of 785 copies

9 x 5⅝; [1-5]⁸, pp [viii], 72, comprising: blank leaf, pp [i-ii]; half-title, verso blank, pp [iii-iv]; title-page as above, with COPYRIGHT, 1926 | WILLIAM EDWIN RUDGE | NEW YORK in center of verso, pp [v-vi]; NOTE (heading and author's initials at end in red), verso blank, pp [vii-viii]; text (with large decorative initials at start of each chapter, shoulder headlines throughout, and typographic ornaments at end of each chapter, all in red) pp 1-[69]; colophon as below, p [70]; pp [71-72] blank; off-white endpapers, matching text paper; all edges untrimmed; red and gold head

---

2. "NOTE: In my narrative of Héloïse and Abélard it is related | that Héloïse wrote a story in French prose entitled Peronnik | the Fool so that she might teach her son French (he had | been away in Brittany for a long time and come back to her | speaking Breton). But the story, had it been included in | the published book, would have distracted the reader's at- | tention from Héloïse's own story. It may be that in some | future edition of Héloïse and Abélard the story will be in- | cluded. — G.M." This same note was appended to the story when it was published in THE DIAL with the final sentence continuing, "but it will be easier for me to make up my mind if it would be wise to do this after reading Peronnik the Fool in print, and it is for this reason that I now offer it to the public through the medium of a review."

3. Other versions of the story in English have appeared as "Peronnik the Jester," "Silly Peter," etc.

and foot bands; bound in blue paper-covered boards, front and back covers decorated in an all-over pattern of red and tan, tan paper label on flat spine, lettered up in red: Peronnik the Fool

Colophon:

[*thistle*] Bruce Rogers [*both initials large swag letters in red*] | DE-SIGNED THIS BOOK: OF WHICH 785 COPIES | WERE PRINTED AT THE PRESS OF | WILLIAM EDWIN RUDGE | MOUNT VERNON | NEW YORK | [*printer-publisher's monogram device, in red*]

Contents:

Same as first edition (a above).

b Continental edition, revised:

PERONNIK | THE FOOL | BY | GEORGE MOORE | (Revised Edition) | The Hours Press | Chapelle-Réanville, Eure, France | 1928

Published 20 December at 42/- in an edition of 200 copies

8⅞ x 5½; [ ]⁴ (endpapers and binder's leaves), [1]² (tipped in), [2-9]⁴, [ ]⁴ (binder's leaves and endpapers); pp [4], iv, 64, [4], comprising: two blank binder's leaves conjugate with endpapers, not paginated; half-title, with notice of limitation as below on verso, pp [i-ii]; title-page as above, verso blank, pp [iii-iv]; text pp [1]-63; colophon as below p [64]; two blank binder's leaves conjugate with endpapers, not paginated; all edges untrimmed; bound in blue buckram, back cover and spine plain, front cover gilt stamped PERONNIK THE FOOL | GEORGE MOORE

Notice of limitation:

200 COPIES OF THIS BOOK | SET BY HAND AND PRIVATELY | PRINTED ON HAND-PRESS | EACH COPY HAS BEEN | SIGNED BY THE AUTHOR | THIS IS NO [*numbered in ink*] | George Moore [*signed in ink*]

Colophon:⁴

This book was finished printing | December 11, 1928, by Nancy | Cunard and Maurice Lévy | and is the first volume of | THE HOURS PRESS.

Contents:

As stated on title-page, this is a revised edition.

2b First English (Uniform) edition:

THE | PASTORAL LOVES OF | DAPHNIS AND CHLOE | Done into English by | GEORGE MOORE | together with | PERONNIK THE FOOL | [*vignette*] | London | William Heinemann Ltd. | 1933

4. Further details regarding the printing of this edition can be found (pp 175-80) in *GM: Memories of George Moore* (B26), by Nancy Cunard, and in "The Hours Press," also by Miss Cunard, in THE BOOK COLLECTOR, Winter 1964. In both, however, her memory apparently played her false, as she lists the price of the volume at £2, but in the original prospectus of The Hours Press it says, "PERONNIK THE FOOL . . . Price 2 guineas Ready at Christmas."

Published June at 6/-

9 x 5½; [A] ^{8}, B-H ^{8}, I ^{4}, I* ^{8} (inserted between I$_2$ and I$_3$); pp [vi], 146, comprising: half-title, with list of other GM works PREVIOUSLY PUB-LISHED IN THE SAME FORMAT on verso, pp [i-ii]; title-page as above, with accurate listing of previous publication of both titles on verso, pp [iii-iv]; fly-title, verso blank, p [v-vi]; INTRODUCTION pp 1-17; PROEM-IAL p 18; text of DAPHNIS AND CHLOE pp 19-98; fly-title, verso blank, pp [99-100]; text of PERONNIK THE FOOL pp 101-144; pp [145-46] blank, with extra spine label tipped to lower right corner of verso; white endpapers; all edges untrimmed; brown cloth spine, with marbled paper-covered board sides, white paper label on spine lettered in brown: Daphnis and | Chloe | [dash] | Peronnik | the Fool | George | Moore | Heinemann

Contents:

"Introduction," "Proemial," and *The Pastoral Loves of Daphnis and Chloe* same as A48-a; *Peronnik the Fool*, same as Hours Press edition (b above).

This edition previously noted as A49-4a. Reissued in a different binding as:

2b2 — Ebury Edition, Heinemann, March 1937, previously noted as A49-4a2.

3b Second English edition, illustrated:

Peronnik the Fool | by George Moore | with Engravings by | Stephen Gooden | [*chalice and arrow*] | LONDON | George G. Harrap & C^O L^{TD} | 1933 [*all engraved*]

Published November at 84/- in an edition of 525 copies; distributed in the U.S. by Lippincott at $25

8⅞ x 6½; [A]^4, B-I^4, K^6; pp 1-36, [2], 37-58, [2], 59-80 (=84), com-prising: half-title, with engraving on verso, pp [1-2]; engraved title-page as above, with "Printed in Great Britain" at foot of verso, pp [3-4]; divisional title p [5]; text pp 6-77, with engraved headpieces pp 6, 26, 50, and 66, pp [24] and [64] blank, divisional titles pp [25], 49, and [65], page engravings ^{5} (not paginated) facing pp 36 and 58, versos blank, and engraved tail-piece p 77; colophon as below p [78]; pp [79-80] blank; white endpapers, with notice of limitations as below on verso of free front endpaper; top edges gilt, fore and bottom edges untrimmed; red and gold headband; chartreuse place marker; bound in cream vellum, back cover plain, front cover gilt stamped PERONNIK | THE FOOL and spine stamped in gilt PER- | ON- | NIK | THE FOOL | GEORGE | MOORE | MCM | XXXIII

Notice of limitation:

This edition of "Peronnik the Fool" is limited to | 525 copies for sale

5. See nos. 95-102 in *An Iconography of the Engravings of Stephen Gooden*, by Campbell Dodgson, London, 1944.

and presentation, of which this | copy is Number [*numbered in ink*] | George Moore [*signed in ink*][6] | Stephen Gooden [*signed in ink*]

Colophon:

Published 1933 | By GEORGE G. HARAP & CO. LTD. | 39-41 Parker Street, Kingsway, London, W.C.2 | Printed by WALTER LEWIS, M.A., at the | University Press, Cambridge

Contents:

Text same as b above.

A51

Ulick and Soracha

a First edition:

Ulick and Soracha | by | George Moore | [*printer's ornament*] | mcmxxvi | the Nonesuch Press | 16 Great James Street, London [*all within border of printer's ornaments*]

Published 28 June 1926 at 42/- in an edition of 1,250 copies

$9\frac{1}{8}$ x $5\frac{3}{4}$; [a]^4 ([a]$_2$ and [a]$_3$ singletons, not conjugate), A-S^8; pp [viii], 288, comprising: blank leaf pp [i-ii]; title-page as above, verso blank, pp [iii-iv]; "Author's Note" followed by "Publisher's Note" as below, with dedication to Lady Cunard signed at end in ink "George Moore" on verso, pp [v-vi]; copper-plate engraving, verso blank, pp [vii-viii]; text pp 1-286; pp [287-88] blank; cream endpapers; all edges untrimmed; bound in cream buckram over beveled boards, back and front covers plain, spine gilt lettered: Ulick and | Soracha | by | George Moore | Issued with loose parchment wrapper, lettered on spine in red as on book, and with design in red on front.

Publisher's note:

THIS EDITION OF ULICK AND | Soracha consists of twelve hundred and | fifty copies, printed on japon vellum for | the Nonesuch Press by T. & A. Constable | Ltd., at the University Press, Edinburgh, | for sale in England. The copper-plate | engraving accompanying the dedica- | tion has been designed and engraved | by Stephen Gooden, and printed by | A. Alexander & Sons. The design for the | loose cover is by Marion V. Dorn. | This is number | [*numbered in ink*]

Contents:

Previously unpublished.

2a First American edition:

ULICK AND SORACHA | BY | GEORGE MOORE | [*three printer's*

---

6. Signed by GM prior to his death earlier in the year.

ornaments, two above and one below] | ISSUED FOR SUBSCRIBERS ONLY | BY BONI AND LIVERIGHT | NEW YORK [*space*] 1926

Published 15 October at $10 in an edition of 1,250 copies

8⅞ x 5⅜; [1]², [2]¹ (both folded around and sewn with [3]), [3-17]⁸; pp [x], 236, comprising: half-title, with notice of limitation as below on verso, pp [i-ii]; title-page as above, with "COPYRIGHT, 1926, BY | BONI AND LIVERIGHT, INC. | All Rights Reserved" above center and PRINTED IN THE UNITED STATES OF AMERICA at foot of verso, pp [iii-iv]; blank page, with steel engraving by Stephen Gooden as in first edition on verso, pp [v-vi]; tissue guard sheet, not paginated; dedication, verso blank, pp [vii-viii]; fly-title, verso blank, pp [ix-x]; text p 1-235; p [236] blank; bluish-gray endpapers; all edges untrimmed; white parchment spine, with bluish-gray paper-covered board sides, matching endpapers, white paper label on spine, lettered in black, except as noted: Ulick & | Soracha | [*decorative rule*] | George Moore [*in red*] | [*decorative rule*] | Limited | Edition [*two plain rules with decorative rule between, all in red, at top and bottom of label*]¹

Notice of limitation:

This edition of ULICK AND SORACHA | is strictly limited to Twelve Hundred | and Fifty Copies Numbered and Signed | This Copy is Number [*numbered in ink*] | George Moore [*signed in ink*]

Contents:

Same as first edition (a above).

A revised version of *Ulick and Soracha* is included as chapters XLIV-LVII of the 1928 and subsequent editions of *A Story-Teller's Holiday* (A37-b et seq.).

A52

Celibate Lives

a First (Uniform) edition with new title:

CELIBATE | LIVES | BY | GEORGE MOORE | [*vignette*] | London | William Heinemann Ltd. | 1927

Published January at 10/6

8½ x 5¼; [a]⁴, a2² (inserted between [a]₂ and [a]₃), A-M⁸, N⁴; pp xii, 200, comprising: half-title, with list of twenty-four WORKS BY GEORGE MOORE on verso, pp [i-ii]; title-page as above, with "Printed in Great Britain by T. and A. CONSTABLE LTD. | at the University Press, Edin-

---

1. Format of this edition matches volumes in Carra Edition, and unnumbered and unsigned copies were issued with remainder sets of it.

burgh" at foot of verso, pp [iii-iv]; ADVERTISEMENT p [v]-ix; p [x] blank; table of CONTENTS, verso blank, pp [xi-xii]; text pp [1]-200, extra spine label tipped in on lower left corner of recto of free rear endpaper; white endpapers; all edges untrimmed; brown cloth spine with marbled paper-covered board sides, white label on spine, lettered in brown: Celibate | Lives | George | Moore | Heinemann

Contents:

"Advertisement" previously unpublished; "Wilfred Holmes" reprinted from *In Single Strictness* (A44); "Priscilla and Emily Lofft" reprinted from *In Single Strictness*; "Albert Nobbs" reprinted from first edition of *A Story-Teller's Holiday* (A37-a); "Henrietta Marr" reprinted from *In Single Strictness*; "Sarah Gwynn" reprinted from *In Single Strictness*.

Reissued in a different binding as:

a2 — Ebury Edition, Heinemann, London, February 1938. An offset impression, reproduced slightly reduced from sheets of this edition, but with "Advertisement" omitted, was issued in:

a3 — The Landmark Library, No. 2, Chatto & Windus, London, 26 September 1968.

2a First American edition:

CELIBATE LIVES | BY | GEORGE MOORE | [*publisher's device*] | NEW YORK | BONI & LIVERIGHT | 1927

Published 10 September at $2.50

8 x 5½; [1-15]⁸; pp xiv, 15-240, comprising: half-title, verso blank, pp [i-ii]; title-page as above, with "Copyright, 1922, by | Boni and Liveright, Inc., | under the Title | IN SINGLE STRICTNESS | [*rule*] | Copyright, 1927, by | Boni and Liveright, Inc. | All Rights Reserved" in center and "Printed in the United States of America" at foot of verso, pp [iii-iv]; ADVERTISEMENT pp v-ix; p [x] blank; table of CONTENTS, verso blank, pp [xi-xii]; fly-title, verso blank, pp [xiii-xiv]; text pp 15-237; pp [238-40] blank; white endpapers; top edges trimmed, fore and bottom edges untrimmed; bound in glazed black cloth,¹ back and front covers plain, publisher's device in blind below center of spine, with white paper label at top, printed in black, except as noted [*eight printer's ornaments in blue, forming decorative border*] | [*rule*] | [*blue rule*] | Celibate | Lives | [*blue rule*] | GEORGE | MOORE | [*blue rule*] | [*publisher's device in black, flanked by three printer's ornaments on each side in blue, matching top border, underlined with blue rule*]

Contents:

Same as first edition (a above). This text also used for:

1. Matching Boni and Liveright trade editions of *Avowals* (A38-3a2), *Héloïse and Abélard* (A40-2b2), *Conversations in Ebury Street* (A46-2a2), and *An Anthology of Pure Poetry* (A47-2a2).

3a — Collection of British Authors, No. 4793, issued in both red cloth and customary paper wrappers, Bernhard Tauchnitz, Leipzig, 1927.

See D:Ge-17 for a German translation of "Albert Nobbs," and D:Sp-1 for Spanish translations of "Henrietta Marr" and "Wilfred Holmes."

A53
The Making of an Immortal

a First edition:

The Making of an | Immortal [*both lines of title in terra-cotta colored ink*] | A Play in One Act | By George Moore | [*terra-cotta colored trellis-like decoration, incorporating within a box the motto* Non Sanz Droict *and a bust of Shakespeare*] | New York | THE BOWLING GREEN PRESS | London: Faber & Gwyer, Ltd. | Mcmxxvii [*in terra-cotta colored ink*] | [*all within single-rule border*]

Published 8 December 1927[1] at $15 in an edition of 1,240 copies, plus 15 special copies (see below)

8⅛ x 4⅞; [1]⁴ ([1]₁ and [1]₂ are paste-down and free front endpapers, not counted in pagination), [2-8]⁴, [9]⁴ ([9]₃ and [9]₄ are free and paste-down rear endpapers, not counted in pagination); pp [ii], 62, comprising: blank page, with notice of limitation as below on verso, p [i-ii]; half-title, verso blank, pp [1-2]; title-page as above, with COPYRIGHT 1927 | BY THE BOWLING GREEN PRESS, INC. | PRINTED IN THE UNITED STATES | OF AMERICA on verso, pp [3-4]; "Preface Dedicatory" pp 5-7; list of "Characters in the Play" p [8]; text pp 9-59 (with title at head of text, p 9, in terra-cotta colored ink); pp [60-62] blank; bound in light brown paper-covered boards, front and back covers plain, red leather label on flat spine, gilt lettered up: The Making of an Immortal

Notice of limitation:

TWELVE HUNDRED AND FORTY COPIES | PRINTED AT THE PRINTING HOUSE OF | WILLIAM EDWIN RUDGE, MOUNT VER- | NON, NEW YORK, AUGUST, 1927. DEC- | ORATIONS BY CLAIRE BRUCE. EACH | COPY SIGNED BY THE AUTHOR. THIS | IS NUM- BER [*numbered in red ink*] | George Moore [*signed in blue ink*]

1. Date of publication from copyright data in Library of Congress. Will Ransom, however, gives "August 1927" as the publication date in *Private Presses and Their Books*, New York, 1929, from information supplied him by James R. Wells, president of the Bowling Green Press. In the notice of limitation August is given as the date of printing.

There are two states: (a) As above. (b) Fifteen copies printed on green paper, as above except notice of limitation on p [ii] is omitted and the page is blank; instead there is a handwritten notice of limitation in green ink below the half-title on p [1]: Number one [*or* two *to* fifteen *as the case may be*] of fifteen copies | printed on green paper | George Moore [*signed in black ink*]

Contents:

The idea for this short play was given GM (circa 1902) by AE, according to Oliver St. John Gogarty, who relates[2] " 'Suppose,' AE went on, 'you were to write a play making Shakespeare merely the mouth-piece for Elizabethan courtiers who feared to write under their own names: Bacon, the Earl of Oxford, Wriothesley — anyone. When Shakespeare has covered their identity in a few plays and finds them a success, he runs off with the credit and the true author finds himself in a position where to prosecute would only make him more suspected and embarrassed. So Shakespeare becomes immortal.' " John Butler Yeats on 11 July 1902 wrote[3] his son, William Butler Yeats, "I hear George Moore is interested in the question of Bacon and Shakespeare — Fancy it!" When GM readied the manuscript for publication John Eglinton assisted him, and 11 March 1927 GM wrote him that he ". . . appreciated your editing on every page."

The Making of an Immortal was produced 1 April 1928 at the Arts Theatre in London, with incidental music by Sir Thomas Beecham, and with Malcolm Keen as Burbage, Leslie Faber as Bacon, Charles Carson as Shakespeare, Brion Glennie as the boy-Juliet Prenny Lister, Sybil Thorndike as Queen Elizabeth, Charles Laughton[4] as Jonson, and Edmund Gwenn, Edward Chapman, and D. Hay Petrie in other roles. Another production was presented in 1929 by the Illyrian Pastoral Players at Beckenham, England.

See D:Fr-25 for a French translation.

2. In "Next Door to George Moore" in SATURDAY REVIEW OF LITERATURE, 18 July 1936.

3. *J.B. Yeats: Letters to His Son W.B. Yeats and Others*, London, 1944; New York, 1946.

4. When questioned by me in 1946 about this production, Mr. Laughton stated that the play was "incredibly bad" and "embarrassing" to the cast. The production, however, received several good notices from the critics. Charles Morgan wrote in THE TIMES (London), "To read the play had been charming, full of humorous sketches of character, decorated with a luminous fancy, enriched with a prose which, even in its lightest lines, belongs to Moore and none other. How would it be in performance? . . . The play is not at its best till it is brought on the stage."

A54

Letters to Dujardin

a First edition:

Letters | FROM GEORGE MOORE | TO ED. DUJARDIN | 1886-1922 | [*steel-blue device of ram, flanked by letters* C *and* G] | CROSBY GAIGE : New York | 1929

Published 28 February at $15 in an edition of 668 copies, distributed in Great Britain by the Cayme Press at 63/-

8½ x 5⅜; [1]^{10}, [2-6]^{8}, [7]^{10}; pp 120, comprising: half-title, followed by signature "George Moore" in ink, verso blank, pp [1-2]; title-page as above, with "Copyright 1929 by The Fountain Press | Printed in the United States of America" in center of verso, pp [3-4]; INTRODUCTION pp 5-17; p [18] blank; text of letters pp 19-116; blank page, with colophon as below on verso, pp [117-18]; pp [119-20] blank; white endpapers; top edges trimmed, fore and bottom edges untrimmed; cream head and foot bands; cream cloth spine with gray paper-covered board sides, back and front plain, light green paper label on flat spine, lettered in black [*heavy and light rules*] | Letters | FROM | GEORGE | MOORE | TO ED. | DUJARDIN | [*light and heavy rules*]

Colophon:

Printed by James Hendrickson | AT THE PRESS OF M.J. WIDTMAN | UTICA, NEW YORK. SIX HUNDRED | AND SIXTY EIGHT COPIES OF WHICH | SIX HUNDRED AND TWENTY SIX ARE | FOR SALE. THREE HUNDRED COP- | IES FOR AMERICA DISTRIBUTED BY | RANDOM HOUSE AND THREE HUN- | DRED AND TWENTY SIX RESERVED | FOR ENGLAND. EACH COPY SIGNED | BY THE AUTHOR. | THIS IS NUMBER [*numbered in ink*]

Contents:

"Introduction," by John Eglinton who selected, edited and translated the 124 letters, originally written in French, from GM to Edouard Dujardin, the first dated "November 10, 1886," and the last "December 16, 1922."

A55

The Passing of the Essenes

a First edition with new title:

The PASSING of | the ESSENES | A DRAMA | IN THREE ACTS | By | GEORGE MOORE | London | William Heinemann Ltd. | 1930

Published 20 September at 42/- in an edition of 775 copies

8⅞ x 5⅝; [ ]⁴ (-[ ]₄), A-M⁴, N² (tipped in); pp [vi], 100, comprising: half-title, with notice of limitation as below on verso, pp [i-ii]; title-page as above, with "Printed in Great Britain by The Riverside Press Limited | Edinburgh" at foot of verso, pp [iii-iv]; blank page, with list of "CHARACTERS in the PLAY" on verso, pp [v-vi]; text pp [1]-96 with sectional titles, verso blank, pp [1-2, 33-34, and 67-68]; music for CHANT FOR PSALMS ON PAGES 17 AND 18 by Gustav Holst p [97]; pp [98-100] blank; off-white endpapers; top edges gilt, fore and bottom edges untrimmed; red and gold silk headband; bound in vellum over beveled boards, back cover plain, vignette¹ in gilt on front cover, spine gilt lettered THE | PASSING | OF THE | ESSENES | GEORGE | MOORE | HEINEMANN

Notice of limitation:

This edition is limited to 775 | copies, of which 750 are for sale | in Great Britain and Ireland and | 25 are for presentation. | This is No. . . . . . [*numbered in ink*] | George Moore [*signed in ink*]

Contents:

This is a further revision of *The Apostle* (A30), and in its present form was produced in London at the Arts Theatre, 1 October 1930, with Ian Fleming as Jesus, H.R. Hignett as Hazael, and John Laurie as Paul.²

2a First American edition:

The PASSING of | the ESSENES | A DRAMA | IN THREE ACTS | By | GEORGE MOORE | New York | The Macmillan Company | 1930

Published 1 October at $5.00 in an edition of 500 copies

9⅜ x 6¼; [1]⁴, [2-7]⁸; pp [viii], 96, comprising: notice of limitation as below, verso blank, pp [i-ii]; half-title, verso blank, pp [iii-iv]; title-page as above, with "COPYRIGHT, 1930, | By GEORGE MOORE. | [*rule*] | All rights reserved — no part of this book may be reproduced | in any form without permission in writing | from the publisher." in center and PRINTED IN THE UNITED STATES OF AMERICA at bottom of verso, pp [v-vi]; list of "CHARACTERS in the PLAY," verso blank, pp [vii-viii]; text pp [1]-96, with sectional titles, versos blank, pp [1-2, 33-34, and 67-68]; white endpapers; top edges trimmed, fore and bottom edges untrimmed; red and gold head and tail bands; bound in plum colored paper-covered boards, back cover plain, front cover gilt stamped THE PASSING OF THE ESSENES | [*printer's ornament*] | GEORGE MOORE and spine gilt lettered THE | PASSING | OF | THE | ESSENES | [*dot*] | GEORGE | MOORE

Notice of limitation:

OF THIS EDITION OF "THE PASSING | OF THE ESSENES," FIVE

---

1. Same as that used on title-pages of several other of GM's books (see A44-n1).

2. Apparently GM was not pleased with the production, for in a letter to John Eglinton, dated 30 October 1930, he wrote, "I found the play infinitely tedious on the stage when I saw it on Tuesday."

HUNDRED | COPIES HAVE BEEN PRINTED FROM | TYPE AND THE TYPE DESTROYED. | THIS IS NUMBER . . . . . [*numbered in ink*]

Contents:

Same as first edition (a above), this printing being an almost line by line resetting of that edition, except that the Holst music at the end is not included.

b Second English (Uniform) edition:

THE PASSING OF | THE ESSENES | A DRAMA | IN THREE ACTS | BY | GEORGE MOORE | [*vignette*] | London | William Heinemann Ltd. | 1931

Published July at 6/-

9 x 5½; [A]⁸, B-F⁸, G⁴; pp [2], viii, 94, comprising: blank leaf, not paginated; half-title, with list of seven titles by GM "PREVIOUSLY PUB-LISHED IN | THE SAME FORMAT" on verso, pp [i-ii]; title-page as above, with "First published, in a Limited Edition, 1930 | New and Revised Edition, 1931" in center and "Printed in Great Britain at | The Windmill Press, Kingswood, Surrey" at foot of verso, pp [iii-iv]; PREFACE TO THE SECOND EDITION pp v-vi; list of "CHARACTERS in the PLAY," verso blank, pp [vii-viii]; text pp [1]-92, with sectional titles, versos blank, pp [1-2], [33-34], and [65-66]; music as in first edition (a above), verso blank, pp [93-94]; extra spine label tipped in on lower right corner p [94]; white endpapers; all edges untrimmed; brown cloth spine, marbled paper-covered board sides, back and front covers plain, white paper label on spine, lettered in brown: The | Passing | of the | Essenes | George | Moore | Heinemann

Contents:

The "Preface" is a letter to the editor reprinted from TIMES LITERARY SUPPLEMENT, 30 October 1930; the text of *The Passing of the Essenes* revised from first edition (a above). Reissued in a different binding as:

b2 — Ebury Edition, Heinemann, London, March 1938.

A56

Aphrodite in Aulis

a First edition:

GEORGE MOORE | APHRODITE [*in red*] | IN AULIS [*in red*] | [*vignette*] | LONDON | WILLIAM HEINEMANN LTD. | NEW YORK : THE FOUNTAIN PRESS

Published 1 December 1930 at 63/- in an edition of 1,825 copies; distributed in the United States by Random House at $20

10⅛ x 6⅜; [a]¹ (tipped in), [b]², A-X⁸, Y⁴; pp vi, 344, comprising: half-title, with notice of limitation as below on verso, pp [i-ii]; title-page as above, with "First published 1930" in center and PRINTED IN GREAT BRITAIN at foot of verso, pp [iii-iv]; dedicatory letter to SIR JOHN THOMSON WALKER p v-vi; text pp 1-340; "Printed in Great Britain | by The Riverside Press Limited | Edinburgh" in center p [341]; pp [342-44] blank; white endpapers; all edges untrimmed; brown head and tail bands; bound in natural vellum over beveled boards, back cover plain, title-page vignette stamped in gilt on center of front cover, spine gilt stamped GEORGE MOORE | APHRODITE | IN AULIS | [column-like ornament]

Notice of limitation:

This, the first edition of Aphrodite | in Aulis is limited to 1825 copies of which | numbers 1 to 900 are for sale in Great | Britain and Ireland, numbers 901 to | 1800 are for sale in the United States of | America, and numbers 1801 to 1825 | are for presentation. | The book is printed by the Riverside | Press, Edinburgh, from hand-set type on | English handmade paper. | This is No. . . . . . [numbered in ink] | George Moore [signed in ink]

Contents:

Chapter I revised from "Aphrodite in Aulis: A Modernist Evokes the Spirit of Ancient Greece in a Fable of a Journey from Athens to Aulis" in VANITY FAIR, February 1929. Chapter II revised from "Aphrodite in Aulis: A Wandering Athenian Is Welcomed to Aulis and There Tells of Two Helens of Troy" in VANITY FAIR, March 1929. Chapters III-XXIII previously unpublished.

b Second American edition, revised:

APHRODITE [small diamond] IN [small diamond] AULIS | GEORGE [small diamond] MOORE | [drawing of statue of Aphrodite in terra-cotta colored ink] | BRENTANO'S [small diamond] NEW [small diamond] YORK [all within box of single rules, resembling a Greek column]

Published 16 March 1931 at $2.50

8⅛ x 5¼; [1-20]⁸; pp [2], vi, 312, comprising: blank leaf, not paginated; half-title, verso blank, pp [i-ii]; title-page as above, with "Copyright 1931 by George Moore | Manufactured in the United States | of America" above center of verso, pp [iii-iv]; dedicatory letter to Sir John Thomson Walker pp v-vi; fly-title, verso blank, pp [1-2]; text pp 3-311; list of seven "Other Books by Mr. Moore" at top and colophon as below at bottom p [312]; white endpapers, matching text paper; top edge trimmed and stained reddish-brown, fore and bottom edges untrimmed; bound in light gray cloth, back cover plain, drawing of Aphrodite statue on title-page repeated on front cover in terra-cotta, spine lettered in terra-cotta APHRODITE | IN AULIS | GEORGE | MOORE | BRENTANO'S

Colophon:

This book has been printed in Fournier type | on Warren's Egg Shell Laid paper by The | Plimpton Press, Norwood, Massachusetts. | Typography by Ronald Freelander. Title | page by Howard Simon.

Contents:

Text revised and chapter Twenty-two rewritten, replacing chapters XXII and XXIII of the first edition (a above).

Part of second printing, noted on verso of title-leaf, remaindered in dark blue cloth binding, stamped in yellow.

2b Second English (Uniform) edition:

APHRODITE | IN AULIS | BY | GEORGE MOORE | [*vignette*] | London | William Heinemann Ltd. | 1931

Published August 1931 at 8/6

9 x 5½; [A]^8, B-S^8, R^2, R*^{4} (inserted between R$_1$ and R$_2$); pp [2], vi, 260, comprising: blank leaf, not paginated, half-title, with list of eight titles by GM "PREVIOUSLY PUBLISHED IN | THE SAME FORMAT" on verso, pp [i-ii]; title-page as above, with "First published, in a Limited Edition, 1930 | New and Revised Edition, 1931" in center and "Printed in Great Britain at | The Windmill Press, Kingswood, Surrey" at foot of verso, pp [iii-iv]; dedicatory letter to SIR JOHN THOMSON WALKER pp v[vi] (the latter misnumbered v);[1] text pp 1-260; white endpapers, with extra spine label tipped on lower right corner of verso of free rear endpaper; all edges untrimmed; brown cloth spine, marbled paper-covered board sides, with white paper label on spine, lettered in brown: Aphrodite | in | Aulis | George | Moore | Heinemann

Contents:

Same as second American edition (b above); second impression September 1931. Reissued in a different binding as:

2b2 — Ebury Edition, Heinemann, London, March 1938.

A57

A Flood

a First edition:

A FLOOD [*in red*] | BY GEORGE MOORE | NEW YORK | G.C. at The Harbor Press | MCMXXX

Published 8 December 1930 at $15 in an edition of 185 copies; distributed in Great Britain by Douglas Cleverdon, Bristol, at 63/-

7¾ x 4¾; [1-6]^4; pp [x], 38, comprising: two blank leaves pp [i-iv]; half-

1. Corrected in subsequent impressions.

title, verso blank, pp [v-vi]; notice of limitation as below, verso blank, pp [vii-viii]; title-page as above, with "Copyright 1930 by Groff Conklin" above center of verso, pp [ix-x]; text pp [1]-33; p [34] blank; device of seahorse and printer's ornaments in double-rule box, p [35]; pp [36-38] blank; off-white endpapers, matching text paper; all edges untrimmed; bound in red buckram, back and front covers plain, lettered up flat spine in gilt A FLOOD [*printer's ornament*] GEORGE MOORE

Notice of limitation:

Of this edition 185 copies have been printed | This is number [*numbered in ink*] | George Moore [*signed in ink*]

Contents:

This is a revised version of the short story originally published in the first issue of THE IRISH REVIEW, March 1911, reprinted in LIVING AGE, 27 May 1911, and again reprinted, without indication of previous publication, in THE SMART SET,[1] November 1913.

A58
The Talking Pine

a First edition:

THE TALKING | PINE | BY | GEORGE MOORE | THE HOURS PRESS | PARIS 1931

Printed May[1] in an edition of 500 copies

10 x 6½; [ ]⁴; pp [8], comprising: blank leaf pp [1-2]; title-page as above, p [3]; text pp [4-5]; notice of limitation as below p [6]; blank leaf pp [7-8]; printed in brown throughout; single white front and rear endpapers, with MADE AND PRINTED IN FRANCE stamped in blue in lower left corner of recto of rear endpaper in some copies; stitched with white silk cord; tan wrappers folded over endpapers to form heavier cover, back cover blank, front cover lettered in brown as on title-page.

1. (A57). In a letter to Groff Conklin, publisher of the above edition, dated "30th October, 1929," GM wrote, "The text published by *The Smart Set* was inferior, or shall I say inadequate. I have rewritten the story, and hope to publish it myself in a volume sometime next year; but if you care to pay for it, you can have the new text."

1. (A58). By Nancy Cunard, who tells something of its printing in *GM: Memories of George Moore* (B26), but says this "plaquette . . . never saw its public," as it was withdrawn due to a misunderstanding between her and GM about his signing the copies, which he refused to do. Some copies, however, must have been issued commercially as it is noted in *The English Catalogue* at 3s, January '32, with Simpkin Marshall listed as publisher or distributor.

Notice of limitation:

500 copies hand-set | & printed on Maillol | hand-made paper of | which this is No. [*numbered in blue ink*]

Previously unpublished, but what may be an earlier text, with three differences in wording, was published as "The Dream" in a publisher's advertising periodical, BOOKS FROM THE HOUSE OF ALEXANDER OUSLEY, No. 1, December 1931. In a letter, quoted in the same issue, GM refers to this "prose poem" as "The Poet and the Pine."

2a First American edition:

THE TALKING PINE | BY | GEORGE MOORE | [*sombrero device*] | TEMPE | EDWIN B. HILL | 1948

7 x 5; [ ]²; pp [4], comprising: title-page as above, verso blank, pp [1-2]; text p [3]; p [4] blank; printed on cream colored paper.²

Contents:

Same as first edition (a above).

Reprinted in both *The Silver Ship* (B25) and *GM: Memories of George Moore* (B26).

A59

George Moore in Quest of Locale

a First edition:

George Moore | In Quest of | Locale | HARVEST [*in an arc over device of a sickle and three stalks of grain*] | PRESS

Printed December 1931 in an edition of 75 copies for private distribution

9 x 6; [ ]⁸; pp [16], comprising: two blank leaves, pp [1-4]; half-title GEORGE MOORE | IN QUEST OF | LOCALE | TWO LETTERS | TO | W. T. STEAD, verso blank, pp [5-6]; title-page as above, verso blank, pp [7-8]; introduction pp [9-11]; text of letters pp [12-14], with notice of limitation as below at foot of p [14]; blank leaf pp [15-16]; all edges trimmed; wire stapled; issued in blue overlapping wrappers, back cover blank, front cover lettered in black: George Moore | In Quest of | Locale [*same type as on title-page*]

Notice of limitation:

Of this pamphlet seventy-five copies only have been printed | from hand set 12-point Bodoni Bold by James D. Hart at The | Harvest Press for Christmas 1931. This is copy number [*numbered in ink*]

2. This is one of a series of leaflets printed by Edwin B. Hill on his private press in Tempe, Arizona. His daughter, Miss Gertrude Hill of Los Angeles, kindly supplied copies of this printing but could furnish no information regarding the number printed.

Contents:

Introduction by John McClelland regarding the two letters, circa 1895, in which GM seeks an introduction to a nun or former nun who could give him first-hand information on life in a convent. The letters were in the possession of Mr. Hart at the time he printed them.

The two letters are also printed, with differences in transcription, in *Memories of a Misspent Youth* (B37), by Grant Richards, and quotations from them, again with a difference in transcription, are used (p 205) by Hone (B44).

A60
A Communication to My Friends

a First edition:

A | Communication | to | my friends | BY | George Moore | [*publisher's device in reddish-brown*] | The Nonesuch Press | 1933 [*all within border of printer's ornament*]

Published 13 June at 18/- in an edition of 1,000 copies

9⅛ x 5½; [1-6]⁸; pp [4], 92, comprising: two blank leaves, not paginated; half-title, verso blank, pp [1-2]; title-page as above, verso blank, pp [3-4]; Note, verso blank, pp [5-6]; text¹ pp [7]-86; colophon as below, p [87]; pp [88-92] blank; cream endpapers, matching text paper; all edges untrimmed; Heritage brown calf spine, with Ingres tan paper-covered board sides, both plain, gilt lettered up spine [*ornament*] George Moore: A Communication to my friends [*ornament*]

Colophon:

This edition consists of 1000 copies, of which 800 copies | are for sale in England by the Nonesuch Press and 200 | are for sale in the United States by Random House Inc. | The device on the title page was designed by Stephen | Gooden. Francis Meynell planned the book. Ernest Ingham | printed and made it in England at the Fanfare Press. | NUMBER | [*numbered in ink*]

Contents:

The "Note" on page [5] by C.D. Medley, GM's literary executor, relates, "When arrangements were made for the completion of the uniform edition of his works, George Moore proposed to write a general introduction to be published with 'A Mummer's Wife' which he had designated as volume I.

1. Printed "in Monotype Goudy Modern on Pannekoek mould-made paper," according to Francis Meynell in *The Nonesuch Century*, London, 1936.

As the writing of this introduction progressed the work grew under his hand, his interest and his enthusiasm increased . . . so that he foresaw a separate publication . . . of what he had at first only intended as an introduction to the uniform edition. [At the time] of his death . . . [he had] written only one half of what he had in mind and a third of that [from p 64 on] had not been revised."

In accordance with GM's intention, *A Communication to My Friends*[2] was used as the introduction to the Uniform Edition and was printed with *A Mummer's Wife* (A6-4c), the earliest of his writings to appear in that edition.

A61
The Lilacs Are in Bloom

a First edition:

The LILACS | ARE IN BLOOM | Song for Voice & Piano | By | MILDRED LUND TYSON | [*two musical notations* | *with arrow indicating* High *or* Low] | Price, 50 cents, net in U.S.A. | G. SCHIRMER, INC.–New York [*design of lilacs and leaves with hovering butterfly, printed in lilac and green, with all lettering in lilac, and all within arched green border*]

Published 1934

11¾ x 9; [a]², [b]¹ (inserted between [a]₁ and [a]₂); pp 6, comprising: title-page as above, p [1]; words and music pp 2-5, with "Copyright, 1934, by G. Schirmer (Inc.) | International Copyright Secured | Printed in the U. S. A." at foot p 2; advertisement for "Two Songs by Kathleen Lockhart Manning" p [6]

Later impressions omit word "net" in price line on title-page, and the advertisement on p [6] is for "SONGS BY | American Composers | SERIES THREE." A still later impression has title-page as above omitted, and in place of it "SONGS BY | American Composers | SERIES FOUR" are listed with an arrow pointing to title of this song. According to the composer, the song "is also published in a 3 part choral arrangement for women's voices."

Contents:

This is a musical setting of GM's poem first published in MAYFAIR MAGAZINE, May 1884, and later as one of the "Two Rondels" in *Ballades and Rondeaus* (B4).

2. A title previously used by Richard Wagner, a fact that could hardly have escaped GM, a great admirer of the German composer.

A62
Letters of George Moore

a First edition:

LETTERS | of | GEORGE MOORE | With an Introduction by JOHN EGLINTON, | to whom they were written

Published October 1942 at 10/6 in an edition of 250 copies

8½ x 5⅜; [1-6]⁸ ([1]₁ and [1]₂ are front paste-down and free endpapers and [6]₇ and [6]₈ are rear free and paste-down endpapers, not paginated); pp 88, comprising: title-page as above, with "Printed and Published¹ by | SYDENHAM & CO. (Est. 1840) LTD. | Oxford Road, Bournemouth, England." at foot of verso,² pp [1-2]; blank leaf pp [3-4]; INTRODUCTION pp 5-16; text of letters pp 17-88; all edges trimmed; tan cloth spine, with blue or green cloth sides, back cover and spine plain, front cover lettered in lower right corner in black: LETTERS | of | GEORGE | MOORE

Contents:

"Introduction" by John Eglinton, plus 119 letters, dated from 1909 to 1932, being a selection from the "five or six hundred" written by GM to Eglinton.

A63
George Moore on Authorship

a First separate edition:

George Moore On Authorship | [*quill pen and manuscript ornament*] | elg Press | 1950

Printed December in an edition of 30 copies for private distribution

6 x 4¼; [ ]⁶; pp 12, comprising: half-title, verso blank, p [1-2]; title-page as above, verso blank, pp [3-4]; printer's NOTE:, verso blank, pp [5-6]; text pp 7-9; p [10] blank; notice of limitation as below, verso blank, pp [11-12]; heavy olive green endpapers; bound¹ with dark green cloth spine

---

1. (A62). Printed for William K. Magee (John Eglinton) and sold for him by the printers.

2. Some copies also have the date 1942 in center of page. According to Mr. Magee, the earliest copies printed were undated, but sometime during the printing the date was added. It is uncertain how many copies are undated, but the presence or absence of the date and the color of the cloth sides have no bearing on priority of issue.

1. (A63). The printer, being far from satisfied with his efforts, bound only a few copies and the balance, sewn and ready for binding, remain unbound.

and natural linen sides, with white paper label on front cover lettered in black: George Moore | [*ornament as on title-page*] | On Authorship [*within double-rule border with box corners*]

Notice of limitation:

Thirty Copies | have been hand set, printed, | and bound, by Edwin Gilcher | for private distribution | December 1950.

Contents:

Reprint of a portion of a GM letter previously published in *The Art of Authorship* (B5).

A64
Diarmuid and Grania

a First edition:

DIARMUID AND GRANIA | A Play in Three Acts | BY | GEORGE MOORE | AND | W.B. YEATS | Now first printed | With an introductory note | BY | William Becker | [*rule*] | [Reprinted from *The Dublin Magazine*, APRIL-JUNE, 1951]

Issued April 1951 in an edition of 25 copies for private distribution[1]

9½ x 7; [A]^8, B^8, C^4, [D]^1; pp 42, comprising: title-page as above, p [1]; introductory note by the editor pp 2-4; text pp [5]-41; p [42] blank; no endpapers; all edges trimmed; wire stapled; issued in light gray[2] overlapping wrappers, back and spine plain, lettered in black on front DIARMUID AND GRANIA | A PLAY IN THREE ACTS | BY GEORGE MOORE AND | W. B. YEATS : : : : : | Reprinted from THE DUBLIN MAGAZINE | VOL. XXVI. (New Series), April-June, 1951

Contents:

A letter from GM to Yeats (8 August 1901) is included in the editor's introductory note. The text of the play is from a typescript,[3] with manuscript

---

1. By Dr. James Starkey, who as Seumas O'Sullivan edited THE DUBLIN MAGAZINE.

2. Which in some cases has discolored to a light tan.

3. Two other typescripts with numerous manuscript corrections, many of them in the handwriting of GM or Yeats, are in the library of the University of Texas at Austin, and were used by Ray Small as the basis of a critical edition of *Diarmuid and Grania* in an unpublished University of Texas doctoral thesis. Dr. Small informs me that his "final text does not differ a great deal" from the above. He does not, however, agree with Mr. Becker's attribution of the original scenario of the play to Lady Gregory, and presents evidence in his thesis that Yeats wrote the scenario in collaboration with GM, conclusively demonstrating that "Yeats supplied the story, that the construction and dialogue were primarily Moore's work, and that Yeats made the final decisions concerning revisions."

corrections by both GM and Yeats, which had been given to Mr. J. Millward, its present owner, by Lady Cunard, who presumably had it from GM. The play was presented by the F. R. Benson Company at the Gaiety Theatre in Dublin, 21 October 1901, for the Irish Literary Theatre. The song, "There Are Seven that Pull the Thread" with words by Yeats and music by Edward Elgar, published in 1902, is not present in this version. GM in *Ave* (A31:I-a) and Yeats in *Dramatis Personae 1896-1902* (New York, and London, 1936) have left accounts of their collaboration. GM gives six pages of the dialogue as written by him in French, to be translated into Gaelic and thence into English, "to convince the reader that two such literary lunatics as Yeats and myself existed," he explains. The scene given in *Ave* is also missing from this text. In the first issue of SAMHAIN, October 1901, Yeats stated, in writing of the forthcoming production of *Diarmuid and Grania*, "the first scene is in the great banqueting hall of Tara, and the second and third on the slopes of Ben Bulben in Sligo." As printed here, the first and last scenes are as noted by Yeats, but the second one is "Diarmuid's house."

2a — This version of *Diarmuid and Grania*, including the editor's introductory note, is included (pp 1168-1222) in *The Variorum Edition of the Plays of W. B. Yeats*, edited by Russell K. Alspach, Macmillan & Co., Ltd., London, and The Macmillan Company, New York, 1966.

A65
Letters to Lady Cunard

a First edition:

GEORGE | MOORE | Letters to Lady Cunard | 1895-1933 | Edited | with an introduction and notes | by Rupert Hart-Davis | [*publisher's device*] | Rupert Hart-Davis | Soho Square London | 1957

Published 20 September at 27/6 in an edition of 3,000 copies, 220 of which were distributed in the United States by Macmillan Co. at $5.50

8½ x 5½; [1]⁸, 2-13⁸; pp 208, comprising: half-title, verso blank, pp [1-2]; inserted frontispiece, not counted in pagination; title-page as above, with PRINTED AND BOUND IN ENGLAND BY | HAZELL WATSON AND VINEY LTD | AYLESBURY AND LONDON at foot of verso, pp [3-4]; list of ILLUSTRATIONS, verso blank, pp [5-6]; INTRODUCTION pp 7-20; THE LETTERS pp 21-195; HÉLOÏSE AND ABÉLARD | FROM CHAPTER XXII pp 196-200; EPILOGUE pp 201-3; p [204] blank; INDEX pp 205-8; inserted illustrations, not counted in pagination, facing pp 30, 40, 54, 56, 94, 131, 172; white endpapers; all edges trimmed, top edges stained blue; plain blue cloth sides and white parchment spine, gilt lettered: George | Moore | LETTERS | TO | LADY | CUNARD [*title within fancy braces*] | Rupert | Hart-Davis

Contents:

The "Introduction" by the editor, Rupert Hart-Davis, outlines the relationship between GM and Lady Cunard, with extensive quotations from "Theme and Variations" in the Tauchnitz edition of *Memoirs of My Dead Life* (A29-b) and the privately printed preliminary version of that section (A45); The Letters include 247 of the 276 surviving from the possible thousands sent by GM to Lady Cunard during a period of nearly forty years; also included (pp 78-80) is an article, "Mr. George Moore's Escape," reprinted from the CONTINENTAL DAILY MAIL, 6 September 1910, which gives, largely in GM's own words, the account of an accident in which he and Lady Cunard were involved as they left the Munich opera; a selection from chapter XXII of *Héloïse and Abélard* which relates the love of Caucelm d'Arembert for the Lady Malberge and seems to echo GM's deep and lasting affection for Lady Cunard; the "Epilogue" by the editor includes quotations from THE TIMES (London) obituary notice of Lady Cunard and a tribute to her by Sacheverell Sitwell in the same paper.

Among the illustrations are reproductions of an oil painting of GM by William Orpen, facing p 30; a letter from GM dated "July 13th 1905," facing p 40; Max Beerbohm's caricature, "George Moore, Preacher to Lord Howard de Walden," facing p 54; a photograph of GM in Dublin, 1908, by Alvin Langdon Coburn, facing p 56; a portion of an illustrated letter from Henry Tonks to Mrs. Charles Hunter with a caricature of GM, facing p 94; and an oil painting by John Lavery of GM and Lady Cunard, facing p 131.

A66

George Moore in Transition
Letters to T. Fisher Unwin and Lena Milman, 1894-1910

a First edition:

GEORGE MOORE | IN TRANSITION | Letters to T. Fisher Unwin and | Lena Milman, 1894-1910 | edited with a commentary by | Helmut E. Gerber, PURDUE UNIVERSITY | Wayne State University Press, Detroit, 1968

Published 19 April at $12 in an edition of 2,176 copies

9 x 5⅞; [1-7]¹⁶, [8]⁴, [9-10]¹⁶, [11]⁸, [12]¹⁶; pp 344, comprising: half-title, with reproduction of Tonks's drawing of GM previously used as frontis-

piece in first edition of *Sister Teresa* (A25-a) on verso, pp [1-2]; title-page as above, with copyright, etc., on verso, pp [3-4]; dedication, verso blank, pp [5-6]; table of "Contents," verso blank, pp [7-8]; "Preface" pp 9-15; p [16] blank; "Acknowledgements" pp 17-19; p [20] blank; "Abbreviations," verso blank, pp 21-[22]; sectional-title, verso blank, pp [23-24]; commentary and text of letters pp 25-333, with pp [48], [100], [120], [228] blank, and sectional-title, verso blank, pp [321-22]; p [334] blank; "Index of Names" pp 335-42; note on editor, type design and printing, verso blank, pp [343-44]; black endpapers; white head and tail bands; bound in purple cloth, back and front covers plain, lettered down spine: Gerber [*gilt*] GEORGE MOORE IN TRANSITION [*white*] | [*horizontally within oval*] Wayne [*white*]

Contents:

In addition to the extended commentary by the editor there are 298 letters, excerpts and telegrams from GM, including 183 to Unwin, 94 to Miss Milman, and 21 to various other correspondents. There are also two letters from J.E. Blanche to Unwin about a portrait of GM being considered as a frontispiece to one of his books; and excerpts from other letters by GM to various correspondents are included in the commentary.

II

Contributions

B1
Walnuts and Wine

a First edition:

WALNUTS [*final six letters underlined with fancy rule*] | AND | WINE:
[*final three letters and colon underlined with fancy rule*] | A Christmas An-
nual. | [*double rule*] | EDITED BY | AUGUSTUS M. MOORE | [*double
rule*] | LONDON: | THE STRAND PUBLISHING COMPANY. | 172,
STRAND

Published December 1883 [1] at 1/-

10⅛ x 7½; [1-9]⁴; pp [x], 62; no endpapers; all edges untrimmed; parchment wrappers, folded over first and last leaves, with commercial advertisement on back, and front cover lettered in wine red and black: Price One
Shilling [*in wine red*] | Walnuts | and | Wine [*last two words to right of a
glass of red wine and above three walnuts*] | Edited by Augustus M. Moore
[*in wine red*]

Contributions by GM:

"Dolorida" p 3, an English translation of a poem in French by Algernon
Charles Swinburne;[2] "A Russian Husband" pp 18-21, a short story, never
reprinted.

1. Incorrectly dated 1885 in British Museum Library Catalogue. It is presumably
this annual that Charles Morgan had in mind when in his *Epitaph on George Moore*
(p 11) he speaks of "a collection of stories, one signed 'George Moore', which under
the general title of *Wine, Women and Nuts* is on the shelves of the British Museum,"
but which is not listed in the BML Catalogue.
2. Swinburne denied authorship of the poem in a letter in the PALL MALL GA-
ZETTE, 25 December 1883. Thomas J. Wise, whose statements must always be taken
with a grain of salt, discusses this at length in his *A Bibliography of the Writings in
Prose and Verse of Algernon Charles Swinburne* (B17), and gives facsimiles of
three manuscripts of the poem, supposedly in Swinburne's hand, as well as GM's
translation from *Walnuts and Wine* and another made by GM for Edmund Gosse.

149

B2

Piping Hot

a First edition:

PIPING HOT! | (POT-BOUILLE). | A REALISTIC NOVEL. | BY | ÉMILE ZOLA. | TRANSLATED FROM THE 63RD FRENCH EDITION. | Illustrated with Sixteen Page Engravings, | FROM DESIGNS BY GEORGES BELLINGER. | LONDON: | VIZETELLY & CO., 42 CATHERINE STREET, STRAND. | 1885.

Published autumn 1884 at 6/-

7½ x 5; a[8], A[6], B-2A[8]: pp [2], xviii, 9-384, plus fourteen inserted engravings not paginated; followed by an inserted 20-page publisher's catalogue dated DECEMBER, 1884.; endpapers brown flowered where facing; all edges untrimmed; bound in blue[1] cloth, back cover plain except for triple-rule border in blind, front cover gilt stamped PIPING HOT! | A REALISTIC NOVEL | [*illustration on red background within an ornamental frame in black*] | BY ÉMILE ZOLA. | ILLUSTRATED. and spine stamped with four red rules at top and bottom, gilt lettered PIPING | HOT! | ÉMILE ZOLA | ILLUSTRATED | VIZETELLY & CO.

Contribution by GM:

"Preface" [2] pp v-xviii.

The translation, including the GM "Preface," was reissued by Vizetelly in a number of different bindings, some without the inserted illustrations.

2a — In 1886 a new edition[3] at 7/6, "Illustrated with 104 Engravings and Designs by French Artists," was published by Vizetelly in a larger format (9⅝ x 6½) from a new setting of type; [a][2] (tipped in), A-O[8], P[2] (tipped in), [Q][1] (tipped in), plus 47 inserted plates counted in pagination; pp xvi, 314.

3a — *Lesson in Love* by Émile Zola, "a newly abridged translation of *Pot-Bouille*," 288 pages, padded, paperbound, Pyramid Books, New York, September 1961, reprints the GM "Preface" as an "Introduction" with all references to *Piping Hot* changed to *Lesson in Love* and, in abridged form, the translation of the first edition text (a above).

---

1. Brown according to Danielson, but no copy in brown has been located.

2. In addition to having written the "Preface," there is also the possibility that GM may have translated the book. Albert J. Farmer in "George Moore et les influences françaises," a chapter in his book *Le Movement Esthetique et "Decadent" en Angleterre*, Paris, 1931, says (p 87), without giving a source for his statement, that GM translated *Pot-Bouille* for Vizetelly and in the book's bibliography (p 396) also lists *Rush for the Spoil* as having been translated by GM. Further, Hone, in discussing the prosecution of Vizetelly for publishing *Nana, The Soil,* and *Piping Hot* says (p 157), also without giving a source for his statement, that GM "was the author of one of the translations." As *Piping Hot* appears to be the only one of the three with which GM had any connection, it seems reasonable that, if in fact he did make

B3

The Rush for the Spoil

a First edition:

THE | RUSH FOR THE SPOIL | (LA CURÉE). | A REALISTIC
NOVEL. | BY | ÉMILE ZOLA. | TRANSLATED WITHOUT ABRIDGE-
MENT FROM THE 34TH FRENCH EDITION. | Illustrated with Twelve
Page Engravings. | London: | VIZETELLY & CO., 42 CATHERINE
STREET, STRAND. | 1886.

Published late 1885[1] at 6/-

7⅜ x 5; [a]² (tipped in), A-S⁸, T² (tipped in); pp [4], viii, 9-292, plus
ten inserted engravings not paginated; followed by inserted 24-page publisher's catalogue dated "November, 1885"; endpapers flowered where
facing; all edges untrimmed; bound in olive green cloth, publisher's monogram in center of back cover and three-rule border at outer edge, all in
blind, front cover gilt stamped THE | RUSH FOR THE SPOIL [*fancy rules
underlining last three letters of first and last words, which are larger than
middle two*] | [*same illustration as frontispiece on red background within an
ornamental green frame*] | BY ÉMILE ZOLA. | ILLUSTRATED. | and
spine stamped with four red rules at top and bottom, gilt lettered THE |
RUSH | FOR THE | SPOIL | ÉMILE ZOLA | ILLUSTRATED | VIZE-
TELLY & CO.

Contribution by GM:

"Preface" p i-viii.

The Rush for the Spoil was reissued[2] in a number of different bindings,
including:

a2 — An issue using sheets of the first edition in a binding similar to the
1887 impression (see Note 1) but with different stamping and having a
tipped-in slip (1¼ x 4¾) lettered VIZETELLY'S ORIGINAL | 5s. NON-
ILLUSTRATED EDITION | covering the line: Illustrated with Twelve
Page Engravings. | on title-page.

---

one of the translations, this must be it. Also the article on GM in Volume III of
Chamber's Cyclopedia of English Literature says, "In 1885 a translation of Zola's
Pot Bouille expressly avowed the direction which Moore's artistic and literary sym-
pathies had now taken."

3. For a more detailed description see No. 48 in Danielson (p 48).

1. Danielson (No. 48) gives 1885 as the date on the title-page in his description,
which also differs in several other particulars, including no mention of an inserted
catalogue, and royal blue binding with front cover lettered in red THE RUSH
FOR | THE SPOIL | A REALISTIC NOVEL | ÉMILE ZOLA. No copy agreeing
with this description has been located except a later impression dated 1887 on title-
page, which also has "NEW EDITION." added above the publisher's imprint.

2. An unlocated American edition is advertised in one issue of *An Actor's Wife*
(A6-2b), but with no indication if the GM "Preface" is included.

B4

Ballades and Rondeaus

a First edition:

BALLADES AND RONDEAUS, [*in red*] | CHANTS ROYAL, SESTI-NAS, | VILLANELLES, &c., SELECTED, | WITH CHAPTER ON THE | VARIOUS FORMS, BY GLEESON | WHITE. | LONDON: | WALTER SCOTT, 24, WARWICK LANE, | AND NEWCASTLE-ON-TYNE. | 1887. [*all within single rule (4½ x 3) border in red*]

Published at 1/-, 2/6, or 4/6 depending on binding

5½ x 4; [a]⁸, b-e⁸, 263-281⁸; pp lxxx, 296, [8]; issued in several different bindings including tan cloth with white paper label on spine; brown cloth with red edges; red roan with gilt edges; and silk plush with gilt edges; the latter three, all with edges trimmed, are slightly smaller (5¼ x 3⅞). All are bindings of the Canterbury Poets series, this title being No. 43.

Contributions by GM:

"The Ballade of Lovelace" pp 86-87, originally printed as "Ballad of a Lover of Life" in *Pagan Poems* (A3); "Rondels" p 143, listed as "not previously published," but "I. The lilacs are in bloom" previously printed in Mayfair Magazine, May 1884. "II. Summer has seen decay" appeared here for the first time.

Plates of this edition were used for an American impression:

a2 — D. Appleton and Company, New York, 1892.

The first rondel, "The lilacs are in bloom," was set to music by Mildred Lund Tyson (A61).

B5

The Art of Authorship

a First edition:

THE | ART OF AUTHORSHIP | Literary Reminiscences, | Methods of Work, and Advice to Young Beginners, | PERSONALLY CONTRIBUTED BY | LEADING AUTHORS OF THE DAY. | COMPILED AND EDITED BY | GEORGE BAINTON. | LONDON: | JAMES CLARKE & CO., 13 & 14, FLEET STREET. | [*dash*] | 1890.

Published April at 5/-

7½ x 5; [ ]⁶, 1-22⁸, [23]² (tipped in); pp xii, 356, plus an 8-page inserted publisher's catalogue; issued in olive-brown cloth stamped on front cover and spine in gilt and red-brown.[1]

1. Leon Edel and Dan H. Laurence, in *A Bibliography of Henry James*, Rupert Hart-Davis, London, 1957, note a variant binding in blue cloth with black blocking in place of the red-brown noted above.

Contribution by GM:

An extract from a letter,[2] elicited for use in connection with a school course in composition and not authorized for publication, is printed pp 73-75 under the general heading "Methods: Conscious and Unconscious."

Sheets of this edition, with new title-page and minor rearrangement of contents, were used for an American edition:

2a — D. Appleton and Company, New York, 5 June 1890.

GM's contribution reprinted as *George Moore on Authorship* (A63).

B6

The Yellow Book — Volume I

a First edition:

The Yellow Book | An Illustrated Quarterly | Volume I April 1894 | London: Elkin Mathews | & John Lane | Boston: Copeland & | Day [*all on right of page, with Aubrey Beardsley drawing of standing woman playing a pianoforte, with trees in background on left of page*]

Published April at 5/-

7⅞ x 6¼; [A]⁸, B-P⁸, Q⁴, R⁸; pp 272 (with 14 inserted plates, each protected by a tissue guard sheet, 13 of which are counted in pagination), 18 (publisher's announcements), followed by an inserted 16-page catalogue of additional publisher's announcements; white endpapers; all edges untrimmed; bound in yellow cloth stamped in black, Beardsley drawing with list of "Letterpress" and "Pictures" on back cover, front cover divided into three boxes: The Yellow Book | An Illustrated Quarterly | Volume I April 1894 | in upper box; Beardsley drawing in center box; | London: Elkin Mathews & John Lane | Boston: Copeland & Day | in left compartment of lower box, | Price | 5/- | Net | in small right compartment; all three boxes within single-rule border, and spine stamped: The | Yellow | Book | [*flower ornament*] | An | Illustrated | Quarterly | [*flower ornament*] | Vol. I | April 1894 | [*flower ornament*] | 5/- | Net | [*flower ornament*] | Elkin | Mathews | & John | Lane

Contribution by GM:

"The Fool's Hour, the First Act of a Comedy by John Oliver Hobbes[1]

2. The original letter, dated "September 15th, 1888," is in the Special Collections Department, University of Kansas Library, Lawrence, Kansas.

1. Pen name of Mrs. Pearl Craigie, who appears as "Agate," a character in "Lui et Elles" in three editions of *Memoirs of My Dead Life* (A29-d, A29-2d, and A29-3d). GM and Mrs. Craigie also collaborated on two other plays, "Journeys End in Lovers Meeting" (B11) and an early version of *Elizabeth Cooper* (A33-n1).

and George Moore" pp [253]-272. Only the first act was published. In writing[2] later of the play and his collaboration with Mrs. Craigie, GM said, "The first act was published in *The Yellow Book* and much admired, and it would have been strange if it had not been, for it is as witty as anything she ever wrote. The second act was better still. It was the third act that decided her not to go on with the play."

a2 Second edition:

"The Fool's Hour" is reprinted (pp [353]-372) in *The Yellow Book: A Selection*, compiled by Norman Denny, London and New York, 1950.

Among the illustrations included at the end of the volume is a reproduction of Walter Sickert's "Portrait of George Moore" originally included in Volume IV of *The Yellow Book*.

B7

Poor Folk

a First edition:

Poor Folk [*in red*] | translated | from | the Russian | of | F. Dostoievsky | by | Lena Milman | with an | Introduction | by | George Moore | London | Elkin Mathews | and John Lane | [*rule*] | Roberts Brothers | Boston | 1894 [*all on right of page, Beardsley drawing of woman standing behind parapet of roof with drain pipe and part of window and blind showing below, at left*]

Published June at 3/6 in an edition of 1,100 copies

7⅝ x 4⅝; [a]⁸, b² (tipped in), A-M⁸; pp xx, 192, followed by 16-page catalogue of publisher's announcements, dated March 1894, on same paper as text; white endpapers; all edges untrimmed; bound in yellow cloth, back cover stamped in black "18 [*key device*] 94," front cover stamped in black on right: Poor Folk | a Novel | by | Fedor Dostoievsky | Translated | from the Russian | by | Lena Milman | With | A Critical Introduction | by | George Moore | and on left Beardsley drawing as on title-page, spine gilt lettered: Poor | Folk | [*dot*] | Fedor | Dostoievsky | [*key device, in black*] | [*square*] ELKIN | MATHEWS | [*vertical dash*] AND JOHN | LANE [*oblong*]

Contribution by GM:

"Preface" pp vii-xx.

2a First American edition:

Poor Folk [*in red*] | translated | from | the | Russian | of | F. Dostoievsky |

2. To Mrs. Craigie's father, John Morgan Richards, in a letter dated December 4, 1909, and published by Richards in the second impression of *The Life of John Oliver Hobbes* (B12).

by | Lena | Milman | With an Introduction | by | George Moore | BOSTON | ROBERTS BROTHERS | LONDON | ELKIN MATHEWS AND JOHN LANE | 1894 [*all on right side of page, Beardsley drawing, as in first edition, at left*]

Published at $1.00

6¾ x 4½; [1]² (tipped in), [2]⁶, [3-14]⁸, [15]² (tipped in); pp xvi, 196; white endpapers; all edges trimmed; bound in rust-colored cloth, black key device in center of back cover, front cover lettered in black on right: Poor Folk | [*rule*] | Dostoievsky | with Beardsley drawing, as on title-page, on left, spine gilt stamped: Poor | Folk | [*ornament*] | Fedor | Dostoievsky | ROBERTS | BROTHERS

Contribution by GM:

"Preface" pp [v]-xvi, same as first edition (a above).

B8
The Heather Field and Maeve

a First edition:

THE HEATHER FIELD | AND | MAEVE | BY | EDWARD MARTYN | AUTHOR OF "MORGANTE THE LESSER" | WITH AN INTRODUC-TION BY | GEORGE MOORE | [*publisher's device*] | LONDON | DUCK-WORTH & CO. | 3 HENRIETTA STREET, W.C. | MDCCCXCIX

Published January 1899

7⅞ x 5½; [a]⁶, b⁸, [A]⁸, B-H⁸, I² (tipped in); pp xxviii, 132; white endpapers; top edges untrimmed, fore and bottom edges trimmed; bound in blue¹ cloth, with publisher's device in dark blue on back cover, front cover stamped in dark blue THE HEATHER FIELD | AND MAEVE [*two outline shamrock ornaments*] | BY EDWARD MARTYN | [*three solid shamrock ornaments*] | WITH AN INTRODUCTION BY | GEORGE MOORE [*two ornaments*] | Published | by | Duckworth | and | Company | London | 1899 | and stamped up the flat spine in dark blue [*two outline shamrock ornaments*] THE HEATHER FIELD [*two outline shamrock ornaments*]

Contribution by GM:

"Introduction" pp vii-xxviii.

Three paragraphs of GM's "Introduction" reprinted in BELTAINE, May 1899. See D:Fr-11 for a French translation of the "Introduction."

1. Danielson lists light green binding, brown lettering, and blank back cover.

B9

Ideals in Ireland

a First edition:

IDEALS IN | IRELAND | EDITED BY LADY GREGORY | WRITTEN BY "A. E.," D. P. | MORAN, GEORGE MOORE, | DOUGLAS HYDE, STANDISH | O'GRADY, AND W. B. YEATS | LONDON: AT THE UNICORN | VII CECIL COURT MDCCCCI

Published January 1901

7½ x 5; [1]⁸, 2-7⁸; pp 112, with addendum slip¹ (1 x 3⅞) tipped in facing p [44]; white endpapers; all edges untrimmed; bound in dark blue cloth, back cover plain, cut of rushlight holder stamped in light green in center of front cover, which also has a light green single-rule border with dots at corners, spine stamped in light green IDEALS | IN | IRELAND | UNICORN | PRESS

Contribution by GM:

"Literature and the Irish Language" pp 45-51, an address given in February 1900 at a meeting of the supporters of the Irish Literary Theatre, and printed in THE NEW IRELAND REVIEW, April 1900.

a2 — Sheets of the English edition were used for an American edition, issued in similar style of binding, the only difference being that the words "NEW YORK: M. F. MANSFIELD. 1901" were substituted for the last line on the title-page, and the publisher's imprint at foot of spine changed to MANSFIELD.

B10

A Loan Collection

a First edition:

[*ornament*] A [*ornament*] | Loan Collection | [*wavy rule*] | of Pictures | [*wavy rule*] | BY NATHANIEL HONE, R.H.A. | AND | JOHN BUTLER YEATS, R.H.A. | WILL BE ON VIEW AT | 6 ST. STEPHEN'S GREEN, | October 21st to November 3rd. | [*ornamental design of dash, colon, circle, colon and dash*] | Admission, including Catalogue, One Shilling. | Season Tickets, 2s. 6d. [*all within a triple-rule border*] | R. T. WHITE, PRINTERS, 45, FLEET St.

1. Printed in red: IDEALS IN IRELAND. | Page 45, last three lines:- | Mr. GEORGE MOORE wishes to add that at the | time he wrote this passage he did not know of the | extraordinary revival of the Irish language in Dublin.

Issued October 1901 at 1/-

8 x 5½; [ ]⁸; pp 16; no endpapers; all edges trimmed; no wrappers.

Contribution by GM:

"Modern Landscape Painters. A Propos of Mr. Hone." p [4]-7.

A foreword signed S.P. (Sarah Purser) p 3; "J. B. Yeats an Appreciation" by F. York Powell pp [8]-11; and the exhibition "Catalogue" pp [12]-15 complete the contents.

B11

Tales about Temperaments

a First edition:

TALES ABOUT | TEMPERAMENTS | THE WORM THAT GOD PRE-PARED . | 'TIS AN ILL FLIGHT WITHOUT WINGS | A REPENT-ANCE . . . . . | PRINCE TOTO . . . . . . | JOURNEYS END IN LOVERS MEETING . | BY | JOHN OLIVER HOBBES | LONDON | T. FISHER UNWIN | PATERNOSTER SQUARE | 1902

7⅜ x 4⅞; [ ]⁴, A-K⁸; pp [viii], 160, white endpapers; top edges gilt, fore and bottom edges untrimmed; bound in green cloth, back cover plain, front cover has four vertical rules in gray, of varying lengths, with decoration at top of each, and gilt lettered in upper left corner TALES ABOUT | TEM-PERAMENTS | JOHN OLIVER | HOBBES | and spine lettered in gilt TALES | ABOUT | TEMPER- | AMENTS | JOHN | OLIVER | HOBBES | T. FISHER UNWIN

Contribution by GM:

"Journeys End in Lovers Meeting" pp 135-58. GM collaborated with John Oliver Hobbes (Mrs. Pearl Craigie) on this one-act play, based on a French play by Caraquell, and although his name is not mentioned in this printing, he was listed as co-author on the playbill and in contemporary reviews when it was presented in London by Ellen Terry, 5 June 1894, at Daly's Theatre and later at the Lyceum Theatre. "According to Moore's account he not only provided the idea for the play . . . he wrote it out, dialogue and all, the lady only adding some pretty little epigrams and speeches" (Hone, pp 202-3).

2a First American edition:

TALES ABOUT | TEMPERAMENTS | BY | JOHN OLIVER HOBBES | [*publisher's device*] | NEW YORK | D. APPLETON AND COMPANY | 1902

Published August in Town and Country Library at $1.00 in cloth and 50¢ in wrappers[1]

1. Advertised in wrappers, but no copy located.

7 x 4⅝; [1]⁸, 2-14⁸; pp x, 214²; white endpapers; all edges trimmed; bound in russet cloth, back cover plain, front cover stamped in black and red, with decoration in upper right corner representing overlapping town and country seals with "T&C" in red superimposed over them | [*four red ornaments*] TALES | [*four red ornaments*] ABOUT | TEMPERAMENTS | and spine stamped in black and gilt [*black ornament*] | TALES | ABOUT | TEMPERAMENTS | [*black ornament*] | HOBBES | [*black ornament*] | [*black ornament*] | [*gilt seal-like ornament*] | [*black ornament*] | [*black ornament*] | APPLETONS

Contribution by GM:

"Journeys End in Lovers Meeting" pp 179-207, text same as first edition (a above).

B12

The Life of John Oliver Hobbes

a First edition, second impression (the first to include GM letter):

THE LIFE OF | JOHN OLIVER HOBBES | TOLD IN HER COR-RESPONDENCE | WITH NUMEROUS FRIENDS | WITH A BIO-GRAPHICAL SKETCH BY HER FATHER | JOHN MORGAN RICHARDS | AND AN INTRODUCTION BY | THE RIGHT REV. BISHOP WELLDON | DEAN OF MANCHESTER | WITH PORTRAITS AND ILLUSTRATIONS | LONDON | JOHN MURRAY, ALBEMARLE STREET, W. | 1911

Published June 1911[1]

8½ x 5½; [a]⁸, b¹ (tipped in), 1-23⁸, 24⁸ (-24₈); pp xviii, 382, plus 12 inserted plates, not paginated; white endpapers; top edges gilt, fore and bottom edges trimmed; bound in olive green cloth, back cover plain, gilt device with motto QUI ME CHERCHE TROUVE around edge, surrounded by gilt ornamental frame, single-rule border in blind at edge of front cover, spine gilt stamped THE LIFE | OF | JOHN OLIVER | HOBBES | LONDON | JOHN MURRAY

Contribution by GM:

A letter dated "DUBLIN, December 4, 1909." to "Dear Mr. Richards"

2. The first impression is designated by a small numeral one in parenthesis [(1)] at foot of p 207, the last page of text; later impressions are indicated by succeeding numbers, agreeing with the number of the impression.

1. The first edition of this book was published March 1911, but the GM letter is found only in the second impression, which is indicated on the verso of the title-leaf as "Second Edition." In this impression the first five pages of gathering 6 are reimposed to permit the added material to be printed on the sixth page.

is printed on page 86 in much smaller type than the rest of the book. It tells of GM's meeting with John Oliver Hobbes and his collaboration with her on "The Fool's Hour" (B6) and "Journeys End In Lovers Meeting" (B11).

a2 — Copies of this second impression, containing the GM letter, were issued in the United States with a slip (2 x 4⅞) tipped on the title-page covering the publisher's imprint, and lettered in black IMPORTED BY | E.P. DUTTON & COMPANY | 31 WEST TWENTY-THIRD STREET | NEW YORK

B13
The George Moore Calendar

a First edition:

The | George Moore Calendar [*in red*] | A QUOTATION FROM THE WORKS OF | GEORGE MOORE | FOR EVERY DAY IN THE YEAR | SELECTED BY MARGARET GOUGH | [*device*] | LONDON | FRANK PALMER [*in red*] | 12-14 RED LION COURT [*all in blue, except as noted*]

Published September 1912 at 1/-

6½ x 4⅜; [1]⁸, 2-6⁸, 7⁴; pp 104; no endpapers; all edges trimmed; issued in brown overlapping wrappers, back cover plain, front cover lettered in blue THE [*printed vertically*] GEORGE | MOORE | [*two printer's ornaments*] CALENDAR [*two printer's ornaments*] [*ornaments and word underlined with heavy rules*] A [*dot*] Quotation [*dot*] from | the [*dot*] Works [*dot*] of | GEORGE | MOORE | for [*dot*] every | day [*dot*] in [*dot*] the | Year. | [*device*] | [*colon*] London: Frank Palmer. [*colon*] [*all within elaborate entwined border in red and blue*] and spine lettered down in blue THE GEORGE MOORE CALENDAR

Contents:

Quotations, selected by GM's secretary, without notation of source. The frontispiece is a reproduction of Sarah Harrison's painting of GM, with his facsimile signature below it.

2a First American edition, retitled:

FIVE CENT POCKET SERIES NO. 402 | Edited by E. Haldeman-Julius | Epigrams of | George Moore | HALDEMAN-JULIUS COMPANY | GIRARD, KANSAS

Published 26 September 1923

4⅞ x 3⅜; [ ]³²; pp 64; no endpapers; all edges trimmed; wire stapled in center fold; issued in heavy blue paper wrappers, publisher's announcements on back cover, front cover lettered in black as on title-page, except first line which omits price, and first two and last two lines reset in a different font.

Contents:

These "Epigrams" are the same as the "Quotations" in *The George Moore Calendar* (a above), but without dates and slightly rearranged in order. There is no acknowledgment of previous printing, and very likely this Little Blue Books edition was unauthorized.[1]

B14

An Irish Gentleman

a First edition:

AN IRISH GENTLEMAN [*in blue*] | GEORGE HENRY MOORE [*in blue*] | HIS TRAVELS | HIS RACING | HIS POLITICS | BY | COLONEL MAURICE GEORGE MOORE, C.B. [*in blue*] | WITH A PREFACE | BY | GEORGE MOORE | [*coat of arms with Latin inscription* FORTIS CADERE CEDERE NON POTEST *in scroll at bottom*] | halla na Murac [*in Gaelic characters*] | LONDON | T. WERNER LAURIE LTD. [*in blue*] | CLIFFORD'S INN

Published July 1913 at 16/-

8½ x 4½; [a]⁸, b⁶, A-2A⁸, [2B]¹⁰; pp xxviii, 404; white endpapers; all edges trimmed; bound in red cloth, with publisher's device in blind in center of back cover, front cover gilt stamped AN IRISH GENTLEMAN | GEORGE HENRY MOORE | HIS TRAVELS | HIS RACING | HIS POLITICS | [*shamrock*] | M.G. MOORE [*all within single-rule border*] and spine gilt stamped AN | IRISH | GENTLEMAN | GEORGE | HENRY | MOORE | [*shamrock*] | M.G. MOORE | T. Werner Laurie Lᵗᵈ [*all within single-rule border*]

There are two binding variants: (1) As above, (2) As above, except front and back covers plain and no border on spine.

Contribution by GM:

"Preface" pp vii-xx. GM's intimation in the "Preface" that his father had committed suicide led his brother to have a slip (1½ x 4⅞) inserted between pp [vi] and vii, saying, "What the Prefacer writes regarding the | mode of his father's death must be taken | as expressing his wishes, and not the facts. | The Author."

---

1. In some advertisements for the series this volume is called *Pungent Precepts*, but no copy so titled has been located.

B15

Maxims of George Moore

a First edition:

SESAME BOOKLETS | Maxims | of | George Moore | Selected by | Elsie E. Morton | G. G. Harrap & Co. Ltd. | 2 & 3 Portsmouth St. London [*first line in top of elaborate design, next five lines in red within wreath of flowers, publisher's imprint under wreath and above bottom portion of design which includes an open book in center and artist's name,* W. E. Ashton *in lower right corner*]

Published November 1915 at -/6

3¾ x 2½; [A]⁸, B-D⁸; pp [ii], 62, with HERE ENDS NUMBER FIFTY- | THREE OF SESAME BOOKLETS¹ at foot of p [62]; tan end-papers; all edges untrimmed; issued in cream-colored heavy paper wrappers, back cover has multi-colored design resembling the border of an oriental rug, front cover lettered in black THE MAXIMS OF | GEORGE MOORE [*flower*] on a tan background within single-rule box at top, multi-colored drawing of trees against sky and distant mountains with artist's name "C A WILKINSON" in lower left corner within heavy-rule border, and lettered in black down the spine THE MAXIMS OF GEORGE MOORE

Contents:

A total of 131 short excerpts from GM's books, *Flowers of Passion* (A1) through *Hail and Farewell* (A31), each credited to the book from which it is taken. A note on p [3] says, "The thanks of the Compiler are due | to Mr. George Moore for permission to | print these quotations."

a2 — An American issue listed in *The United States Catalog* as having been published as *Thoughts from George Moore* by McKay, Philadelphia, n.d., and by Crowell, New York, 1927, differs in several particulars from the first edition.² In place of the inserted colored frontispiece of a young woman wearing a large blue hat used in the first edition, there is an inserted frontispiece of a reproduction of the GM portrait by William Strang, used as the frontispiece of the first edition of *Confessions of a Young Man* (A12-a); endpapers are light green; back cover and spine are plain, and front is lettered in black THOUGHTS FROM | GEORGE MOORE within double-rule border above a line drawing in four colors of Father Time, scythe over his shoulder and an hour glass at his feet, pausing at a sign post in a desert-like landscape.

1. A list on verso of half-title, p [ii], lists this booklet as "46."
2. The only located copy was formerly in the collection of the late P. S. O'Hegarty of Dublin, who kindly loaned it to me for examination. It is now in the Special Collections Department of the University of Kansas Library at Lawrence.

B16

The Life of Algernon Charles Swinburne

a First edition:

THE LIFE | OF | ALGERNON CHARLES | SWINBURNE | BY | ED-MUND GOSSE, C.B. | MACMILLAN AND CO., LIMITED | ST. MARTIN'S STREET, LONDON | 1917

Published 3 April

8⅞ x 5⅝; [A]^6, B-Z^8, 2A^6; pp xii, 364, plus seven inserted plates, not paginated; white endpapers; all edges untrimmed; bound in dark green cloth, back and front covers plain, spine gilt lettered ALGERNON | CHARLES | SWINBURNE | EDMUND | GOSSE | MACMILLAN & C^O

Further impressions May and July 1917

Contribution by GM:

"Swinburne and Mallarmé" pp 327-30, is a letter to Gosse dated "2nd December, 1912," written specially for this volume, relating Mallarmé's alterations in a French poem by Swinburne, and GM's one visit to, and abrupt view of, the English poet.

B17

A Bibliography ... of ... Swinburne

a First edition:

A | BIBLIOGRAPHY | OF | THE WRITINGS IN PROSE AND VERSE | OF | ALGERNON CHARLES SWINBURNE | BY | THOMAS J. WISE | VOL. I | LONDON: | PRINTED FOR PRIVATE CIRCULATION ONLY | BY RICHARD CLAY & SONS, LTD. | 1919

8⅝ x 6½; [A-B]^8, C-KK^8; pp xvi, 512, with many illustrations included in pagination; white endpapers; all edges untrimmed; bound in light blue paper-covered boards, back cover plain, front cover lettered as on title-page, and spine lettered: A | BIBLIOGRAPHY | OF | THE WRITINGS OF | A.C. SWINBURNE | BY | THOMAS J. WISE | VOL. I | LONDON | 1919

Notice of limitation p [vii]:

OF THIS BOOK | ONE HUNDRED AND TWENTY-FIVE COPIES ONLY | HAVE BEEN PRINTED.

Contribution by GM:

"Dolorida" pp 340 and 347, two translations of a French poem by Swinburne, the first reprinted from *Walnuts and Wine* (B1) and the second made for Edmund Gosse in 1915.[1]

1. Several versions are given in letters to Gosse, dated 28 April, 20, and 21 June 1915, now in Duke University Library at Durham, North Carolina.

B18

The Genius of the Marne

a First edition:

THE | GENIUS OF THE MARNE | A PLAY IN THREE SCENES | BY | JOHN LLOYD BALDERSTON | WITH AN INTRODUCTION | BY | GEORGE MOORE | NICHOLAS L. BROWN | NEW YORK – – – – – MCMXIX

Published 31 December 1919

7½ x 5; [1-7]⁸; pp [2], xx, 90; white endpapers; top edges trimmed, fore and bottom edges untrimmed; bound tan paper-covered boards, back cover plain, white label on upper right corner of front cover, lettered in black THE GENIUS | OF THE | MARNE | [*rule*] | JOHN L. | BALDERSTON | [*rule*] | Introduction | by | GEORGE MOORE [*all within single-rule border*] and white label on spine lettered in black [*heavy rule*] | THE | GENIUS | OF | THE | MARNE | [*short rule*] | BALDERSTON | [*light rule*] | N. L. BROWN | [*heavy rule*]

Contribution by GM:

"Introduction" pp ix-xv.

a2 — Sheets of the first edition (a above) were issued in Great Britain with a white slip (1⅞ x 4¼) tipped in at title-page, covering the publisher's imprint, lettered in red "This Book is now published by | GEORGE ALLEN & UNWIN, LTD. | Ruskin House, | 40, MUSEUM STREET, | LONDON, W.C."; white endpapers; all edges trimmed; bound in charcoal-colored paper-covered boards, back cover plain, fleur-de-lis in all-over pattern stamped in blind on front cover, with double-rule double boxes in blind in center around light blue paper label, lettered in dark blue THE | GENIUS | OF THE | MARNE | JOHN L. BALDERSTON | Introduction by | GEORGE MOORE | and five fleur-de-lis vertically blind stamped on spine with light blue paper label between top two, lettered in dark blue [*rule*] | THE | GENIUS | OF THE | MARNE | Balderston | George Allen | & Unwin Ltd. | [*rule*]

B19

Bibliographies of Modern Authors

BIBLIOGRAPHIES OF | MODERN AUTHORS | No. 3 | GEORGE MOORE | COMPILED BY | I.A. WILLIAMS | With a Prefatory Letter by | GEORGE MOORE | Leslie Chaundy & Co. | 40 Maddox Street | London | The Brick Row Book Shop, Inc. | New Haven, New York, and Princeton. | 1921

7 x 5½; [ ]¹²; pp [viii], 16; white paste-down endpapers; bound in heavy tan wrappers, with white label on front cover lettered same as first four lines of title-page. Issued in both ordinary and limited editions, the latter with limitation notice as below printed on front paste-down endpaper.

Notice of limitation:

Only fifty copies of this edition | have been printed on hand-made | paper of which this is No. — [*numbered in ink*]

The bibliography is expanded and reprinted from LONDON MERCURY, April 1921.

Contribution by GM:

"Prefatory Letter" p [vii].

B20

Et Cetera

a First edition:

ET CETERA [*in red*] | A Collector's | Scrap-Book | [*publisher's device in red*] | CHICAGO | PASCAL COVICI [*printer's ornament*] Publisher | 1924 [*all within decorative medieval woodcut-type border*]

9⅛ x 6⅛; [1-18]⁸; pp [xviii], 254; mottled gray endpapers; linen headband; top edges trimmed and gilt, fore and bottom edges untrimmed; bound in mottled gray paper-covered board sides, matching endpapers, and natural linen extended from spine, with gray paper label on spine lettered: Et Cetera | A Collector's | Scrap-Book | with border above and below of printer's ornaments, and publisher's device stamped in gilt at foot of spine.

Notice of limitation, p [viii]:

This Edition is Limited to | Six Hundred and Twenty-five Copies | Of Which This is [*numbered in purple ink*]

Contribution by GM:

"Reply to an Invitation | [*ornament*] | (A letter to the Lord Chancellor of England in reply to | an invitation to attend the dinner to Sir Leslie Ward — | 'Spy' — at the Savoy Hotel, November 21, 1921.)" pp 199-202, originally published as "What is Art? Mr. George Moore's Satire. 'Aristocratic Patter' " in THE SUNDAY TIMES (London), 20 November 1921, and reprinted in the first number of THE WAVE (Chicago), January 1922, which was edited by Vincent Starrett, who also edited this volume. Both printings were unauthorized, as apparently was a subsequent one in TWO WORLDS MONTHLY (New York), Volume II, No. 3, 1927.

B21

The Letters of Abélard and Héloïse

a First edition:

THE LETTERS OF ABELARD AND HELOISE | NOW FIRST TRANS-
LATED FROM THE | LATIN BY C. K. SCOTT MONCRIEFF | LON-
DON: GUY CHAPMAN | MCMXXV

Published 20 October 1925

11½ x 9; [1]² (tipped in), [2-58]⁴; pp xx, 212, with printer's device and
"Printed by Walter Lewis | at the | Cambridge University | Press" p [212];
off-white heavy endpapers; all edges untrimmed; bound in black buckram[1]
over beveled boards, back cover plain, front cover gilt stamped THE
LETTERS | of | ABELARD AND HELOISE | within single-rule border
at edge with a bird with outspread wings in each corner, spine gilt stamped
[*rule*] | The | LETTERS | of | ABELARD | and | HELOISE | GUY |
CHAPMAN | [*rule*]

Colophon and notice of limitation p [iii]:

This edition is printed in the Monotype reproductions of the roman type |
designed by Francesco Griffo of Bologna for Aldus Manutius, | and of the
cursive of Antonio Blado. It is limited to 750 copies, | of which 18, num-
bered I to XVIII, are specially bound in vellum, | and 732, numbered 19
to 750, are bound in buckram. | The type has been distributed. | This copy
is No. [*numbered in ink*]

Contribution by GM:

Prefatory letter pp xiii-xviii, addressed to "My dear Moncrieff" and dated
at end "121, Ebury Street, | London, S.W.I, | May 14th, 1925." The book
is dedicated (p [vii]) "To my friend | GEORGE MOORE | who has made
these dry | bones live" followed (pp x-xii) by a dedicatory letter to him.

2a First American edition:

THE LETTERS OF | ABELARD AND HELOISE [*title in red*] | Trans-
lated from the Latin by | C. K. SCOTT MONCRIEFF | with a prefatory
letter by | GEORGE MOORE | [*publisher's device in red in frame of
printer's ornaments in black*] | NEW YORK | ALFRED A. KNOPF | 1926
[*all within a border of printer's ornaments*]

Published 19 February at $3.00 in The Blue Jade Library

8 x 5⅜; [1-18]⁸; pp xiv, 264; white endpapers with over-all design of
printer's ornaments in red where facing; top edges trimmed and stained red,
fore and bottom edges untrimmed; bound with purple cloth sides, publisher's
device in blind in lower right corner of back cover, series device in blind
in lower right corner of front cover, and red cloth spine gilt stamped THE |

---

1. Also eighteen copies bound in vellum (see notice of limitation).

LETTERS | OF | ABELARD | AND | HELOISE | [*rule and printer's ornaments*] | ALFRED A. KNOPF [*with design at top and bottom of rule, printer's ornaments and rule*]

Contribution by GM:

Prefatory letter same as in first edition (a above).

GM's letter is omitted from all subsequent printings and editions of the Scott Moncrieff translation of *The Letters of Abelard and Heloise*, both in England and the United States.

B22

The Best Poems of 1926

a First edition:

The | BEST POEMS | of 1926 | [*publisher's device*] | Selected by | THOMAS MOULT | & decorated by | JOHN AUSTEN | LONDON | Jonathan Cape, Thirty Bedford Square | 1927

7⅜ x 5; [A]⁸, B-H⁸, [I]⁴; pp xiv, 120, [2]; white endpapers with artist's decorations where facing; top edges trimmed, fore and bottom edges untrimmed; bound in red and black decorated paper-covered boards, white paper label on spine lettered in black: The | BEST | POEMS | of | 1926

Contribution by GM:

"Argenteuil, 1128" p 99, reprinted from THE OBSERVER, August.

a2 — Sheets of the first edition (a above), including endpapers, were used for an American edition, with cancel title-leaf exactly as in English edition except publisher's imprint on recto changed to "NEW YORK | Harcourt, Brace & Company | 383 Madison Avenue"; top edges trimmed and stained blue, bound in black and gold decorated paper-covered board sides, with cream cloth spine, white label on spine stamped in blue: The | BEST | POEMS | of 1926 | Selected by | T. MOULT | [*rule*] | Harcourt, | Brace & Co. [*double rule, light and heavy at top and bottom*]

B23

Conversations with George Moore

a First edition:

Geraint Goodwin | CONVERSATIONS | with | GEORGE MOORE | LONDON | ERNEST BENN LIMITED | 1929

Published 15 November at 10/6

8¾ x 5⅝; [A]⁸, B-K⁸, L¹⁰; pp 180; white endpapers; top edges gilt, fore and bottom edges untrimmed; dark green head and tail bands with dark green ribbon marker; bound with green leather spine and corners and green decorative paper-covered board sides, spine gilt stamped CONVER- | SA- TIONS | WITH | GEORGE | MOORE | [*printer's ornament*] GERAINT | GOODWIN | BENN

There are two issues of the first edition: (1) Limited issue, as above, with a notice of limitation on p [2]: "This edition is limited to | 110 num- bered copies, signed by the author & Mr. Moore | of which a hundred are for sale | THIS IS COPY NO. . . . . . [*numbered in ink*] | George Moore [*signed in ink*] | Geraint Goodwin [*signed in ink*]" (2) Regular issue, with fore and bottom edges also trimmed making a slightly smaller format (8⁷⁄₁₆ x 5⅜), notice of limitation omitted; bound with decorative red paper-covered board sides and dark red cloth spine, gilt stamped as above.

Contributions by GM:

Letter to publisher Sir Ernest Benn, dated "26th July 1929" pp 11-[12]; "Obiter Dicta" pp 167-[180], not credited to GM, but in the "Preface" to the New Library Edition (3a below) Goodwin says, "One chapter, how- ever, is his [GM's] own work, and it is so transparently obvious that I will not attempt to point it out."

2a First American edition:

Geraint Goodwin | CONVERSATIONS | with | GEORGE MOORE | NEW YORK | ALFRED A. KNOPF | 1930

Published 28 March

8⅛ x 5; [1]⁸, (±[1]₃), [2-12]⁸; pp [4], x, 3-180; white endpapers; top edges trimmed and stained brown, fore and bottom edges untrimmed; orange paper-covered board sides, black cloth spine with orange paper stamped in black [*printer's ornaments*] | [*rule*] | Conversations | WITH | GEORGE MOORE | [*printer's ornament*] | Geraint | Goodwin | [*rule*] | [*printer's ornaments*]

Text same as first edition (a above) and is set in close approximation of that printing. Same text also used for:

3a — The New Library, No. 5, Jonathan Cape, London, 1937, with a "PREFACE TO THE NEW | EDITION" by Geraint Goodwin and "A LETTER AS POSTSCRIPT" (to the "Preface") by G. Bernard Shaw.

B24

The Life and Letters of Sir Edmund Gosse

a First edition:

THE LIFE | AND LETTERS OF | SIR EDMUND GOSSE | by | THE
HON. EVAN CHARTERIS, K.C. | [*publisher's windmill device, flanked
by letters* W *and* H] | LONDON | WILLIAM HEINEMANN LTD
    Published 1931 at 25/
    10 x 6; [a]⁶, A-II⁸; pp [xii], 626, plus eighteen inserted plates not pagi-
nated; white endpapers; all edges trimmed; bound in dark blue cloth, publisher's device in blind in lower right corner of back cover, front cover plain,
spine gilt lettered THE | LIFE & LETTERS | OF | SIR EDMUND | GOSSE
| EVAN | CHARTERIS | HEINEMANN
    Contribution by GM:
    An account in his own words of his suggestion to Gosse for the writing
of *Father and Son*,¹ pp 308-10.
    Among the illustrations is a photograph of GM, Gosse and Haddon
Chambers "In William Heinemann's Garden at Ockham, 1919" facing p
424 and a caricature, "Presentation of the Bust," by Max Beerbohm, which
includes GM among its subjects, facing p 444.

B25

The Silver Ship

a First edition:

    "The Silver Ship . ." | [*drawing of ship within circular frame, signed at
bottom*:] A. H. Watson | New Stories, Poems, & Pictures | for Children. |
collected by | Lady Cynthia Asquith. | Putnam. | London & New York [*all
reproduced from hand lettering*]
    Published October 1932
    9¾ x 7¼; [A]⁶, B-P⁸, Q⁴; pp xii, 232, plus four inserted colored illustra-
tions, not paginated; light blue endpapers with printed book-plate on recto
of front free and back paste-down endpapers; all edges trimmed; bound in
light blue cloth, back cover plain, front cover stamped in dark blue THE |

---

    1. Samuel C. Chew in *A Literary History of England*, Appleton-Century-Crofts,
New York, 1948, says (p 1604) that Gosse "was aided in its composition by George
Moore," but Charles Burkhart in "George Moore and *Father and Son*" in NINETEENTH-
CENTURY FICTION, June 1960, demonstrates, by quotations from GM's letters to Gosse,
"that Moore's share in the writing . . . was limited to very active encouragement
and to generally unheeded advice."

SILVER | SHIP [*title reproduced from hand lettering*] | LADY CYNTHIA | ASQUITH | [*cornucopia*] and spine lettered in dark blue THE | SILVER | SHIP [*title reproduced from hand lettering*] | LADY | CYNTHIA | AS- QUITH | PUTNAM

Contribution by GM:

The Talking Pine p 65, first English book publication; text of Hours Press edition (A58) is used, and it is illustrated with two drawings, one of a tall tree and the other of a high-masted sailing ship, both seemingly by A. H. Watson.

B26

GM: Memories of George Moore

a First edition:

G M | Memories of George Moore | by Nancy Cunard | [*publisher's device*] | Rupert Hart-Davis | Soho Square London | 1956

Published 21 September at 25/-

8½ x 5½; [A]^8, B-N^8; pp 208, with nine inserted illustrations not pagi- nated; white endpapers; all edges trimmed, top edges stained orange-brown; bound in plain brown cloth sides, with white parchment spine gilt lettered: G M | Nancy | Cunard [*title and author's name within double-rule elliptical border*] | Rupert | Hart-Davis

Contributions by GM:

Synopsis of a suggested poem, pp 132-33; a rondel "For Nancy Who Is About To Leave Us," pp 140-41; *The Talking Pine* (A58) reprinted p 192; and letters and excerpts, 1909-1928, pp 44, 90-91, 106, 120, 128-29, 136- 37, 141-42, 146-48, 157-60, 168, 177-80 (two previously published in *The Life of George Moore*, B43).

Among the illustrations is a reproduction of a painting of GM by S.C. Harrison, frontispiece; facsimile of inscription on half-title of a presentation copy of *Daphnis and Chloe*, p [6]; caricature of GM by Montague Eliot, facing p 56; caricature of GM by an unknown artist, facing p 82; photograph of GM at Hill Hall facing p 120; and photograph of GM and Miss Cunard at Sanary, facing p 134.

PART II
Letters and Excerpts

During GM's lifetime and since his death a sizable number of his letters or excerpts, not primarily intended for publication, have appeared in various books, and those noted in the course of compiling this bibliography are listed[1] here for the sake of completeness:

B27 *Song of Songs* by Hermann Sudermann, translated by Beatrice Marshall, John Lane, London, 1913.

Letter, p xx, to President of the Society of Authors, "in reality addressed to [Thomas] Hardy."[2]

B28 *Contemporary Portraits: Second Series* by Frank Harris, published by the author, New York, 1919.

Letter to Harris, circa 1916, pp 134-35 in article, "George Moore and Jesus," reprinted from PEARSON'S MAGAZINE, December 1916 and January 1917; also printed as second letter in *Moore Versus Harris* (A42).

Facing first page (p 107) of the article is a reproduction of a drawing of GM apparently made from the 1907 oil portrait by S. C. Harrison.

B29 *Jurgen and the Censor*, privately printed, New York, 1920, in an edition of 458 numbered copies, of which 50 are signed by James Branch Cabell.

Two letters, dated 22 April, and 27 May 1920, p 55; these, with two subsequent letters, reprinted in "Mon Ami Moore," by E. H. Bierstadt, in THE BOOKMAN (New York), February 1923.

B30 *Steeplejack*, Volume II, by James Gibbons Huneker, Scribners, New York, 1920.

Excerpts from letters, dated 2 April 1904, 26 October 1906, and others undated, pp 227-32; *Steeplejack* previously serialized in daily installments in THE PHILADELPHIA PRESS, 9 June through 9 November 1918; complete text of the letters in "Irish Author and American Critic: George Moore and

---

1. Not listed are the many auction, dealer, and other catalogues, as well as several books containing extremely fragmentary excerpts, including *The Pathos of Distance* by James Huneker, New York, 1913; *Graphology for All* by Graphique, London, 1916; *Theatre and Friendship* by Elizabeth Robins, London, and New York, 1932; *The Wild Geese* by Gerald Griffin, London, 1938; *A. J. A. Symons* by Julian Symons, London, 1950; *The Life and Death of a Newspaper* by J. Robertson Scott, London, 1952; *Portrait of Britain 2*, Austin, Texas, 1961, containing "Authors I Have Known" by David Garnett; etc.

2. Page 316, *Thomas Hardy: A Bibliographical Study*, by Richard Little Purdy, Oxford University Press, London, 1954.

James Huneker," by Arnold T. Schwab, in NINETEENTH-CENTURY FICTION, March and June 1954.

B31 *The Library of Edmund Gosse*, compiled by E. H. M. Cox, Dulau & Company, London, 1924.

Inscriptions in presentation copies and inserted letters quoted pp 185-87.

B32 *Are They the Same at Home?* by Beverley Nichols, Cape, London, 1927; Doran, New York, 1927.

Letter in "Author's Note," p 17 Cape edition, p 9 Doran edition.

B33 *The Main Stream* by Stuart Sherman, Scribners, New York, 1927.

Portion of letter, pp 192-93, in "George Moore: An Irish Epicure," quoted from a Burton Rascoe column (circa 1918) in the CHICAGO TRIBUNE, on Sherman's 1917 article, "The Aesthetic Naturalism of George Moore."

B34 *The Colvins and Their Friends* by E.V. Lucas, Methuen, London, 1928; Dutton, New York, 1928.

Two letters to Sidney Colvin, dated "March 8th," and "March 15th, 1917," pp 145-47.

B35 *Pays Parisiens* by Daniel Halévy, 12th edition, Grasset, Paris, 1932.

Two letters, dated 18 aôut 1931 and 1er septembre [1931], and an excerpt from a third, undated, in "Appendix II," pp 280-85; reprinted in *Lettres De Degas*, Paris, translated as *Degas Letters* (B54).

B36 *Work and Days, from the Journal of Michael Field*, edited by T. and D.C. Sturge Moore, Murray, London, 1933.

Excerpts from three undated letters pp 194-97.

B37 *Memories of a Misspent Youth* by Grant Richards, Heinemann, London, 1932; Harper, New York, 1933.

Two letters to W.T. Stead, circa 1895, pp 264-65; previously published as *George Moore in Quest of Locale* (A59).

Among the illustrations is a caricature of GM by "Sic" [Walter Sickert], originally published 21 January 1897 as a supplement to VANITY FAIR, facing p 264.

B38 *Men and Memories*, Volume II, by William Rothenstein, Faber, London, 1932; Coward-McCann, New York, 1932.

Letter to Alice Rothenstein, circa 1912, pp 264-65.

Among the illustrations in Volume I is a reproduction of a pastel of GM, 1895, by Rothenstein, facing p 241.

B39 *Essays of the Year 1933-1934*, Argonaut Press, London, 1934.

Excerpts from three letters, the first dated 18 April 1932, in "A Visit from George Moore" by Philip Gosse, pp 165-82, previously published in LONDON MERCURY, March 1933; reprinted separately as a pamphlet, *A Visit from George Moore*, Saint Helena, 1937, in an edition of 100 copies.

B40   *Author Hunting* by Grant Richards, The Unicorn Press, London, 1934; Coward-McCann, New York, 1934.

Letter to the editor, "Mr. Andrew Lang as Critic," p 90, reprinted from THE SATURDAY REVIEW, 5 December 1896 [not 1897 as stated here].

Among the illustrations is a black and white reproduction of an unpublished water-color, "The Annunciation of Esther Waters," by Ilbery Lynch, p 293.

B41   *Call Back Yesterday* by Geraint Goodwin, Cape, London, 1935.

Letters pp 179, 181, 191, 193-94, 196-97, and 200-201.

B42   *English Years* by James Whitall, Harcourt, Brace and Company, New York, 1935.

Eight letters pp 92, 120-22, 132-33, 256, 307-8.

B43   *Irish Literary Portraits* by John Eglinton, Macmillan, London, 1935.

Excerpt pp 103-4.

B44   *The Life of George Moore* by Joseph Hone, Gollancz, London, 1936; Macmillan, New York, 1936.

Letters and excerpts pp 23, 26-27, 33, 49, 51-52, 56-59, 68-69, 75, 77, 81, 93-94, 96, 101, 103, 107-8, 110, 112, 114-16, 123, 126-28, 133, 136-39, 148, 150, 155, 159, 162-63, 167, 169-70, 172, 183-84, 186-87, 194, 202, 204, 211, 221, 224, 226, 229, 233, 239-40, 245, 253-54, 256, 258, 269, 271, 273, 276-77, 281-82, 284-85, 293, 296, 301, 304-6, 309, 311, 313, 317, 320-21, 328, 331, 335, 340, 344, 348, 352-56, 358-60, 362-63, 365, 383, 385-86, 391, 393, 395-97, 401-4, 411-13, 416, 418-20, 423-25, 427, 432-34, 436, 440-41, 444, 447, 449-50, 493-97.

Among the illustrations are a daguerreotype of GM, aged 9, frontispiece; photograph of GM, circa 1873-75, facing p 48; reproduction of a drawing of GM by Manet, facing p 66; photograph of GM, circa 1880, facing p 96; reproduction of a painting of GM by (Walter) Richard Sickert, facing p 184; reproduction of the painting "Homage À Manet" by William Orpen, facing p 270; photograph of GM and an unidentified young woman in Dujardin's garden facing p 400; reproduction of the water color "The Conversation then Turned on Tonks" by Henry Tonks, facing p 406 (Macmillan edition only); reproduction of the painting "Saturday Evening at the Vale" by Henry Tonks, facing p 406 (Gollancz edition) and p 442 (Macmillan edition); reproduction of the pastel "The Red Dressing-Gown" by Henry Tonks, facing p 432 (Macmillan edition) and p 442 (Gollancz edition); and GM's last passport photograph,[1] facing p 456.

B45 *Letters from Limbo* by Ernest Rhys, Dent, London, 1936.

Two letters to Will Dircks about proofs of *Esther Waters*, circa 1894, pp 73 and 75, with first also reproduced in facsimile p [74].

B46 *Their Moods and Mine* by Reginald Pound, Chapman and Hall, London, 1937.

Letter and note, pp 112 and 114.

B47 *Portraits of a Lifetime* by Jacques-Emile Blanche, Dent, London, 1937; Coward-McCann, New York, 1938.

Eleven letters, 1885-89, pp 290-98 in Appendix, and portions quoted in text, pp 140-42.

Among the illustrations is a reproduction of the Blanche 1887 portrait of GM in the Musée de Rouen, facing p 147.

B48 *The Moores of Moore Hall* by Joseph Hone, Cape, London, 1939.

Letters and excerpts to various members of the Moore family, pp 169, 179, 205, 210, 219, 221-22, 224, and 237-38.

Among the illustrations is a reproduction of J. L. Forain's painting "George Moore Leaving the Opera" in the Fogg Art Museum at Harvard University, facing p 232.

B49 *Autobiography with Letters* by William Lyon Phelps, Oxford, New York and London, 1939.

Letter p 827.

B50 *Since Fifty* by William Rothenstein, Faber, London, 1939; Coward-McCann, New York, 1939.

Two letters, circa 1920 and 1928, pp 116-17 and 123.

B51 *The Life of Henry Tonks* by Joseph Hone, Heinemann, London, 1939.

Excerpts from two letters to Tonks, 1903 and 6 December 1932, pp 70-72; brief excerpt from letter to Mrs. Williamson, p 92; and long excerpt from letter to Tonks, circa late December 1917, pp 139-41.

Among the illustrations are a caricature, "The Unknown God," of Roger Fry lecturing and with GM in the front row of the audience, facing p 100;

1. Taken from the photograph of GM, Gosse, and Haddon Chambers in Heinemann's garden used as an illustration in *The Life and Letters of Sir Edmund Gosse* (B24).

and a reproduction of Tonks's water-color "The Conversation then Turned on Tonks," facing p 335.

B52   *W. B. Yeats* by Joseph Hone, Macmillan, London, 1943; Macmillan, New York, 1943.

Excerpt from letter, circa 1899, pp 140-41 London edition and p 147 New York edition.

B53   *Of Making Many Books* by Roger Burlingame, Scribners, New York, 1946.

Excerpts from two letters, circa 1893, pp 84-85.

B54   *Degas Letters*, translated by Marguerite Kay, Cassirer, Oxford, 1949; Studio, New York, 1949.

Two letters and excerpt from a third to Daniel Halévy, pp 236-41, originally published in *Pays Parisiens* (B35).

B55   *Fruit Among the Leaves, An Anniversary Anthology*, edited with a historical introduction by Samuel C. Chew, Appleton-Century-Crofts, New York, 1950.

Excerpt from letter to Appleton's, November 1924, p. 57; and brief excerpts from *Hail and Farewell*, pp 200-203.

B56   *Robert Ross: Friend of Friends*, edited by Margery Ross, Cape, London, 1952.

Eighteen letters 26 June 1915 to 15 December 1917, pp 242-43, 269-70, 272, 276-78,[1] 296-98, 313-16, and 321.

B57   *Edward Martyn and the Irish Theatre* by Sister Marie-Thérèse Courtney, Vantage Press, New York, 1956.

Letter, 14 September [1901], referring to an interview with GM in THE FREEMAN, 13 September 1901, in Appendix D, p 170.

B58   *George Moore et la France* by Georges-Paul Collet, Librairie E. Droz, Genève, and Librairie Minard, Paris, 1957.

Letters and excerpts, some previously unpublished, pp 13, 15-16, 19, 21, 28-29, 41-42, 46-50, 55-56, 63, 65-66, 70, 80, 85, 93, 123, 127, 133, 138, 145, 158, 162, 174, 177, 193, 195-97, 200-201, and 203; also two of GM's French poems, the sonnet "La Chair est bonne de l'alose" from *Fragments from "Heloise & Abelard"* (A41), and "Les Dormeuses" from the 1904 and subsequent editions of *Confessions of a Young Man* (A12-c et seq.), reprinted pp 101 and 195.

1. In a note to letter 1 January 1916 the editor states that *A Mummer's Wife* (A6) was "not republished"; however, a revised edition, dedicated to Robert Ross, was published in the United States in 1917 (A6-c) and in England in 1918 (A6-2c).

B59   *A Biography of Edward Marsh* by Christopher Hassall, Longmans, Green, London, 1959; Harcourt, Brace, New York, 1959.

Excerpt, circa August 1916, pp 400-401.

B60   *George Moore: l'Homme et l'Oeuvre (1852-1933)* by Jean C. Noel, Etudes Anglaises 24, Didier, Paris, 1966.

Brief excerpts, several previously unpublished, pp 229, 277, 279-80, 285, 287, 296, 409, 410, 450, 456; as well as quotations of varying length from most of GM's works.

III

Periodical Appearances

1880

"The Love of the Past"

THE SPECTATOR, 11 December

Poem, revised and used as a portion of "A Modern Poem" in *Pagan Poems* (A3) and reprinted as "The Sweetness of the Past" in *Confessions of a Young Man* (A12).

1881

"Mr. Swinburne's 'Studies in Song' "

THE SPECTATOR, 5 March

Unsigned[1] review.

Review of John Payne's translation of *Poems of Master Villon of Paris.*

"The New Playground"

THE SPECTATOR, 7 May

Review of Alexander A. Knox's book on Algeria.

"A Visit to M. Zola"

ST. JAMES'S GAZETTE, 26 May

Unsigned[2] article.

1. Identified as being by GM in the article, "The Spectator Records 1874-1894," by Robert H. Tener, in THE VICTORIAN NEWSLETTER, Spring 1960. In the article, which is based on seven notebooks of Richard Holt Hutton, editor of THE SPECTATOR, and called by him "Record of Articles." Mr. Tener also identifies the unsigned contributions of 7 May, and 24 December 1881, as being by GM, as well as the 11 December 1880 and the 15 October 1881 poems. In *Confessions of a Young Man,* GM writes of "seven or eight critical articles" in THE SPECTATOR, and some of these may have been brief reviews not identified in the Hutton "Record."

2. Identified by Mrs. Marilyn B. Saveson in her 1955 Cambridge University thesis,

"Looking Back"
> THE SPECTATOR, 15 October
> Unsigned poem, reprinted as "Nostalgia" in *Confessions of a Young Man* (A12).

"A Mediaeval Poet"
> THE SPECTATOR, 24 December

1882

"Under the Fan"
> TINSLEY'S MAGAZINE, February
> Earliest published story by GM, never reprinted.

1884

"Rondels: 1. The Lilacs Are in Bloom. 2. Our Rose Horizons Fade"
> MAYFAIR MAGAZINE, May
> First rondel reprinted in *Ballades and Rondeaus* (B4) and later set to music by Mildred Tyson (A61); second one never reprinted.

"Topics of the Day by the Heroes of the Hour: My New Novel by Emile Zola"
> PALL MALL GAZETTE, 3 May
> Unsigned[3] interview.

"A Breakfast with Edmond de Goncourt"
> ST. JAMES'S GAZETTE, 13 May

"A Curious Book"
> PALL MALL GAZETTE, 2 September
> Review of *A Rebours*, by Huysmans.

"A New Censorship of Literature"
> PALL MALL GAZETTE, 10 December
> Never reprinted, but same argument continued in *Literature at Nurse* (A7).

"The Influence of Emile Zola upon the Theory and Practice of Some English Novelists of His Time [James, Moore, Gissing, and Bennett]."

3. Identified by Noël from a reference in letter of 19 May 1884 from GM to Zola, now in the Bibliotheque Nationale in Paris.

1885

"Can the Nineteenth Century Produce a Dramatic Literature?"
THE BAT, 28 April
Unsigned, but answering description of article summarized by GM in "Theatre Libre" in *Impressions and Opinions* (A15).

"M. Zola's New Work
THE BAT, 10 November
Review of *L'Oeuvre*, unsigned, but stated to be by GM on another page.

"Dried Fruit"
COURT AND SOCIETY REVIEW, Christmas number, December
Short story, never reprinted, but synopsis given by Hone (p 116).

"Mr. George Moore on 'A Drama in Muslin' "
COURT AND SOCIETY REVIEW, 24 December
Letter to the editor.

1886

"A Drama in Muslin"
COURT AND SOCIETY REVIEW, 14 January through 1 July
Serialization of the novel published later in the year in book form (A9). With the 4 February issue a six-page supplement was included, which reprinted the first chapter, articles from THE TABLET and WEEKLY REGISTER regarding the story, and letters from GM and others about it.

[Letter]
THE BAT, 26 January
Quoted in section, "Playhouse without Plays," regarding a visit by GM to the convent used as a setting for the opening pages of *A Drama in Muslin* (A9).

"Serenade"
COURT AND SOCIETY REVIEW, 20 May
Poem.

"Half-a-Dozen Enthusiasts"
THE BAT, 25 May
Unsigned art criticism, but seemingly by GM as the section on Degas is strikingly similar to passages in the article "Degas" in *Impressions and Opinions* (A15).

"Mr. George Moore and the Circulating Libraries"
THE TIMES (London), 12 August
Letter to the editor about the rejection of *A Drama in Muslin* (A9)
by the circulating libraries.

"Two Poems: A Vau-l'Eau, Une Crise"
COURT AND SOCIETY REVIEW, 9 December

"Cheap Tripping to Parnassus"
THE BAT, 28 December
Unsigned, but portions of it are so similar to "Meissonier and the
Salon Julian" in FORTNIGHTLY REVIEW, July 1890, that it is very
likely an early version of that article.

1887

"A Farewell to 1886"
THE BAT, 4 January
Verse.
"Parody as a Fine Art"
COURT AND SOCIETY REVIEW, 5 January

"Les Decadents"
COURT AND SOCIETY REVIEW, 19 January
Unsigned, but as it includes two translations from Mallarmé reprinted
the next year in *Confessions of a Young Man* (A12) it is undoubtedly
by GM.

"Françillon"
THE HOUR GLASS, March
Review of the play by Dumas Fils; reprinted in THE HAWK, 7 August
1888.

"Defensio pro scriptis meis"
TIME, March
Article explaining the writing of *A Drama in Muslin* (A9)

"An Evening at Alphonse Daudet's"
THE BAT, 1 March
Unsigned but likely by GM as portions of the article, about the Pierrot
pantomime, are used, in an abbreviated form, in chapter III of *Mike
Fletcher* (A14).

"Can Mr. Rider Haggard Write?"
COURT AND SOCIETY REVIEW, 30 March
Letter.

"Two Men, A Railway Story"
> COURT AND SOCIETY REVIEW, 20 April
> Unsigned, but credited to GM in the next issue. This is the story previously published in French as "Le Sinistre de Tonbridge" in LA REVUE INDEPENDANTE, March (D:Fr-6).

"Confessions of a Young Man"
> TIME, July through November
> Serialization, published in book form (A12) 1888.

"Intensely Virginal Indeed"
> PALL MALL GAZETTE, 21 July
> Letter, in reply to George Bernard Shaw's unsigned review of *A Mere Accident* (A10) in the 19 July issue.

"Grandmother's Wedding Gown"
> LADY'S PICTORIAL, Christmas number, December
> Revised as "The Wedding Gown" in ENGLISH ILLUSTRATED MAGAZINE, June 1902, and again revised for inclusion in *The Untilled Field* (A26).

1888

"Turgueneff"
> FORTNIGHTLY REVIEW, 1 February
> Reprinted in *Impressions and Opinions* (A15).

"Spring Days"
> EVENING NEWS, 3 April through 31 May
> Published in book form later in the year (A13).

"Play Producing"
> EVENING NEWS, 14 April
> Letter about amateur actors (see M8).

"The Salon of 1888"
> THE HAWK, 8 May

"Two French Plays"
> THE HAWK, 5 June
> Reviews of "Le Flibustier," by Richepin, and "Le Baiser," by Scribe.

"Plays of the Week"
> THE HAWK, 7 August
> Reprinting of GM's review, unsigned, of "Françillon" originally published in THE HOUR GLASS, March 1887 (see above).

"Mummer Worship"
> UNIVERSAL REVIEW, September
> Reprinted in *Impressions and Opinions* (A15) "redeemed from certain emendations introduced into it by Mr. Quilter," the UNIVERSAL REVIEW editor.

"A Plea for a Literary Censorship"
> ST. JAMES'S GAZETTE, 22 September
> Letter.

"M. Zola 'On the Side of the Angels' "
> ST. JAMES'S GAZETTE, 2 November
> Review of *Le Rêve*, reprinted as "Le Rêve" in the first edition of *Impressions and Opinions* (A15-a).

"British Authors and American Publishers"
> ATHENAEUM, 8 December
> Letter about Brentano edition of *Confessions of a Young Man* (A12-2a), answered by George Haven Putnam 5 January 1889.

1889

"American Publishers"
> ATHENAEUM, 12 January
> Letter continuing controversy started in letter of 8 December 1888 (see above), and again answered by George Haven Putnam, 9 February.

"The Pirates at Bay: An Interview with Mr. George Moore"
> PALL MALL GAZETTE, 24 January

"Le Rêve"
> ST. JAMES'S GAZETTE, April

"Is Buchanan Still Possible?"
> TRUTH, 4 April
> Unsigned, but this and article of 6 June acknowledged by GM in "Bye-Bye, Buchanan" in THE HAWK, 19 November.

"No! Buchanan Is Not Still Possible"
> TRUTH, 6 June
> Unsigned, but later acknowledged by GM to have been by him.

"Art for the Villa"
> MAGAZINE OF ART, July
> Reprinted in first edition of *Impressions and Opinions* (A15-a).

"The New Censorship of Literature"
  NEW YORK HERALD, London edition, 28 July

"Mr. Harry Quilter and Mr. George Moore"
  PALL MALL GAZETTE, 27 September
  Letter.

"Some of Balzac's Minor Pieces"
  FORTNIGHTLY REVIEW, 1 October
  Revised and expanded "to nearly three times its original length" as
  "Balzac" in *Impressions and Opinions* (A15).

"A Strange Death"
  THE HAWK, 22 and 29 October
  Story, possibly based on one by Villiers de l'Isle Adam.

"Our Dramatists and Their Literature"
  FORTNIGHTLY REVIEW, November
  Short extracts reprinted in POET LORE, Vol. II, No. 1, 1890; complete
  article, plus two other articles, reprinted under same title in *Impressions and Opinions* (A15).

"Anonymity" by Tighe Hopkins
  THE NEW REVIEW, November, and March 1890
  Includes two quotations from a GM letter to the author on the subject
  of signed articles in the press.

"The Master of Ballantrae"
  THE HAWK, 5 November

"My Article and My Critics"
  THE HAWK, 12 November

"Bye-Bye, Buchanan!"
  THE HAWK, 19 November

"There Are Many Roads to Rome"
  THE HAWK, 3 December

"Dante Gabriel Rossetti"
  THE HAWK, 10 December

"Impressionism"
  THE HAWK, 17 December

"From the Naked Model"
  THE HAWK, 24 December
  A passage from this article is incorporated in "Meissonier and the
  Salon Julian" in *Impressions and Opinions* (A15)

"Three Books"
> THE HAWK, 31 December
> Reviews of *At the Roots of the Mountains*, Walter Pater's *Appreciations*, and some translations from Balzac.

1890

"Literature and Art"
> THE HAWK, 7 January

"Pictures"
> THE HAWK, 14 January
> On Old Masters at the Royal Academy.

"Baboonacy"
> THE HAWK, 21 January
> On Rider Haggard and Walter Besant.

"Le Revers d'un Grande Homme"
> THE HAWK, 28 January
> Reprinted in *Impressions and Opinions* (A15)

"Sport in Art"
> THE HAWK, 4 February

"Notes and Sensations"
> THE HAWK, 11 February
> Revised as "Moods and Memories III" in DANA, June 1904, and LIPPINCOTT'S MAGAZINE, July 1904, and included as "A Waitress" in *Memoirs of My Dead Life* (A29).

"Notes and Sensations"
> THE HAWK, 18 February
> Genesis of "Bring in the Lamp" in *Memoirs of My Dead Life* (A29).

"A Great Poet"
> THE HAWK, 25 February
> Reprinted in *Impressions and Opinions* (A15).

"Buy the Tryon!"
> THE HAWK, 4 March
> Revised passages are incorporated in "The New Pictures in the National Gallery" in *Impressions and Opinions* (A15).

"Notes and Sensations"
> THE HAWK, 11 March
> Revised as "Moods and Memories VI" in DANA, September, and

October 1904, and LIPPINCOTT'S MAGAZINE, August 1904, and January 1905; and included as "The End of Marie Pellegrin" in *Memoirs of My Dead Life* (A29).

"The Human Animal"
THE HAWK, 18 March
Review of *La Bête Humaine* by Émile Zola.

"Pruriency"
THE HAWK, 25 March
Review of *The Kreutzer Sonata* by Leo Tolstoy.

"The New English Art Club"
THE HAWK, 1 April

"London in April"
THE HAWK, 8 April
Revised as "Spring in London" in PALL MALL BUDGET, 5 April 1894; again revised as "Moods and Memories I" in DANA, May 1904, and LIPPINCOTT'S MAGAZINE, June 1904; and once again revised as "Spring in London" in *Memoirs of My Dead Life* (A29).

"Advertised Incompetency"
THE HAWK, 15 April
Review of *The Bondman* by Hall Caine.

"In Blue Silk and Brass"
THE HAWK, 22 April
Short story, never reprinted.

"The Secret of Immortality"
THE HAWK, 29 April
Reprinted as the final portion of "Our Dramatists and Their Literature" in *Impressions and Opinions* (A15).

"The Royal Academy"
THE HAWK, 6 May

"The Grosvenor Gallery"
THE HAWK, 13 May

"The New Gallery"
THE HAWK, 20 May

"Mr. Philip Gower and Two Ladies"
THE HAWK, 27 May
Short story, never reprinted.

"To Paris and Back"
THE HAWK, 3 June
Revised as "Flowering Normandy" in THE SPEAKER, 25 May 1895;

again revised as "Moods and Memories II" in DANA, May 1904, and LIPPINCOTT'S MAGAZINE, June 1904, and included as "Flowering Normandy" in *Memoirs of My Dead Life* (A29).

"Private Theatricals in Paris"
THE HAWK, 10 June
Includes a translation of a scene from a play by Henri Meilhac.

"Le Théâtre Libre"
THE HAWK, 17 June
Reprinted as "Note on 'Ghosts' " in *Impressions and Opinions* (A15).

"The New Théâtre Libre"
THE HAWK, 24 June, 1 and 8 July
First section reprinted as "Théâtre Libre" and third section reprinted as "On the Necessity of an English Théâtre Libre" in *Impressions and Opinions* (A15).

"Meissonier and the Salon Julian"
FORTNIGHTLY REVIEW, 1 July
Revised and reprinted in *Impressions and Opinions* (A15); probably based on the unsigned article, "Cheap Tripping to Parnassus," in THE BAT, 28 December 1886, which is strikingly similar to the first portion of this article.

"Malbrouk s'en Va"
THE HAWK, 15 July
On an article in THE NEW REVIEW by the Duke of Marlborough about art.

"A London 'Théâtre Libre' "
ST. JAMES'S GAZETTE, 19 July
Letter, in the course of which GM notes that he is responsible for nothing in THE HAWK except his signed weekly articles.

"An Actress of the Eighteenth Century"
THE HAWK, 22 July
Reprinted in *Impressions and Opinions* (A15).

"Notes and Sensations"
THE HAWK, 29 July
Genesis of "Ninon's Table d'Hôte" in *Memoirs of My Dead Life* (A29).

"A Little Excursion"
THE HAWK, 5 August
On the Dulwich Gallery.

"The Legal Laundry"
THE HAWK, 12 August
On the Dunlo divorce case.

"Michael Field and 'The Tragic Mary' "
ST. JAMES'S GAZETTE, 18 August

"Is 'Judah' Literature?"
THE HAWK, 26 August
Incorporated in "Our Dramatists and Their Literature" in *Impressions and Opinions* (A15).

"Mr. Dumpty's Ideal"
ST. JAMES'S GAZETTE, 3 September
Revised and printed in Gaelic (D:Ga-3) and in English as "Mr. Dumpty's Quest" in THE NEW IRELAND REVIEW, November 1902; the latter revised and retitled "The Clerk's Quest" for inclusion in *The Untilled Field* (A26).

"Notes and Sensations"
THE HAWK, 9 September
Revised as "Moods and Memories V" in LIPPINCOTT'S MAGAZINE, July 1904, and DANA, August 1904, and included as the first section of "Spent Love" in *Memoirs of My Dead Life* (A29).

"Is Education Worth Having?"
ST. JAMES'S GAZETTE, 10 September

"Notes and Sensations"
THE HAWK, 16 September
Revised as "Moods and Memories IV" in DANA, July 1904, and LIPPINCOTT'S MAGAZINE, July 1904; and included as "La Butte" in *Memoirs of My Dead Life* (A29).

"Notes and Sensations"
THE HAWK, 23 September
Reprinted as "Two Unknown Poets" in *Impressions and Opinions* (A15).

"Notes and Sensations"
THE HAWK, 30 September
Relating a rendezvous in Paddington Station.

"The Dramatic Censorship"
THE NEW REVIEW, October
Defending official censorship of the theater, if trial by jury and summary police action be the alternative.

"The New Pictures in the National Gallery"
FORTNIGHTLY REVIEW, October
Reprinted in *Impressions and Opinions* (A15).

"Degas: The Painter of Modern Life"
MAGAZINE OF ART, November
Reprinted as "Degas" in *Impressions and Opinions* (A15) and later included in the Carra Edition of *Modern Painting* (A17-c).

"Mr. Tree's Monday Mights"
FORTNIGHTLY REVIEW, October
Signed "X," but GM's authorship disclosed in correspondence in PALL MALL GAZETTE, 17 September 1891, occasioned by GM's article, "Our Dramatic Critics," in the issues of 9 and 10 September (see below).

1891

"The Independent Theatre"
THE TIMES (London), 18 March
Letter.

"A Lesser Light"
THE SPEAKER, 21 March
On an exhibition of the works of Diaz in Bond Street.

"A Great Artist"
THE SPEAKER, 4 April
Reprinted in *Modern Painting* (A17).

"A Modern Artist"
THE SPEAKER, 11 April

"The New English Art Club"
THE SPEAKER, 18 April

"Another View of 'Hedda Gabler' "
ST. JAMES'S BUDGET, 24 April

"The Royal Academy"
THE SPEAKER, 2 May

"The New Gallery"
THE SPEAKER, 9 May

"The Camera in Art"
THE SPEAKER, 16 May
Reprinted in *Modern Painting* (A17).

"The Paris Salon"
THE SPEAKER, 23 May

"Le Champs de Mars"
THE SPEAKER, 30 May

"The Louvre Revisited"
THE SPEAKER, 6 and 13 June

"The Intelligence of Actors"
NATIONAL OBSERVER, 13 June

"The Early English Masters"
THE SPEAKER, 20 June

"Art Patrons"
THE SPEAKER, 27 June
Reprinted in *Modern Painting* (A17).

"Money in Art"
THE SPEAKER, 4 July

"Vain Fortune"
LADY'S PICTORIAL, 4 July through 17 October
Serialized as by "Lady Rhone"; revised and published in November in
book form with GM's name as the author (see A16-n3).

"The Society of Portrait Painters"
THE SPEAKER, 11 and 18 July
A portion of the first article incorporated in "Whistler" in *Modern
Painting* (A17).

"A Remembrance"
THE NEW REVIEW, August
Reprinted in LIVING AGE, 10 October. Reprinted in *Memoirs of My
Dead Life* (A29).

"Our Dramatic Critics"
PALL MALL GAZETTE, 9 and 10 September
Correspondence on these articles in issues of 12, 15, 17, 22 and 26
September.

"Honour to Whom Honour Is Due"
PALL MALL GAZETTE, 22 September
Letter replying to James Glover letter, 17 September, concerning
acknowledgment of sources.

"The Independent Theatre"
THE TIMES (London), 13 October
Letter.

"The British Artists"
THE SPEAKER, 31 October

"Institute of Painters in Oil Colours"
THE SPEAKER, 7 November

"The Subject"
THE SPEAKER, 14 November
Incorporated in "The Failure of the Nineteenth Century" in *Modern Painting* (A17).

"Curiosity in Art"
THE SPEAKER, 21 November
Incorporated in "The Failure of the Nineteenth Century" in *Modern Painting* (A17).

"Religiosity in Art"
THE SPEAKER, 28 November
Reprinted in *Modern Painting* (A17).

"The New English Art Club"
THE SPEAKER, 5 December

"Royalty in Art"
THE SPEAKER, 12 December
Reprinted in *Modern Painting* (A17).

"How England Lost Her Pictures"
THE SPEAKER, 19 December

"Two Landscape Painters"
THE SPEAKER, 26 December

1892

"Degas in Bond Street"
THE SPEAKER, 2 January

"The Masters of Old Time"
THE SPEAKER, 16 January

"Guy de Maupassant"
ILLUSTRATED LONDON NEWS, 16 January

"A Modern Among the Ancients"
THE SPEAKER, 23 January

"Artistic Education"
THE SPEAKER, 30 January

"More About Artistic Education"
THE SPEAKER, 6 February
Incorporated in "Artistic Education in France and England" in *Modern Painting* (A17).

"The Proposed Destruction of the National Gallery"
THE SPEAKER, 13 February

"A Book About Bastien-Lepage"
THE SPEAKER, 20 February

"Spielmann and Valhalla"
THE SPEAKER, 27 February
Reply to M. H. Spielmann's letter, "G. M. and the Gallery of British Art," a comment on GM's article of 13 February; Spielmann replied to this article in another letter, "A National Gallery of British Art," in the 5 March issue.

"The Zoo in Art"
THE SPEAKER, 5 March

"Free Trade in Art"
THE SPEAKER, 12 March

"Art and Science"
THE SPEAKER, 19 March
Reprinted in *Modern Painting* (A17).

"Mr. Whistler: The Man and his Art"
THE SPEAKER, 26 March
Incorporated in "Whistler" in *Modern Painting* (A17).

"Is Mr. Tate a Public Benefactor? No."
ILLUSTRATED LONDON NEWS, 26 March
Reply to 19 March article by M. H. Spielmann, who posed the same question, but answered it "Yes."

"Mr. Whistler's Portraits"
THE SPEAKER, 2 and 9 April
Incorporated in "Whistler" in *Modern Painting* (A17).

"The New English Art Club"
THE SPEAKER, 16 April

"A Faithful Heart"
THE SPEAKER, 16 and 23 April
Story, never reprinted.

"The Royal Academy"
THE SPEAKER, 23 April

"An 'Average' Academy"
THE SPEAKER, 30 April

"The New Gallery"
THE SPEAKER, 7 May

"The New Architecture"
THE SPEAKER, 14 May

"The New English Art Club and the Academy"
THE SPEAKER, 21 May

"A Select Few"
THE SPEAKER, 28 May

"The Royal Academy Exhibition"
FORTNIGHTLY REVIEW, June
Incorporated in "Our Academicians" in *Modern Painting* (A17).

"The Organization of Art"
THE SPEAKER, 4 June

"Facts and Ideas"
THE SPEAKER, 11 June

"Sex in Art"
THE SPEAKER, 18 and 25 June
Reprinted in *Modern Painting* (A17).

"The Society of Portrait Painters"
THE SPEAKER, 2 July

"Some Picture Exhibitions"
THE SPEAKER, 9 July

"Art (Manet)"
THE SPEAKER, 16 July
Incorporated in "Chavannes, Millet, and Manet" in *Modern Painting* (A17).

"Handling"
THE SPEAKER, 30 July
Incorporated in "Chavannes, Millet, and Manet" in *Modern Painting* (A17).

"La Débâcle"
FORTNIGHTLY REVIEW, August
Review of Zola's novel; short excerpts reprinted in REVIEW OF REVIEWS (New York) September.

"A Hint for Manchester and Glasgow"
THE SPEAKER, 6 August

Incorporated in "Chavannes, Millet and Manet" in *Modern Painting* (A17).

"A Popular Error"
THE SPEAKER, 13 August

"Corot"
THE SPEAKER, 20 August
Incorporated in "Ingres and Corot" in *Modern Painting* (A17).

"Values"
THE SPEAKER, 27 August
Incorporated in "Ingres and Corot" in *Modern Painting* (A17).

"Decadence"
THE SPEAKER, 3 September
Incorporated in "Monet, Sisley, Pissaro and the Decadence" in *Modern Painting* (A17).

"Why I Don't Write Plays"
PALL MALL GAZETTE, 7 September
Letter, one of a series by various authors.

"The Division of the Tones"
THE SPEAKER, 10 September
Incorporated in "Monet, Sisley, Pissaro and the Decadence" in *Modern Painting* (A17).

"The Organisation of Art"
THE SPEAKER, 17 September
Incorporated in the article by the same name in *Modern Painting* (A17).

"Our Michaelmas Goose"
THE SPEAKER, 24 September

"An Autumn Outing"
THE SPEAKER, 1 October

"The New Gallery"
THE SPEAKER, 8 October

"Rival Cities"
THE SPEAKER, 15 October
Incorporated in "The Alderman in Art" in *Modern Painting* (A17).

"The Alderman in Art"
THE SPEAKER, 22 October
Incorporated in article by the same name in *Modern Painting* (A17).

"On the Necessity for a Director of Fine Arts"
THE SPEAKER, 29 October
Incorporated in "The Alderman in Art" in *Modern Painting* (A17).

"Picture Dealers"
THE SPEAKER, 12 November
Reprinted in *Modern Painting* (A17).

"Mr. G. F. Watts"
THE SPEAKER, 19 November
Incorporated in "Our Academicians" in *Modern Painting* (A17).

"To the Editor of 'The Speaker'"
THE SPEAKER, 26 November
Letter, replying to the letter of "R. I." in the issue of 19 November, and both reprinted as "Mr. Burne-Jones and the Academy" in *Modern Painting* (A17).

"New English Art Club"
THE SPEAKER, 26 November, and 3 December
Partially incorporated in article by the same name in *Modern Painting* (A17).

"The Glasgow School"
THE SPEAKER, 10 December
Partially incorporated in "The New English Art Club" in *Modern Painting* (A17).

"Mr. Brabazon"
THE SPEAKER, 17 December
Incorporated in "The New English Art Club" in *Modern Painting* (A17).

1893

"Mr. Burne-Jones"
THE SPEAKER, 7 January

"The Old Masters"
THE SPEAKER, 21 January

"The Grafton Gallery"
THE SPEAKER, 25 February, and 4 March

"New Art Criticism"
THE SPEAKER, 25 March, 1 and 8 April
Incorporated in article by same name in *Modern Painting* (A17).

"The New English Art Club"
THE SPEAKER, 15 April

"Meissonier"
THE SPEAKER, 22 April

"The Royal Academy"
THE SPEAKER, 29 April

"A Portrait in the New Gallery"
THE SPEAKER, 6 May
Partially reprinted as "A Portrait by Mr. Sargent" in the enlarged edition of *Modern Painting* (A17-b).

"The New Gallery"
THE SPEAKER, 20 May

"Parted"
DAILY CHRONICLE, 22 May
Story, never reprinted.

"Our Academicians and Their Associates"
THE NEW REVIEW, June

"The Grafton Gallery"
THE SPEAKER, 3 June

"The Price of the Masters"
THE SPEAKER, 10 June

"An Orchid by Mr. James"
THE SPEAKER, 17 June
Partially reprinted, with same title, in the enlarged edition of *Modern Painting* (A17-b).

"Half a Dozen Pictures in the Academy"
THE SPEAKER, 22 July

"The Sale at Christie's"
THE SPEAKER, 29 July

"Catholic Critics"
THE SPEAKER, 5 August

"Advice to Critics"
THE SPEAKER, 12 August

"Mr. Whitmore and the National Gallery"
THE SPEAKER, 19 August

"The National Gallery"
THE SPEAKER, 2, 9 and 16 September

A portion of the third section reprinted as "Ingres" in the enlarged edition of *Modern Painting* (A17-b).

"Charity"
THE SKETCH, 13 September
Revised and reprinted in THE SPEAKER, 6 July 1895; again revised and printed in Gaelic (D:Ga-4) and in English as "Alms-giving" in NEW IRELAND REVIEW, December 1902; the latter revised for inclusion in *The Untilled Field* (A26).

"Impressions in St. James's Park"
THE SPEAKER, 30 September
Revised as "Sunday Evening in London" in *Memoirs of My Dead Life* (A29).

"Passages from the Life of a Workgirl"
PALL MALL GAZETTE, 2, 3, 4, 6, 7, 9, 10, 11, 12, 13, and 14 October
Serialization of an early version of chapters XX-XXIII, XV-XVII, and XXIX of *Esther Waters* (A19).

"Arts and Crafts"
THE SPEAKER, 7 October

"The New English Art Club"
THE SPEAKER, 25 November

"Mr. Arthur Tomson's Cats"
THE SPEAKER, 2 December

"A Diary of Moods"
THE SPEAKER, 9 December

"The Whistler Album"
THE SPEAKER, 16 December
Partially reprinted with same title in enlarged edition of *Modern Painting* (A17-b).

1894

"Puvis de Chavannes an ideal wall painting," and "Mr. Moore's opinion of Whistler"
MODERN ART, Winter number
Excerpts from two articles in *Modern Painting* (A17).

"Literary Freedom"
DAILY CHRONICLE, 12 January

Letter on Henry Vizetelly trial; answered 13 January by William Alexander Coote, secretary of the National Vigilance Society.

"The New Gallery"
THE SPEAKER, 13 and 20 January

"Literary Freedom"
DAILY CHRONICLE, 16 January
Letter in reply to Coote's letter of 13 January; in turn answered by Coote 18 January.

"An Episode in Bachelor Life"
THE SKETCH, 24 January
Short story, never reprinted.

"The Grafton Gallery"
THE SPEAKER, 27 January

"My Impressions of Zola"
ENGLISH ILLUSTRATED MAGAZINE, February
Rewritten for the revised edition of *Impressions and Opinions* (A15-b); and retitled "A Visit to Medan" for inclusion in the enlarged edition of *Confessions of a Young Man* (A12-2d2).

"The Genius of Japan"
THE SPEAKER, 3 and 10 February
A portion of second installment reprinted as "Some Japanese Prints" in the enlarged edition of *Modern Painting* (A17-b).

"An Episode in Married Life"
THE SKETCH, 21 February
Short story, never reprinted.

"Mr. Steer's Exhibition"
THE SPEAKER, 3 March
Reprinted in enlarged edition of *Modern Painting* (A17-b).

"M. Duret's Collection"
THE SPEAKER, 17 March

"Spring in London"
PALL MALL BUDGET, 5 April
Revised from "London in April" in THE HAWK, 15 April 1890; again revised and incorporated in "Moods and Memories I" in DANA, May 1904, and LIPPINCOTT'S MAGAZINE, June 1904; and revised as "Spring in London" in *Memoirs of My Dead Life* (A29).

"The New English Art Club"
THE SPEAKER, 14 April

"The Boycotted Book"
> DAILY CHRONICLE, 4 May
> Letter on the banning of *Esther Waters* by Smith's Library.

"The Royal Academy"
> THE SPEAKER, 5 May

"The New Gallery"
> THE SPEAKER, 12 May

"Some Amateur Water Colours"
> SATURDAY REVIEW, 22 December

1895

"Nuit de septembre"
> PALL MALL GAZETTE, 15 January; THE BOOKMAN (New York), October
> Poem, revision of the song in "La Maitress Maternelle" in *Pagan Poems* (A3); included in 1904 and subsequent editions of *Confessions of a Young Man* (A12-c et seq.).

"The Baronet's Indiscretions, or the Voice that Breathed o'er Eden"
> PALL MALL GAZETTE, 12 March
> Letter, with copy of 11 March letter to Whistler.

"An Art Student"
> TODAY, Spring
> Revised as sections XIV-XVII of "Mildred Lawson" in *Celibates* (A21).

"The New Gallery"
> THE SPEAKER, 4 May

"The Royal Academy Exhibition"
> NEW BUDGET, 9 May
> Reprinted as pamphlet, *The Royal Academy 1895* (A20).

"The Royal Academy"
> THE SPEAKER, 11 May

"Flowering Normandy"
> THE SPEAKER, 25 May
> Revision of "To Paris and Back" in THE HAWK, 3 June 1890; again revised as "Moods and Memories II" in DANA, May 1904, and LIPPINCOTT'S MAGAZINE, June 1904, and included as "Flowering Normandy" in *Memoirs of My Dead Life* (A29).

"Claude Monet"
THE SPEAKER, 15 June
Reprinted in the enlarged edition of *Modern Painting* (A17-b).

"Exteriority"
THE SPEAKER, 22 June

"Mr. Mark Fisher"
THE SPEAKER, 29 June
Partially reprinted with same title in the enlarged edition of *Modern Painting* (A17-b).

"Charity"
THE SPEAKER, 6 July
A revision of the story of the same name in THE SKETCH, 13 September 1893; again revised and printed in Gaelic (D:Ga-4) and in English as "Alms-giving" in THE NEW IRELAND REVIEW, December 1902, the latter version once again revised for inclusion in *The Untilled Field* (A26).

"A Reaction"
THE SPEAKER, 13 July
On Wagner.

"Tannhäuser"
THE SPEAKER, 20 July

"The End of the Season"
THE SPEAKER, 27 July

"Mr. Ellis Roberts"
THE SPEAKER, 3 August

"Letter to the Editor"
SATURDAY REVIEW, 2 August
Reply to a review of *Celibates* (A21) by Julia Frankau (Frank Danby) in issue of 27 July; and in turn answered by the reviewer 10 August.

"The New Gallery"
THE SPEAKER, 19 October

"The Joy of London"
THE SPEAKER, 26 October
On Wagner's *Valkyrie*.

"The New English Art Club"
THE SPEAKER, 23 November

"After 'Parsifal' "
THE SPEAKER, Supplement, 30 November

1896

"Les Dormeuses"

PALL MALL GAZETTE, circa early February

Poem, quoted in letter of 13 February 1896 to Edouard Dujardin (A54); revised and reprinted in "Lord Leighton" in COSMOPOLIS, March; and again revised and reprinted as "Pour un Tableau de Lord Leighton" in 1904 and subsequent editions of *Confessions of a Young Man* (A12-c et seq.).

"Lord Leighton"

COSMOPOLIS, March

"The Future Phenomenon"

THE SAVOY, No. 3, July

Translation from Mallarmé; included in 1917 and subsequent editions of *Confessions of a Young Man* (A12-d et seq.).

"Since the Elizabethans"

COSMOPOLIS, 5 December

"Mr. Andrew Lang as Critic"

SATURDAY REVIEW, 5 December

Letter, reprinted in *Author Hunting* (B40), where it is incorrectly dated 1897.

1897

"Mr. Yeats' New Book"

DAILY CHRONICLE, 24 April

Review of *The Secret Rose*, including a "depreciation of Stevenson" which prompted the article, "George Moore as a Critic of Stevenson" by Vernon Blackburn, in the ACADEMY, May.

"Stevenson and the Moral Idea"

DAILY CHRONICLE, 12 May

Reply to the Blackburn article in the May ACADEMY.

"Wagner's 'Jesus of Nazareth' "

THE MUSICIAN, 12 May

"A Tragic Novel"

COSMOPOLIS, July

On Flaubert's *L'Education Sentimentale*.

"Mr. George Moore on Music and Literature"

THE MUSICIAN, 29 September

"A Scenario for an Opera"
THE MUSICIAN, 17 November

1898

"Morality in Literature"
WESTMINSTER GAZETTE, 24 June
Reply by J. A. Steuart, 30 June.

"Primary Ideas in Literature"
WESTMINSTER GAZETTE, 7 July
Reply by J. A. Steuart, 20 July.

"Another Word on Rodin, with special reference to the Balzac monument"
STUDIO, 15 July

1899

"Mr. George Moore Replies"
DAILY CHRONICLE, 25 January
Long letter on William Archer, *The Countess Cathleen*, and *The Heather Field*.

"A Valediction"
DAILY CHRONICLE, 27 January
Letter.

"On the Difficulty of Buying Pictures"
THE PHOENIX, 17 March

"The Heather Field"
BELTAINE, May
Three paragraphs of GM's "Introduction" to *The Heather Field and Maeve* (B8).

"Vers"
DAILY EXPRESS (Dublin), 20 September
Poem.

1900

"Preface to 'The Bending of the Bough' "
FORTNIGHTLY REVIEW, February
Reprinted with the play (A23), and separately as a pamphlet (A24).

"Is the Theatre a Place of Amusement?"
    BELTAINE,[4] February

"The Queen of England's Visit"
    THE UNITED IRISHMAN, 17 March
    Letter.

"The Irish Literary Renaissance and the Irish Language"
    THE NEW IRELAND REVIEW, April
    An address delivered at a meeting of the supporters of the Irish Liter-
    ary Theatre, and reprinted as "Literature and the Irish Language" in
    Ideals in Ireland (B9).

"Some Characteristics of English Fiction"
    NORTH AMERICAN, April

[Letter]
    AN CLADHEAM SOLUIS, 14 July
    On the teaching of Irish.

"On the Irish Language"
    THE TIMES (London), 18 July
    Letter.

1901

"A Plea for the Soul of the Irish People"
    THE NINETEENTH CENTURY AND AFTER, February

"The Culture Hero in Dublin Myths"
    THE LEADER (Dublin), 20 July

"The Irish Literary Theatre"
    SAMHAIN, October

"My Own Funeral"
    LIPPINCOTT'S MAGAZINE, November
    Revised as "Resurgum" in *Memoirs of My Dead Life* (A29).

"On the Thoughtlessness of Critics"
    THE LEADER (Dublin), 9 November

"The Proposed Censorship"
    THE FREEMAN'S JOURNAL, circa mid-November

4. Only three numbers of BELTAINE were issued, and copies of these were bound
together and issued with a special title-page as THE FIRST ANNUAL VOLUME
OF BELTAINE . . . THE ORGAN OF THE IRISH LITERARY THEATRE, London, [1900].

1902

"The Golden Apples"
ENGLISH ILLUSTRATED MAGAZINE, April
Revised as "Julia Cahill's Curse" in *The Untilled Field* (A26).

"Emma Bovary"
LIPPINCOTT'S MAGAZINE, May
Rewritten as "Emily and Priscilla Lofft" for *In Single Strictness* (A44).

"The Wedding Gown"
ENGLISH ILLUSTRATED MAGAZINE, June
Revised from "Grandmother's Wedding Gown" in LADY'S PICTORIAL, December 1887; and again revised for inclusion in *The Untilled Field* (A26).

"The Hill of Tara"
THE TIMES (London), 27 June
Letter, also signed by Douglas Hyde and W. B. Yeats.

"Home-Sickness"
HARPER'S WEEKLY, 16 August, and PALL MALL MAGAZINE, September; reprinted in THE GAEL, April 1903
Revised and included in *The Untilled Field* (A26).

"The Exile"
HARPER'S WEEKLY, 20 September, and PALL MALL MAGAZINE, October
Revised and included in *The Untilled Field* (A26).

"Mr. Dumpty's Quest"
THE NEW IRELAND REVIEW, November
Gaelic (D:Ga-3) and English versions; revised from "Mr. Dumpty's Ideal" in ST. JAMES'S GAZETTE, 3 September 1890; again revised as "The Clerk's Quest" in *The Untilled Field* (A26).

"Alms-giving"
THE NEW IRELAND REVIEW, December
Gaelic (D:Ga-4) and English versions; revised from "Charity" in THE SKETCH, 13 September 1893, and a further revision in THE SPEAKER, 6 July 1895; again revised and included in *The Untilled Field* (A26).

1903

"An Irish Art Gallery, A Protest"
> THE FREEMAN'S JOURNAL, 3 July
> Letter.

"Avowals: Being a New Series of the Confessions of a Young Man"
> LIPPINCOTT'S MAGAZINE, September through February 1904, and revised, without sub-title, PALL MALL MAGAZINE, March through August 1904
> These six articles, revised and expanded, form the basis of chapters IV-XI in *Avowals* (A38).

[Letter]
> THE IRISH TIMES, 24 October
> Regarding GM's profession of Protestantism, discussed in final paragraphs of *Salve* (A31:II-a).

1904

"The Abbe Loisy," by Edouard Dujardin
> DANA, May
> Unsigned translation by GM, acknowledged by him in letter to Dujardin, 17 March.

"Moods and Memories"
> DANA, May through October, and LIPPINCOTT'S MAGAZINE, June, July, August, and January 1905
> Revised from sketches in THE HAWK, 11 February, 11 March, 8 April, 3 June, 9 and 16 September, 1890; THE SPEAKER, 25 May 1895; and PALL MALL BUDGET, 5 April 1894; poem in section III revised from "A une Poitrinaire" in *Pagan Poems* (A3), also used in *Mike Fletcher* (A14), and included in 1904 and subsequent editions of *Confessions of a Young Man* (A12-c et seq.); all revised for inclusion as first 58 pages of *Memoirs of My Dead Life* (A29).

"The Voice of the Mountain"
> THE GAEL, July
> Short story, never reprinted.

"Stage Management in the Irish National Theatre"

5. GM's authorship established by Jack Wayne Weaver, who marshals his evidence in an article, " 'Stage Management in the Irish National Theatre': An Unknown Article

DANA, September
Signed "Paul Ruttledge."[5]

"Preface to a new edition of 'Confessions of a Young Man' "
DANA, November
Included in 1904 edition (A12-c), and revised for subsequent editions.

"The Loan Collection at the Academy"
DAILY EXPRESS (Dublin), 5 December
Letter.

1905

"The Irish Literary Theatre"
THE IRISH TIMES, 13 February

"Art Chats with Mr. George Moore"
EVENING MAIL, 4 August
Telegram, in reply to an interview of 3 August, printed under same title.

"Mr. George Moore and the 'Evening Mail' "
EVENING MAIL, 5 August
Letter, continuing discussion regarding an allegedly false Corot painting presented to the Dublin Modern Art Gallery by the Prince of Wales.

1906

"Reminiscences of the Impressionist Painters"
SCRIBNER'S MAGAZINE, February
Revised and published as a pamphlet (A28); and again revised and included as section VI of *Vale* (A31:III-a).

"The Garret"
THE SATURDAY REVIEW, 23 June
About an exhibition of pictures at the New English Art Club.

---

by George Moore?" in ENGLISH LITERATURE IN TRANSITION, Volume 9, Number 1, 1966.

1908

"Balzac"

PAPYRUS, A MAGAZINE OF INDIVIDUALITY (Mount Vernon, N.Y.), December

Unauthorized printing, without source credit, of a section from chapter VI of *Confessions of a Young Man* (A12).

1909

"Souvenir sur Mallarmé"

"A Memory of Mallarmé"

THE BUTTERFLY QUARTERLY (Philadelphia), No. 7, Summer (15 August)

Article in French reprinted from *Parsifal* (D:Fr-14), with an English translation by Helene Wood.

"A Waitress"

PAPYRUS, A MAGAINE OF INDIVIDUALITY, August-September

Unauthorized printing, without source credit, from *Memoirs of My Dead Life* (A29).

1910

"Overture to 'Hail and Farewell' "

ENGLISH REVIEW, March

Reprinted in *Ave* (A31:I-a)

"The Apostle"

ENGLISH REVIEW, June

Revised and issued in book form (A30-a) 1911, without the "Prefatory Note" included here.

"Mr. George Moore's Escape, Crowd Charged by Motor-Car"

CONTINENTAL DAILY MAIL, 6 September

Article, extensively quoting GM, on a motor-car accident that befell him, Lady Cunard, and a Mrs. [Josephine] Marshall as they were leaving the opera in Munich; reprinted (pp 78-80) in *Letters to Lady Cunard* (A65).

"Une Promenade Sentimentale"

ENGLISH REVIEW, October

Rewritten and included as chapter XII of *Avowals* (A38).

"Immorality in Dublin"
  IRISH TIMES, 28 October
  Letter.

"On the Late Mr. Augustus Moore"
  THE TIMES (London), 30 December
  Letter on religious beliefs of Moore family, refuting statement in
  obituary notice of Augustus Moore that he was from an old Roman
  Catholic family.

1911

"Prefatory Letter on Reading the Bible for the First Time"
  ENGLISH REVIEW, February
  Reprinted in *The Apostle*, 1911 (A30-a).

"A Flood"
  THE IRISH REVIEW, March; reprinted in LIVING AGE, 27 May; and
  again in SMART SET, November 1913
  Revised and published separately in a signed, limited edition (A57).

"La Réponse de Georges Moore à sa Cousine Germaine une Carmelite De-
puis 23 ans qui lui a demandé de Brûler ses Livres"
  THE IRISH REVIEW, April
  Reprinted as concluding section of chapter XV of *Avowals* (A38).

"In Search of Divinity"
  ENGLISH REVIEW, December, and January, and February 1912
  Reprinted as first four sections of *Salve* (A31:II-a).

1912

"From the Beginning"
  THE SUNDAY RECORD-HERALD (Chicago), 4 February [6]
  Published, with articles by Sara Allgood, T. W. Rolleston, Augusta

6. Previously published in BOSTON EVENING TRANSCRIPT (circa late 1911) according to Anna Irene Miller who quotes portions of the article in *The Independent
Theatre in Europe* (New York, 1931). The Irish players opened their American tour
late in 1911 at the Plymouth Theatre in Boston, so it is likely the article appeared
there as publicity for the engagement, and it may also have been printed in papers in
New York and Philadelphia when the company played those cities during the course
of its tour.

Gregory, and W. B. Yeats, under general heading "The Story of the Irish Players."

"The Lord Chamberlain and Mr. Phillpotts' Play"
THE TIMES (London), 14 February
Letter, subtitled "A Protest from Authors," believed to have been written by William Archer and signed by twenty-three authors, including GM, protesting against censoring of Eden Phillpott's play, *The Secret Woman.*

"Jubilation in the Garden"
ENGLISH REVIEW, August
Reprinted as section XI of *Salve* (A31:II-a).

"Rencontre au Salon"
FORTNIGHTLY REVIEW, November
Revision of "Art for the Villa" from the first edition of *Impressions and Opinions* (A15-a) and reprinted in its place in the revised edition (A15-b).

1913

"Elizabeth Cooper"
INTERNATIONAL MAGAZINE, August, September, and October
An act in each issue; previously published in book form (A33).

1914

"Yeats, Lady Gregory, and Synge"
ENGLISH REVIEW, January, and February
Reprinted as section VII of *Vale* (A31:III-a).

"Mr. George Moore and 'Vale' "
THE DAILY TELEGRAPH, circa first week in April
Letter.

"Shakespeare and Balzac"
THE CENTURY MAGAZINE, May
English translation of French lecture published in REVUE BLEUE, 26 February and 5 March 1910 (D:Fr-15). The translation is stated to be by GM, and in a letter to Dujardin, 24 September 1913, he writes of the trouble he is having making the translation, but W. H. Royce

in *A Balzac Bibliography* (Chicago, 1929) states that it was "in reality translated by L. M. Atkinson."

"Imperilled Safeguards?"

THE TIMES (London), 27 June

Letter on Irish Home Rule; establishment of army; and analogy to Irish Nationalist Volunteer Force.

"Euphorian [sic] in Texas"

ENGLISH REVIEW, July

Included in the 1915 and subsequent editions of *Memoirs of My Dead Life* (A29-c et seq.), with spelling of the title changed to "Euphorion"; also printed separately (A43).

"Epistle to the Cymry"

FORTNIGHTLY REVIEW, September

Reprinted in 1926 and subsequent editions of *Confessions of A Young Man* (A12-2d2 et seq.).

1915

[Letter from GM to Kuno Meyer, dated 4 January]

DAILY TELEGRAPH, circa early January; reprinted in MANCHESTER GUARDIAN

Reply to letter from Meyer, dated 8 December 1914, which is also given.

"Correspondence with the Enemy"

VACCINATION INQUIRER, 1 February

Letter, one of several, attacking the anti-vaccinationist point of view.

1916

"Fighting for Inefficiency: A Conversation with George Moore" by John Lloyd Balderston

HARPER'S WEEKLY, 25 March

This, like two subsequent articles, is by GM although signed by Balderston.

"What Shakespeare Has Meant to Me"

WEEKLY DISPATCH, 30 April

Three-paragraph contribution to a symposium.

"Whistle, Whistle, Whistle"
EVENING NEWS, 25 May

[Article on ruins of Dublin]
EVENING NEWS, 5 June
Reprinted in chapter III of *A Story-Teller's Holiday* (A37).

"A June Trip Through Ireland"
EVENING NEWS, 29 June
Reprinted in chapter V of *A Story-Teller's Holiday* (A37).

"The Dusk of the Gods: A Conversation on Art with George Moore" by John Lloyd Balderston
ATLANTIC MONTHLY, August
This, like a previous and a subsequent article, although signed by Balderston is by GM and was rewritten by him for the final chapter of *Avowals* (A38).

"Mr. George Moore on Christ's Divinity"
PALL MALL GAZETTE, 4 September
Letter, used as basis of "Preface" added to second American edition of *The Brook Kerith* (A35-2a2).

"Mr. George Moore and Our Reviewer: A Personal Vindication"
WESTMINSTER GAZETTE, 15 September
Letter, followed by others from Robert Ross, L. G. R., Vernon Bartlett, W. Horsley, and F. W. W.

[Letter to the editor]
NEW YORK SUN, 10 October
Reply to James Huneker's review of *The Brook Kerith*, particularly in regard to GM's ascribed conversion from Roman Catholicism.

"Mr. George Moore's Reply"
WESTMINSTER GAZETTE, 16 October
Letter.

1917

"Mr. George Moore on the Literary Law"
WESTMINSTER GAZETTE, circa Mid-April
Letter.

"Freedom of the Pen: A Conversation with George Moore" by John Lloyd Balderston
FORTNIGHTLY REVIEW, October
Like the two previous "Conversations" signed by Balderston, this is by

GM, and with slight revisions was republished under his name as "Literature and Morals" in THE CENTURY MAGAZINE, May 1919.

"An Irish Essayist"
> THE OBSERVER, 4 November
> Review of *Anglo-Irish Essays* by John Eglinton.

"Senilis"
> THE OBSERVER, 25 November
> Review of the book by Cicely Hamilton.

1918

"Fromentin, Poet and Painter"
> THE OBSERVER, 27 January
> Review of *Eugène Fromentin: Lettres de Jeunesse.*

"Memories of Degas"
> BURLINGTON MAGAZINE, January and February

"A Leave-Taking: Preface to *A Story-Teller's Holiday*"
> TIMES LITERARY SUPPLEMENT, 21 March
> Included in the book (A37).

"James Stephens as Poet"
> THE OBSERVER, 9 June

"My Friendship with George Moore, Three Thousand Miles Away," by the Marquise Clara Lanza
> THE BOOKMAN (New York), July
> Includes quotations from GM's letters to her.

"Imaginary Conversations: Gosse and Moore"
> FORTNIGHTLY REVIEW, October, and November; and THE DIAL, 5, 19 October, and 2 November.
> Reprinted as chapter I of *Avowals* (A38).

1919

"Imaginary Conversations: Gosse and Moore, Second Conversation"
> FORTNIGHTLY REVIEW, January, and February; and THE DIAL, 22 March, 5 and 19 April
> Reprinted as chapter II of *Avowals* (A38).

"The Psychology of Juliet"
THE OBSERVER, 9 March
Letter.

"Ireland: A Solution"
THE TIMES (London), 17 April
Letter on Ireland and Home Rule.

"The Irish Question"
THE TIMES (London), 1 May
Letter, more on Home Rule.

"My Irish Solution"
SUNDAY CHRONICLE, 4 May

"Literature and Morals"
THE CENTURY MAGAZINE, May
Revision of "Freedom of the Pen" by John Lloyd Balderston in FORT-
NIGHTLY REVIEW, October 1917; and is a reworking of the material
in the early pamphlet, *Literature at Nurse* (A7); again rewritten for
chapter III of *Avowals* (A38).

"Ireland's Choice"
THE TIMES (London), 8 July
Letter, still more on Home Rule.

"Ireland and British Commerce"
THE TIMES (London), 5 August
Letter on the western harbor scheme; and like several other letters of
this period, although signed by GM, actually written by T. W. Rolleston and acknowledged to be by him in the dedication to the 1920
revised edition of *Esther Waters* (A19-c).

[Letter to the Editor]
THE TIMES (London), 15 August
On labor, railwaymen's wages, standard rates, etc.; a letter to Sir A.
Geddes, signed by GM but written by T. W. Rolleston.

"The Happy Author. 'Interview' with Mr. George Moore. Two types of
Novelist. 'Best Seller' Recipes. The Fallacy of Cheap Literature."
THE OBSERVER, circa October
Gives verbatim the "Interview" as dictated by GM.

"Nineness in the Oneness"
CHESTERIAN, N.S., No. 1, September; and THE CENTURY MAGAZINE,
November

[Article or letter]
IRISH STATESMAN, 8 November

"The Problem of a Peasantry"
THE OBSERVER, 21 December

1920

"George Moore Interviews Himself," by Joseph Gollomb
THE EVENING POST — BOOK REVIEW, 21 February

"The Coming of Gabrielle"
ENGLISH REVIEW, March, April, and May
An act in each issue; published December in book form (A39). Act I
in March issue is preceded by a letter to Austin Harrison dated 10
February.

"La réponse de Georges Moore en forme de sonnet à son ami Edouard
Dujardin . . ."
FORTNIGHTLY REVIEW, September, and THE DIAL, July 1921
Reprinted, with revisions, in *Fragments from Héloise & Abélard*
(A41); in section XIII of *Conversations in Ebury Street* (A46); and
in letter of "May 20, 1920" in *Letters from George Moore to Ed.
Dujardin 1886-1922* (A54).

"Héloise and Abélard"
FORTNIGHTLY REVIEW, September, and October
Reprinted as chapters VII, VIII, and IX in *Héloïse and Abélard*
(A40).

"Héloise First Meets Abélard"
THE CENTURY MAGAZINE, October
Reprinted as final portion of chapter VI, chapter VII, and a portion
of chapter VIII in *Héloïse and Abélard* (A40).

[Letter to the Editor]
THE TIMES (London), 22 October

"How Héloise passed the winter of 1117 with her uncle, Canon Fulbert of
Notre Dame, and his good servant, Madelon"
THE DIAL, November
Reprinted as final portion of chapter V and beginning of chapter VI
of *Héloïse and Abélard* (A40).

"Preface to 'The Coming of Gabrielle' "
FORTNIGHTLY REVIEW, December; and omitting first five and last two
paragraphs, reprinted as:

"Decline of the Drama"
> THE DIAL, January 1921
> Included complete with the play (A39).

1921

"Outlaws"
> THE OBSERVER, 27 February
> Review of Nancy Cunard's book.

"A Communication to Book Collectors"
> TIMES LITERARY SUPPLEMENT, 10 March
> On hand-set books; letters on same subject by Henry Tonks, Chas. T. Jacobi, and Gerard T. Meynell, 17 March.

"History or Myth?"
> SUNDAY TIMES, 13 March
> On Edmund Goose's 6 March review of *Héloïse and Abélard* (A40).

[Letter]
> TIMES LITERARY SUPPLEMENT, 17 March
> To R. D. Main on printing of limited edition of *Esther Waters* (A19-c2).

"Héloise and Abélard"
> THE OBSERVER, 20 March
> Letter on alleged anachronisms; followed by others from J. C. Squire, and Percival M. Fraser, 27 March.

" 'Anachronisms' Mr. George Moore replies to criticism"
> THE OBSERVER, 3 April
> Letter, continuation of correspondence of 20, and 27 March; followed by a letter from J. C. Squire in same issue — correspondence closed.

"Photography Old and New. A Preface"
> THE OBSERVER, 10 April

"Prelude to 'Memoirs of My Dead Life' "
> THE OBSERVER, 26 June
> Included in Moore Hall and subsequent editions of *Memoirs of My Dead Life* (A29-2d et seq.).

"The Tenth Muse"
> THE OBSERVER, 26 June
> Article in form of an interview on the Phoenix Society and its productions of sixteenth- and seventeenth-century plays.

"The Irrepressible George Moore"
NEW YORK HERALD, 6 August
Letter to Helen Louise Cohen.

"George Moore and Mr. Ervine"
NEW YORK TIMES, 22 August
Letter to editor dated 9 August 1921.

"Revised Texts. Mr. George Moore's Reply to Mr. Gosse"
SUNDAY TIMES, 28 August
Letter regarding Gosse's review of *Fragments from Héloïse & Abélard* (A41) in issue of 21 August.

"Peronnik the Fool"
LONDON MERCURY, September, and October; and THE DIAL, November
Reprinted in Volume XXI of Carra Edition (A50-a).

" 'The Brook Kerith' Mr. George Moore's New Preface. How St. Paul Died"
SUNDAY TIMES, 6 November
Excerpts from "Preface" to 1921 edition of *The Brook Kerith* (A35-a3).

"What is Art? Mr. George Moore's Satire. 'Aristocratic Patter' "
SUNDAY TIMES, 20 November
Letter in reply to an invitation to a dinner honoring Sir Leslie Ward ("Spy"); reprinted in THE WAVE, January 1922, and in *Et Cetera* (B20), both edited by Vincent Starrett; and in TWO WORLDS MONTHLY, Volume II, Number 3, 1927.

"Mr. Moore and His Play"
NEW YORK TIMES, 29 November
Extensive excerpts from letter sent to London newspapers by GM regarding Nigel Playfair's production, then in rehearsal, of *The Coming of Gabrielle* (A39).

"Works of St. Paul. Authorship of the Acts. The Internal Evidence"
SUNDAY TIMES, 25 December; reprinted in LIVING AGE, 11 February 1922.

1922

"Wilfred Holmes"
LONDON MERCURY, February
Included in *In Single Strictness* (A44), which was reissued as *Celibate Lives* (A52).

"Conversation in Ebury Street"
> LONDON MERCURY, August; and ATLANTIC MONTHLY, September
> Revised for first chapter of *Conversations in Ebury Street* (A46).

"Apologia pro scriptis meis"
> FORTNIGHTLY REVIEW, October
> Slightly expanded for use as preface of Carra Edition, where it is included in Volume I, *Lewis Seymour and Some Women* (A36-4a).

1923

"Mon Ami Moore," by E.H. Bierstadt
> THE BOOKMAN (New York), February
> Includes excerpts from four letters, two of which were previously printed in *Jurgen and the Censor* (B29).

[Letter to the Editor]
> THE TIMES (London), 5 February
> On the burning of Moore Hall.

"The Burning of Moore Hall"
> THE OBSERVER, 11 February
> Letter.

[Letter to the Editor]
> THE TIMES (London), 20 February
> On Kensington Square and threatened business encroachment.

"The Cinderella of Literature"
> FORTNIGHTLY REVIEW, April; and as:

"Mr. Moore Talks to Mr. Gosse"
> ATLANTIC MONTHLY, April
> Reprinted as chapter XVI in first edition of *Conversations in Ebury Street* (A46) and as chapter XVII in subsequent editions.

"The Apostle"
> THE DIAL, June, and July
> Published in June in book form (A30-b).

"George Moore and Granville Barker"
> FORTNIGHTLY REVIEW, July; and THE DIAL, August
> Reprinted as chapter XVII in first edition of *Conversations in Ebury Street* (A46) and as chapter XVIII in subsequent editions.

"George Moore and John Freeman"
> THE DIAL, October

Revised and reprinted as chapters IV and V in the English editions of *Conversations in Ebury Street* (A46), and as chapters V and VI in the American editions.

"Sunt lacrimae rerum"
> FORTNIGHTLY REVIEW, December
> Reprinted as final chapter of *Conversations in Ebury Street* (A46).

1924

"The Savagery of Electric Sky-Signs. A Conversation with George Moore," by A.B. (Alan Bott)
> THE WORLD TODAY, February; and under sub-title in NEW YORK TIMES MAGAZINE, 3 February.

1925

"Art Without the Artist"
> FORTNIGHTLY REVIEW, March
> Reprinted as the preface to the revised editions of *Hail and Farewell* (A31-c).

"Abélard and Héloise"
> TIMES LITERARY SUPPLEMENT, 10 December
> Letter, reprinted as *A Letter to the Editor of the TIMES* (A48); answered by C.K. Scott Moncrieff in issue of 24 December.

[Letter to the Editor]
> TIMES LITERARY SUPPLEMENT, 31 December
> In reply to Scott Moncrieff's letter in issue of 24 December.

1926

[Letter to the Editor]
> THE TIMES (London), 12 April
> On traffic inconvenience.

"Argenteuil, 1128: Astrolabe"
> THE OBSERVER, August
> Reprinted in *The Best Poems of 1926* (B22).

"Secret of Making Good Coffee"
BEAU MAGAZINE, October
Short excerpt from final section of *Avowals* (A38).

1927

"The Hermit's Love Story"
COSMOPOLITAN, June; and NASH'S MAGAZINE, August
Revised and included as chapter LVIII of the expanded *A Story-Teller's Holiday* (A37-b), where, in the "Preface," it is called "Dinoll and Crede."

"At the Turn of the Road: An Irish Girl's Love Story"
COSMOPOLITAN, July, and NASH'S MAGAZINE, February 1928
Short story, never reprinted.

"The Strange Story of 3 Golden Fishes: A Comedy of a Man Who Always Was Lucky — Especially in Marriage"
COSMOPOLITAN, September, and NASH'S MAGAZINE, November
Short story, never reprinted.

"The Brook Kerith"
THE OBSERVER, 18 December
Letter.

[Letter to the Editor]
THE TIMES (London), 31 December
Reply to a letter in issue of 29 December from A.A. Milne remonstrating with GM for publishing *The Making of an Immortal* (A53) at three guineas.

1929

"Aphrodite in Aulis: A Modernist Evokes the Spirit of Ancient Greece in a Fable of a Journey from Athens to Aulis"
VANITY FAIR, February
Revised for opening chapter of *Aphrodite in Aulis* (A56).

"Aphrodite in Aulis: A Wandering Athenian Is Welcomed to Aulis and There Tells of Two Helens of Troy"
VANITY FAIR, March
Revised for second chapter of *Aphrodite in Aulis* (A56).

"Art and the Camera"
> THE OBSERVER, 18 August
> "A page from *Conversations with George Moore* to be published in the autumn." (See B23, chapter XXVI.)

1930

"Mr. George Moore to M. Halévy: A New Play"
> THE OBSERVER, 2 February
> Letter addressed to Daniel Halévy.

"Preface to Program of 'Passing of the Essenes' "
> THE TIMES (London), 22 September
> Not used in program when play was produced at Arts Theatre, London, 1 October.

[Letter to the Editor]
> TIMES LITERARY SUPPLEMENT, 30 October
> Reply to critics on interpretation of Jesus in *The Passing of the Essenes*; reprinted as "Preface to the Second Edition" (A55-b).

1931

"A Note from George Moore"
> EVENING NEWS, 3 September
> On origin of the 6/- novel.

"The Dream"
> BOOKS FROM THE HOUSE OF ALEXANDER OUSLEY, No. 1, December
> Same, except for three words, as *The Talking Pine* (A58); also called "The Poet and the Pine" in a letter from GM quoted in the same issue.

1932

"Esther Waters and Mr. Moore"
> THE OBSERVER, 21 February
> Reprinted as "A Colloquy: George Moore and Esther Waters" in the Black and Gold Library edition of *Esther Waters* (A19-3c) and in-

cluded in all subsequent editions except Everyman Library editions (A19-5c and A19-5c2)

"Mr. Moore to His Friends"
THE TIMES (London), 1 March
Letter in reply to message of homage and congratulations on the occasion of GM's eightieth birthday published in the TIMES (London), composed by Charles Morgan and signed by friends and admirers of GM's work.

"Recollections of an Anglo-Parisian Bibliophile, II: George Moore in Paris" by George Frederic Lees
THE BOOKMAN (London), September
Contains two short dedicatory poems by GM found inscribed in a copy of *Pagan Poems*, and a letter from GM to Lees about Flaubert, Zola, and *Evelyn Innes*.

1933

"George Moore: His Life and Work, a Last Interview" by G.W. Bishop
SUNDAY TIMES, 8 January
Contains two letters from GM to Bishop.

"A Visit from George Moore" by Philip Gosse
LONDON MERCURY, March; reprinted in *Essays of the Year 1933-1934* (B39), and separately as a pamphlet, St. Helena, 1937.

1934

"Letters from George Moore: The Greek Background of 'Aphrodite in Aulis'," annotated by P.J. Dixon
LONDON MERCURY, November

1935

"Confessions"
GOLDEN BOOK MAGAZINE, April
Excerpts reprinted from *Confessions of a Young Man* (A12).

1936

"George Moore: Letters of His Last Years," with notes by V.M. Crawford
LONDON MERCURY AND BOOKMAN, December

1938

"Moore on Inscriptions: with annotations by the editor [Ben Abramson]"
READING AND COLLECTING, February-March
Letter (15 February 1932) from GM explaining why he cannot meet requests to autograph his books.

1947

"George Moore and Some Correspondents," by J.M. Hone
THE DUBLIN MAGAZINE, January-March
Includes letters from GM to Henry Tonks, Richard Best, and Mrs. Best.

1951

"Diarmuid and Grania, A Play in Three Acts, by George Moore and W.B. Yeats, Now first printed with an introductory note by William Becker"
THE DUBLIN MAGAZINE, April-June
Twenty-five offprints issued (A64).

1954

"Irish Author and American Critic: George Moore and James Huneker" by Arnold T. Schwab
NINETEENTH CENTURY FICTION, March and June
Contains letters from GM, excerpts of which previously had been published in Volume II of Huneker's *Steeplejack* (B30).

1960

"George Moore and *Father and Son*" by Charles Burkhart
NINETEENTH CENTURY FICTION, January
Contains letters from GM to Edmund Gosse.

1962

"George Moore, W.T. Stead, and the Boer War" by Joseph O. Baylen
THE UNIVERSITY OF MISSISSIPPI STUDIES IN ENGLISH, Volume Three
Contains four brief letters (early November 1900–January 1901)
from GM to W.T. Stead.

IV

Translations

Chinese

D:Ch-1   *Memoirs of My Dead Life*, translated by Hsün-mei Shao, published by Shin Tai, Shanghai, at 30 Chinese cents. Not seen.[1]

Czech

D:Cz-1   . . . *Mildred Lawsonova a Jiné Povidký*, Nakladem J. Otty, Prague 1905. 6⅞ x 4⅜; [1], 2-24⁸, 25²; pp XIV, 15-388. Translations by Jos. Bartos of "Mildred Lawson" and "John Norton" from *Celibates* (A21), "The Clerk's Quest," "A Letter from Rome" and "A Play-house in the Waste" from *The Untilled Field* (A26), with an introduction by the translator tracing GM's writing career and translating brief passages from various books, plus a list of the English titles and dates of original publication of GM's books from *Pagan Poems* through *The Untilled Field*.

D:Cz-2   *Moderní Maliři*, péčí Volných Smera, Prague, 1909, Pp 204. Apparently a translation of all or part of *Modern Painting*. Not seen.[1]

D:Cz-3   *Zpovedi Mladeho Muže*, Moderni biblioteka, VIII, 5, 6, Kral. Vinohrady (Prague). 129 pp. Translation by Jan Reichmann of *Confessions of a Young Man* (A12), with preface by Maxe Meyerfelda. Not seen.[2]

D:Cz-4   "Konec Marie Pellegrinove" in "Zenskem Klastere" (Women's

1. Listed in *A Classified Catalogue of Current Chinese Books*, compiled by Ch'u-ts'ang Huang, published by Sheng Huo, Shanghai, 1935.

1. Particulars from New York Public Library catalogue card of copy formerly in Webster Branch, now discarded, as has been the copy listed in Chicago Public Library catalogue.

2. Listed in *Soupis Ceskoslovenske Literatury za Leta 1901-05*, by Noskovsky and Prazak.

Monastery). Translation by Meyrer C.F. Plaztus of "The End of Marie Pellegrin" from *Memoirs of My Dead Life* (A29). Not seen.[2]

D:Cz-5   *Vyzite Lásky* (Outlived Loves), "Všem a všude" (To all and everywhere), 6, Prague, 1921. 192 pp. Translation by H. Jost of an unidentified story or stories (possibly from *Memoirs of My Dead Life?*). Not seen.[2]

Danish

D:Da-1   *Esther Waters*, Copenhagen, 1895. Not seen.[1]

Dutch

D:Du-1   *De Vrouw von den Comediant*, Pytersen's Goedkope Bibliotheek, Vols. 3-5, Sneek, 1886. Translation of *A Mummer's Wife* (A6). Not seen.[1]

D:Du-2   *Een Drama in Neteldoek*, two volumes, Sneek, 1888. Translation of *A Drama in Muslin* (A9). Not seen.[1]

D:Du-3   *Ijdel Geld*, Amsterdam, 1895. Translation by Mme. L. Couperous of *Vain Fortune* (A16), with an introduction by Louis Couperous. Not seen.[2]

French

D:Fr-1   "Zola à l'étranger . . . II — En Angleterre et en Amerique" by Paul Alexis, in LE VOLTAIRE, 1 November 1879. Includes letter from GM, apparently quoted almost in its entirety.

D:Fr-2   "Le Poète Anglais Shelley" in LE FIGARO, 22 May 1886. Article about a London performance of *The Cenci*, some passages foreshadowing the opening chapter of *Confessions of a Young Man* (A12).

1. Listed in *Dansk Bogfurtenneise*, the national bibliography continuing from the early nineteenth century.

1. Listed in Brinkman's *Catalugus van Boekwn 1882-1892*. Also noted, but without particulars, in LITERARY WORLD (Boston), 21 August 1886.

2. In the "Prefatory Note" to the second English edition (A16-c), GM tells of corresponding with "Madam" Couperous regarding this translation, and he says "she pointed out that the two versions [i.e., Henry (A16-a) and Scribner (A16-b)] could be combined . . . and the union of the texts was no doubt accomplished . . . without the alteration of a sentence."

D:Fr-3   "La Femme du Cabotin" in Le Voltaire,[1] 9 July through 18 October 1886, with no installments in issues of 1, 4, 24 August and 11 October; revised and reprinted in book form (D:Fr-8). Translation by "Mme. Judith[2] de la Comédie Française" of the first edition of *A Mummer's Wife* (A6-a).

D:Fr-4   "Lettres sur l'Irlande" in Le Figaro, 31 July, 7, 14, 21, 28 August, and 4 September 1886; reprinted as *Terre D'Irlande* (D:Fr-5). Translation by M.F. Rabbe of a series of articles later published in English as *Parnell and His Island* (A11).

D:Fr-5   *Terre D'Irlande* . . . Charpentier, Paris, March 1887. 7⅜ x 4½; [ ]⁶, 1-24⁶; pp VI, 288. Reprinted from Le Figaro (D:Fr-4).

D:Fr-6   "Le Sinistre de Tonbridge" in La Revue Independante, March 1887. Translation of "Two Men" later published in Court and Society Review, 20 April 1887.

D:Fr-7   "Une Simple Accident" in Revue International, Rome, 25 May, 10, 25 June, 5 July 1887. Translation[3] of *A Mere Accident* (A10).

D:Fr-8   . . . *La Femme du Cabotin* . . . Charpentier, Paris, 1888. 7½ x 4⅜; [ ]², 1-33⁶, [34]⁴; pp [iv], 404. Translation of *A Mummer's Wife* (A6), corrected by Paul Alexis from version serialized in Le Voltaire (D:Fr-3).

D:Fr-9   "Confessions" in La Revue Independante, March through August 1888. Translation of *Confessions of a Young Man* (A12); revised and expanded for publication as *Confessions d'un Jeune Anglais* (D:Fr-10).

D:Fr-10   . . . *Confessions d'un Jeune Anglaise* . . . Savine, Paris, 1889. 7⁵⁄₁₆ x 4¾; [a]¹², b⁴, 1-16¹²ᐟ⁶ ; pp [12], xx, 288. Translation of the expanded English text of *Confessions of a Young Man* (A12-b), revised by Edouard Dujardin from text serialized in La Revue Independante (D:Fr-9). Reprinted in Le Cabinet Cosmopolite Stock, Paris, 1925, in an edition of 2,200 numbered copies; and again reprinted by Stock, Paris, 1935.

D:Fr-11   "Les Conditions actuelles de l'Art Dramatique en Angleterre" in Mercure de France, February 1899. Translation by H.D. Davray of GM's "Introduction" to *The Heather Field and Maeve* (B8).

D:Fr-12   . . . *Esther Waters* . . . Librairie Hachette, Paris, 1907. 7⅜ x 4¾; [a]⁴, [b]² (tipped in), 1-23⁸, 24⁶; pp [6], VI, 380. An abridged translation by Firmin Roz and Emm. Fernard of the first revision of *Esther Waters* (A19-b).

D:Fr-13   "Souvenirs Parisiens: La Mort de Marie Pellegrin" in Revue

1. According to GM in "My Impressions of Zola" in the revised edition of *Impressions and Opinions* (A15-b), the translation was also published in La Vie Populaire, but no file of this periodical has been located.

2. Madame Judith Bernard.

3. Described by GM in a letter to Dujardin, dated "July 2, 1887" as "an infamy: ten times worse than the translation of 'Terre d'Irlande'."

BLEUE, 17 August 1907. Translation[4] by Firmin Roz and Emm. Fernard of "The End of Marie Pellegrin" from *Memoirs of My Dead Life* (A29).

D:Fr-14   "Souvenir sur Mallarmé" in PARSIFAL, April 1909. Reprinted, with an English translation in THE BUTTERFLY QUARTERLY, No. 7, Summer 1909.

D:Fr-15   "Shakespeare et Balzac" in REVUE BLEUE, 26 February and 5 March 1910. Text of lecture delivered 18 February at Salle de l'Agriculture, Paris; an English translation, "Shakespeare and Balzac," published in THE CENTURY MAGAZINE, May 1914; original French text reprinted as chapter XIII of *Avowals* (A33); in Carra and subsequent American editions, it is transferred to *Conversations in Ebury Street* (A46-2a).

D:Fr-16   "Curither et Liadine" in MERCURE DE FRANCE, 18 April 1918. Translation by G. Jean-Aubry of a story from *A Story-Teller's Holiday* (A37).

D:Fr-17   "Memoires de ma vie Morte: Resurgam" in LA REVUE DE GENÈVE, October 1920; reprinted in *Memoires de Ma Vie Morte* (D:Fr-20). Translation by G. Jean-Aubry of "Resurgam" from *Memoirs of My Dead Life* (A29).

D:Fr-18   "Clara Florise, comedie en trois actes," in L''AFRIQUE DU NORD ILLUSTRÉE, supplements 6, 20 November and 4 December 1920. Adaption by Edouard Dujardin of *Elizabeth Cooper* (A33); produced 24 February 1914 at the Comédie Royal in Paris.

D:Fr-19   "Apportez la lampe" in REVUE DE PARIS, 15 October 1922; reprinted in *Memoires de Ma Vie Morte* (D:Fr-20). Translation by G. Jean-Aubry of "Bring in the Lamp" from *Memoirs of My Dead Life* (A29).

D:Fr-20   . . . *Memoires de Ma Vie Morte* . . . Grasset, Paris, 14 October 1922. $7\frac{3}{8}$ x $4\frac{5}{8}$; [A]^8, B^4, 1-15^8, 16^6; pp xxiv, 252. Translation by G. Jean-Aubry of the Moore Hall edition of *Memoirs of My Dead Life* (A29-2d), but with "Lui et Elles" and "The Lovers of Orelay" omitted; and including an "Introduction" by Daniel Halévy and a "Dedicace à George Moore" by the translator. Reprinted 24 April 1928 with slight revisions, including the addition of "Les Amants d'Orelay" and the omission of the "Introduction."

D:Fr-21   . . . *Le Lac* . . . Stock, Paris, 1923. $7\frac{1}{2}$ x $4\frac{5}{8}$; [a]^2, [b]^{16}, 1-19^{16}, 10^8, 11^4; pp xxxvi, 312. Translation by Mme. W. Laparra of "Preface" and text of revised third English edition of *The Lake* (A27-d); with a "Preface à la Presente Edition française" by Emond Jaloux, and the author's dedication in French from English edition.

D:Fr-22   "Walter Pater" in REVUE DE GENEVE, July-August 1923. Translation by G. Jean-Aubry of a section of *Avowals* (A38).

4. Another translation by G. Jean-Aubry, "La Fin de Marie Pellegrin," included in *Memoirs de Ma Vie Morte* (D:Fr-20).

D:Fr-23 "Mes Souvenirs sur Mallarmé" in LE FIGARO, 13 October 1923.

D:Fr-24 . . . *Solitude de Kerith* . . . Cres, Paris, 1927. Two volumes, 7½ x 4⅝; Vol. I, [1]⁸, 2-15⁸, 16⁴; pp [vi], 242; Vol. II, 1⁸, 2-15⁸; pp [vi], 234. Translation by Phillippe Neel of the fifth impression of *The Brook Kerith* (A35-a3). Later in 1927 a one-volume edition was issued, using the plates of the two-volume first edition.

D:Fr-25 "Comment se fait un immortel ou Le Poet malgré lui" in REVUE DES DEUX MONDES, 15 January 1930. Translation by Louis Gillet of *The Making of an Immortal* (A53).

D:Fr-25 . . . *Esther* . . . Catalogne, Paris, 1933. Published in a limited edition of 200 copies. 7¼ x 4½; [1]⁶, 2-27⁸, 28²; pp xii, 420. Translation by Daniel Halévy and Mlle. Laparra of the final revision of *Esther Waters* (A19-c), including the "Epistle Dedicatory" and "A Colloquy: George Moore and Esther Waters" from the Black and Gold Library edition (A19-3c).

D:Fr-27 "Un disciple d'Emile Zola: George Moore — Documents inédits" by Auriant in MERCURE DE FRANCE, 1 May 1940. Included are carelessly transcribed letters from GM to Zola (1880s-1890s), portions of which were previously published in translation in Hone's *Life of George Moore* (B44).

D:Fr-28 "Louis Gillet et George Moore" by Georges-Paul Collet in ETUDES ANGLAISES, August 1953. Includes extracts from GM letters.

Gaelic

D:Ga-1 "An Gúna-Postà" in THE NEW IRELAND REVIEW, January 1902; reprinted in *An T-Úr-Gort* (D:Ga-2). Translation of "The Wedding Gown," later revised and included in *The Untilled Field* (A26).

D:Ga-2 *An T-Úr-Gort* . . . Sealy, Bryers & Walker, Dublin, 1902. 9¼ x 6¼; [a]⁴, [A]², B-H⁸, I²; pp [8], iv, 116. Translation by Pádraig Ó Súilleabáin (Padraic O'Sullivan) of six stories later published in English in *The Untilled Field* (A26); also a dedication in English, and a preface in Gaelic by the translator.

D:Ga-3 "T öir mic vi Diomasuig" in THE NEW IRELAND REVIEW, November 1902. Translation of "Mr. Dumpty's Quest" in same issue; later revised and included in *The Untilled Field* (A26).

D:Ga-4 "An Déirc" in THE NEW IRELAND REVIEW, December 1902. Translation of "Alms-giving" in same issue; later revised and included in *The Untilled Field* (A26).

German

D:Ge-1 "Heimweh" in DIE NATION, 1 February 1902. Translation by Max Meyerfeld of "Home-Sickness," later published in HARPER'S WEEKLY, 16 August 1902, and PALL MALL MAGAZINE, September 1902, and included the next year in *The Untilled Field* (A26).

D:Ge-2 "Das Hochzeitskleid" in DIE NATION, 19 April 1902. Translation by Max Meyerfeld of "The Wedding Gown," later published in ENGLISH ILLUSTRATED MAGAZINE, June 1902, and included the next year in *The Untilled Field* (A26).

D:Ge-3 "Emma Bovary" in DIE NATION, 29 November 1902. Translation by Max Meyerfeld of story by same name in LIPPINCOTT'S MAGAZINE, May 1902.

D:Ge-4 "Ihr Fenster" in DIE NATION, 18 April 1903. Translation by Max Meyerfeld of "The Window," originally published as "Naoim Aiteamail" in *An T-Úr-Gort* (D:Ga-2); later revised and included as section V of "Some Parishioners" in the first edition of *The Untilled Field* (A26-a).

D:Ge-5 *Arbeite und Bete* . . . Egon Fleischel & Co., Berlin, 1904. 7⅜ x 4¾; [a]⁸, [b]² (tipped in), 1-30⁸, 31⁶; pp XX, 492. Translation by Annie Neuman-Hofer of the revised second edition of *Esther Waters* (A19-b), with an introduction by Max Meyerfeld, friend and correspondent of GM, as well as translator of several of his books.

D:Ge-6 *Irdische und Himlische Lieb* . . . Egon Fleischel & Co., Berlin, 1905. In two volumes. Vol. I: 7⅜ x 5; [a]⁴, 1-25⁸, *²; pp viii, 412. Vol. II: 7⅜ x 4⅞; [a]¹ (tipped in), [b]² (tipped in), 1-20⁸, [21]² (tipped in); pp [vi], 324. Translations by Max Meyerfeld from special texts[1] prepared by GM based on revised third edition of *Evelyn Innes* (A22-d) for Vol. I and on revised Tauchnitz edition of *Sister Teresa* (A25-2b) for Vol. II; with a preface by the translator in Vol. I.

D:Ge-7 "Marie Pellegrins Ende" in DIE NATION, 22 September 1906; reprinted in *Aus Toten Tagen* (D:Ge-11) and *Pariser Geschichten* (D:Ge-16). Translation by Max Meyerfeld of "The End of Marie Pellegrin" from *Memoirs of My Dead Life* (A29).

D:Ge-8 "Ein Gedentblatt" in DIE NATION, 17 November 1906; reprinted in *Aus Toten Tagen* (D:Ge-11). Translation by Max Meyerfeld of "A Remembrance" from *Memoirs of My Dead Life* (A29).

D:Ge-9 "Sonntag Abend in London (ein Rhapsodie)" in DIE NATION, 29 December 1906; reprinted in *Aus Toten Tagen* (D:Ge-11). Translation

---

1. A detailed study of the revisions in these texts is given in John Denny Fischer's 1959 doctoral thesis at the University of Illinois, "*Evelyn Innes* and *Sister Teresa* by George Moore: A Variorum Edition."

by Max Meyerfeld of "Sunday Evening in London" from *Memoirs of My Dead Life* (A29).

D:Ge-10   "Eine Kellnerin" in DIE NATION, 23 March 1907; reprinted in *Aus Toten Tagen* (D:Ge-11) and *Pariser Geschichten* (D:Ge-16). Translation by Max Meyerfeld of "A Waitress" from *Memoirs of My Dead Life* (A29).

D:Ge-11   *Aus Toten Tagen* . . . Egon Fleischel & Co., Berlin, 1907. 7½ x 5; [a]² (tipped in), 1-23⁸, *⁴; pp [iv], 376. Translations by Max Meyerfeld of the eleven sections of the Tauchnitz edition of *Memoirs of My Dead Life* (A29-b), and the two sections omitted from that edition translated from the first edition (A29-a); four of the translations previously published in DIE NATION (D:Ge-7, D:Ge-8, D:Ge-9, and D:Ge-10). "Liebesleute in Orelay" reprinted separately (D:Ge-15) and eight other sections reprinted in *Pariser Geschichten* (D:Ge-16).

D:Ge-12   . . . *Erinnerungen an die Impressionisten* . . . **Bruno Cassirer**, Berlin, 1907 [1908]. 7⅞ x 5¾; [1]⁸, [1a]¹ (tipped in between [1]₁ and [1]₂), 2-4⁸, [5]¹ (tipped in); pp [ii], 66. Translation by Max Meyerfeld of dedicatory letter to [Wilson] Steer and text of *Reminiscences of the Impressionist Painters* (A28).

D:Ge-13   *Der Apostle, ein Szenarium* . . . Paul Cassirer, Berlin, 1911. 7⅛ x 4⅝; [1]⁸, 2-5⁸, 6⁴, [7]²; pp 92. Translation by Max Meyerfeld of "The Apostle" from THE ENGLISH REVIEW, June 1910; "Prefatory Letter on Reading the Bible for the First Time" from THE ENGLISH REVIEW, February 1911; and the dedication from the first edition of *The Apostle* (A30-a).

D:Ge-14   *Die Wildgans* . . . Im Insel-Verlag, Leipzig, [1922]. 7⅛ x 4½; [1-5]⁸; pp 80. Translation by Clara Barth and Max Freund of "The Wild Goose" from *The Untilled Field* (A26).

D:Ge-15   *Liebesleute in Orelay* . . . S. Fischer, Berlin, 1925. 6¾ x 4½; [1]⁸, 2-9⁸, 10² (tipped in); pp 148. Translation by Max Meyerfeld of "The Lovers of Orelay" from *Memoirs of My Dead Life* (A29); reprinted from *Aus Toten Tagen* (D:Ge-11).

D:Ge-16   *Pariser Geschichten* . . . S. Fischer, Berlin, 1926. 6¾ x 4½; [1]⁸, 2-10⁸, [11]² (tipped in); pp 164. Reprint of eight of the thirteen translations in *Aus Toten Tagen* (D:Ge-11), with "Thema mit Variations," "Liebesleute in Orelay," "Ein Gedentblatt," "Sonntag Abend in London," and "Resurgam" omitted.

D:Ge-17   *Albert und Hubert* . . . S. Fischer, Berlin, 1928. 7¼ x 4¼; [1]⁸, 2-6⁸, 7⁴; pp 104. Translation by Max Meyerfeld of "Albert Nobbs" from *Celibate Lives* (A52), originally published in first edition as *A Story-Teller's Holiday* (A37).

Italian

D:It-1 . . . *Confessioni di un giovane* . . . Alberto Stock, Rome, 1929. 7¾ x 5⅜; [1]⁸, 2-19⁸, 20⁴; pp 312. Translation by Gian Dàuli of the 1904 edition, including preface, of *Confessions of a Young Man* (A12-c) with a few passages restored from the 1889 edition (A12-b); plus an introduction about GM by the translator and a list of GM's works from 1887 to 1927.

D:It-2 . . . *Il Lago* . . . Rizoli & C., Milano, 1933. 6⅛ x 4; [1]¹⁶, 2-10¹⁶; pp 320. Translation by Mario Casalino of the 1906 Tauchnitz edition of *The Lake* (A27-b). A brief note about GM preceding the text possibly is by the translator.

D:It-3 . . . *Esther Waters* . . . A. Mondadori, Milano, 1934. 6⅝ x 3⅞; [1]⁸, 2-33⁸, 34⁶; pp 540. Translation by Mario Praz of the final revision of *Esther Waters* (A19-c), including the "Epistle Dedicatory," and "A Colloquy: George Moore and Esther Waters" from the Black and Gold library edition (A19-3c).

D:It-4 . . . *Ricordi della mia morta vita* . . . Casa Editrice Bietti, Milano, 1945. 7⅛ x 4¾; [1]⁸, 2-16⁸; pp 256. Translation by Fluffy Mella Mazzucato of the Moore Hall edition of *Memoirs of My Dead Life* (A29-2d), but with "Spring in London," "Lui et Elles," and "A Waitress" omitted. There is a brief preface about GM and his book, possibly by the translator.

D:It-5 *Esther Waters*, Milano, 1959. Pp 360. Translation by Beatrice Boffito Serra. Not seen.[1]

Japanese

D:Ja-1 *Ichi Seinen No Kokuhaku*, Iwanami shoten, Tokyo, 1952. Pp 277. Translation by Seiki Saikiyama of *Confessions of a Young Man* (A12). Not seen.[1]

Norwegian

D:No-1 "Agnes Lahens," Kristiansand, 1895. Translation of "Agnes Lahens" from *Celibates* (A21). Not seen.[1]

1. Listed in *Index Translationum*, Unesco, Paris, 1960.
1. Listed in *Index Translationum*, Unesco, Paris, 1953.
1. Title from Noël.

230

D:No-2 "John Norton," Kristiansand, 1896. Translation by Fernanda Nissen of "John Norton" from *Celibates* (A21). Not seen.[1]

D:No-3 *A Mere Accident*, n.d. Not seen.[2]

Russian[1]

D:Ru-1 "Kiseinaia Drama" in SEVERNYI VESTNIK (Northern Messenger), Nos. 10-12, 1887. Translation of *A Drama in Muslin* (A9). Not seen.[2]

D:Ru-2 "Esters Uoters" in VESTNIK INOSTRANNOI LITERATURY (Messenger of Foreign Literature), Nos. 7-12, 1895. Translation of *Esther Waters* (A19). Not seen.[2]

D:Ru-3 "Mildred Looson" in NABLIUDATEL (Observer), Nos. 4-7, 1897. Translation of "Mildred Lawson" from *Celibates* (A21). Not seen.[2]

Spanish

D:Sp-1 "Henrietta Marr" and "Wilfred Holmes," Barcelona, 1942. Translation by P. Eluas of two stories from *In Single Strictness* (A44) and *Celibate Lives* (A52). Not seen.[1]

Swedish

D:Sw-1 Ester Waters . . . Adolf Bonnier, Stockholm, 1900. 283 pp. An adapted translation (bearbetad öfversättning) of *Esther Waters* (A19); translator not recorded. Not seen.[1]

2. Listed by Prof. Bradford Booth in the GM section of the revised *Cambridge Bibliography of English Literature*. When questioned Professor Booth was unable to supply the source of his information regarding this translation as he had mislaid his notes on it.

1. Transliteration of Russian titles by Library of Congress system.

2. Russian title and particulars from Noël. The first two titles also listed by Prof. Bradford Booth in the GM section he prepared for the revised *CBEL*. He secured information about these translations from the Russian-English bibliographer of the University of Moscow.

1. Title and particulars from Noël.

1. Information supplied by Thomas R. Buckman, director of libraries at the University of Kansas, who at my request examined a copy in the Royal Library in Stockholm.

D:Sw-2   *De Älskande i Orelay och andra Berättelser* . . . Wahlström & Widstrand, Stockholm, 1927. 7⅝ x 5; [1]^8, 2-13^8; pp 208. Translation by Karin Jensen, f. Lidforss of "The Lovers of Orelay," "A Remembrance," "Sunday Evening in London," and "Resurgam" from *Memoirs of My Dead Life* (A29).

V

Miscellanea

In addition to the books, pamphlets, articles, etc., already noted, there are a number of other titles that should be mentioned. These include works begun but never completed; plays written and in some cases produced but never published; and titles which from time to time have been attributed to GM but which actually are not by him.

Not listed are two books, *Two Trips to the Emerald Isles*, London, n.d., and *Cycling*, New Edition, Badminton Library, London, 1896, both of which have illustrations attributed to "George Moore," as any work by GM as an illustrator would be outside the scope of this bibliography. It seems, furthermore, inconceivable that his work in connection with these volumes, if George Moore the well-known author was the illustrator, would not have received contemporary mention, for at least one of the two books was published after he was well established as a writer.

An inquiry to the publisher of *Cycling*, Longmans, Green & Co., produced an answer from G. W. Skinner, dated 27 April 1951. He said, "Unfortunately the greater part of our records were destroyed by enemy action in 1940, but from those remaining we have been unable to trace any connection between 'George Moore' one of the illustrators to the New Edition of Badminton Library 'Cycling' and George Moore, the renowned Anglo-Irish writer. . . . We feel that they were two separate and distinct persons, and George Moore the illustrator, may have been a contributor to 'Badminton Magazine' which we published during the years 1895-1899."

A. E. Popham, keeper of prints and drawings at the British Museum, when questioned about the same time regarding these illustrations, stated it is "very improbable that George Moore, the novelist, worked as an illustrator."

Perhaps a handwriting expert could definitely settle the matter, but to at least one inexperienced eye the signature "G. Moore" on the *Cycling* illustrations does not seem to match other GM signatures of the period, the *G* being unquestionably different.

Also not listed, as it seems to be in the same category as interviews which quote GM, but which were not actually revised or rewritten by him, is a publication which prints testimony given by GM, W. B. Yeats, William Orpen, AE (George William Russell), and others at a hearing in the board room of Leinster House, Dublin, in October 1905.[1] It is the *Report of the Committee of Inquiry into the Work Carried on by the Royal Hibernian Academy, and the Metropolitan School of Art*, Dublin. Parliamentary Papers: Commons. 1906. His Majesty's Stationery Office: Command Publication No. 3256. Issued in paper wrappers, pp xxiv, 98. GM appeared before the committee 11 October 1905, and his testimony is printed pp 27-29 (paragraphs 488-516). As the testimony was extemporaneous and not prepared in advance nor intended for publication, this report is not included in Section II: Contributions.

For the same reason the account of the libel action instituted by Louis N. Seymour on the publication of *Lewis Seymour and Some Women* (A36) is not listed. It can be found in "Seymour vs. Heinemann and Others," in Law Report No. 33, THE TIMES (London), 24 November 1917.

M1

Worldliness

According to the Williams bibliography a comedy, *Worldliness*, was GM's earliest published book, but as far as can be discovered no copy has ever been offered for sale, no contemporary mention of it can be found, there is no record of a copy having been seen, and as the offer of £100 in the October 1921 LONDON MERCURY failed to produce a copy, it seems reasonable to assume that the existence of the play, at least in printed form, is highly improbable.[2]

The comedy is not mentioned by Danielson, and all bibliographic references to it seem to stem from Williams, who gives "London" as the place

---

1. This was called to my attention by Alan Denson, bibliographer of AE and editor of his letters, who supplied the particulars of its publication and tells me that GM's replies are "very amusing" and "deserve reprinting." In his "documented biography," *John Hughes: Sculptor* (published by the author, Kendal, Westmoreland, England, 1969), Mr. Denson quotes the portion of GM's testimony which relates to Hughes.

2. The existence of copies of the play was discussed with Allan Wade, who wrote, "I daresay that you are right in thinking that *Worldliness* may never have existed in print; certainly I have never heard of anybody who has seen a copy. At the same time, it was not unusual, in the days before typescripts, for authors to have their plays put into print in small numbers so that they could be read more easily by theatre-managers than a hand-written copy. . . . If a very small number had been printed he might have destroyed the 'remainder' and it is very unlikely that copies sent to managers would survive; they would probably end in the waste-paper basket!"

of publication, "1874" as the approximate date, and who states it was issued in "pink wrappers." In a letter to Williams dated July 28, 1921, used as a preface to the bibliography, GM mentions that one of the characters was called "Mr. Goldstick" who planned "to marry his mistress to his friend."

Much earlier, in 1887 in the admittedly "purely literary" *Confessions of a Young Man* (A12), GM wrote, "I completed a comedy in three acts entitled 'Worldliness' . . . Is it necessary to say that I did not find a manager to produce my play? A printer was more obtainable, and the correction of proofs amused me for a while." In the final revisions (A12-2d and A12-e), however, this reference to publication was changed, the new text reading, "I learnt among other things that it would be well to have my play copied and the stage directions inscribed in red ink." He seems to have made no further references to the comedy, and in *Vale* (A31:III-a) as well as in other places GM speaks of *Flowers of Passion* (A1) as being his "first" book.

M2
Roses of Midnight

In an undated latter, quoted by Hone (p 75), GM wrote his mother, "My next book is three quarters finished *Roses of Midnight*," which is described in *Confessions of a Young Man* (A12) as being "a set of stories in many various metres," and raises the possibility that it was an early title for *Pagan Poems* (A3).

M3
Aristocracy of Vice

A novel "of the three quarter world," *Aristocracy of Vice*, was also mentioned by GM in the undated letter to his mother noted above (M2), and according to Hone (p 88) it "got completely out of hand and was abandoned [3] in despair."

M4
L'Assommoir

Circa 1882 GM wrote Zola about doing an English version of *L'Assommoir* (Hone, p 93), and although the translation apparently was never pub-

3. See A14-nl.

lished and very likely never completed, at least one chapter survived in a 10-page manuscipt, sold in 1924 at Anderson Galleries, New York, as item 6638 in the sale of the library of John Quinn, the American collector, friend, and patron of many authors of the Irish literary revival.

M5
Le Sycamore

In "Boycotting on the Bookstalls, a Note on George Moore" in COURT AND SOCIETY REVIEW, 15 July 1886, it is stated, "Mr. George Moore has had a play accepted at the Odéon," and in an undated [4] letter to Jacques-Emile Blanche GM wrote, "Avez vous entendu que nous avons avec Alexis une pièce à l'Odéon," both presumably references to *Le Sycamore*, the unpublished translation by GM and Paul Alexis of W.S. Gilbert's play, *Sweethearts*, and so identified by Hone (p 115), who also gives a translation of GM's letter to Blanche. Edward Marsh retells [5] "a rather amusing story" related in 1898 by GM at a gathering at Edmund Gosse's regarding "an English play that he had translated into French" being rehearsed at the Odéon the same day as *A Midsummer Night's Dream* and of his being mistaken by the stage doorman for Shakespeare. According to Noël (p 222), who gives "archives de la Comédie-Française" as his authority, there was a production of *Le Sycamore* 20 September 1894 at "theatre de l'Odéon, Paris."

M6
The Fashionable Beauty

According to J.M. Glover in "George Moore as Librettist" in THE OBSERVER, 18 April 1923, *The Fashionable Beauty*, an unpublished [6] burlesque by GM and Harry Paulton, author of the libretto of *Ermine*, was produced in

4. Dated "Summer 1885" by Blanche (p 290) in *Portraits of a Lifetime* (B47).

5. In a letter to Neville Lytton, quoted (p 86) by Christopher Hassall in *A Biography of Edward Marsh* (B59). A note in THE BAT, 25 May 1886, also tells an anecdote similar to the one related by GM.

6. Allardyce Nicoll in *A History of Late Nineteenth Century Drama*, Cambridge, 1948, says there is a manuscript copy of the play in the Lord Chamberlain's office at St. James's Palace.

1887 [7 April] for a two week's run at the Avenue Theatre, London, by Violet Melnotte.

M7
Defensio pro Scriptis Meis

Defensio pro Scriptis Meis is noted by Hone (pp 118-19) as being "a pamphlet which Swan Sonneschein" published in 1887. It is not listed, however, in the check list appended to the Hone biography, nor is it listed in *The English Catalogue*. A copy catalogued in the New York Public Library proves to be on examination extracted pages of the article from TIME, March 1887, and not a separate offprint or issue.

M8
The Honeymoon in Eclipse

A one-act play, *The Honeymoon in Eclipse*, by George Moore was produced at St. George's Hall, London, 12 April 1888, by "The Strolling Players," who were praised by GM in a letter, "Play Producing," in THE EVENING NEWS, 14 April 1888, in which the amateur actors are favorably compared with professionals. The play was a dramatization of a story by Mrs. G. W. Godfrey, "Ugly Barrington," originally published in THE WORLD.

M9
Extracts Principally from the English Classics . . .

In *This Book-Collecting Game*, 1928, A. Edward Newton gave currency to the legend that GM had compiled the booklet issued as a protest against the legal suppression in England of Zola's works, *Extracts Principally from the English Classics* . . . , London, 1888,[7] and that he was author of the inserted letter to the "Solicitor to the Treasury." A notation by Wilfred

7. Described (p 200) in *A Bibliography of Henry James*, by Leon Edel and Dan H. Laurence, Soho Bibliographies, London, 1957. It should also be noted that Max Harzof, a New York book dealer, issued (circa 1923) a facsimile reprint, on heavier paper, with different type used for the word "Introduction" at head of page [4], and with the board covers trimmed evenly with the book's edges, and not overlapping as

Partington, possibly stemming from Newton's attribution, in the copy of *Extracts* . . . in the library of Stanford University at Palo Alto, California, also credits GM with a hand in the work. By permission of the late Frank Fayant, I quote the inscription in the copy of this book in his collection, "My dear Fayant, I assure you hand on my heart, that I had no hand in the making of this book. Very sincerely yours, George Moore."

M10
Thérèse Raquin

An unpublished[8] translation of Zola's play, *Thérèse Raquin,* by George Moore and Teixeira de Mattos, was presented 9 October 1891 by the Independent Theatre Society at the Royalty Theatre, London. A letter from de Mattos regarding GM's revisions in this play was published in the PALL MALL GAZETTE, 22 February 1893.

M11
Only a Hint

"Only a Hint" by "George Moore," twenty-four lines of light verse dealing with the California gold rush, in CENTURY MAGAZINE, January 1892, has not been listed in the periodical section, as there is general agreement among all consulted that it could not have been written by the Irish George Moore, not because he was incapable of writing such verse, but rather because the meter and subject matter are completely foreign to him.

M12
The Minister's Call

It has been said[9] that GM collaborated with Arthur Symons on a drama-

in the original issue. Other differences are noted in the article, "The Vizetelly Extracts," by William E. Colburn, in THE PRINCETON UNIVERSITY LIBRARY CHRONICLE, Winter 1962.

8. According to Nicoll (see M6-n6), there is a manuscript copy of the play in the Lord Chamberlain's office.

9. In *Frank Harris: A Study in Black and White,* by I.A. Tobin and Elmer Gertz,

tization of "A Modern Idyll" by Frank Harris which was produced 4 March 1892 as *The Minister's Call* by the Independent Theatre Society at the Royalty Theatre in London. Contemporary reviews list only Symons as the adaptor, and his biographer, Prof. Roger Lhombreaud, considered GM as simply an intermediary who secured permission from Harris for Symons to turn the story into a play, and it's likely that was his original role. It appears, however, that as the dramatization proceeded GM became an actual, if anonymous, collaborator, for Symons wrote of the composition of the play in an unpublished manuscript, "Frank Harris," now in the Princeton University Library, which was called to my attention by another Symons scholar, John M. Munro. By permission of the Princeton library I quote the passage: "Just then I had not the faintest idea of how one begins to write a play, how one constructs it, how one sets one's figures in motion, how one contrives the final climax. Night after night I went across to Moore's rooms, showing him the fragments I had composed, which he read and commented upon. We ended by collaborating. Moore refused to have his name put beside mine on the play-bill."

M13

In Minor Keys

In an interview[10] given to John Austin in 1927 GM told of a book of three stories, two already written, which were to "appear in a volume for which I have chosen the nice title 'In Minor Keys.'" In correspondence of the period GM also spoke of the book, and it is possible the two completed stories were "At the Turn of the Road: An Irish Girl's Love Story" and "The Strange Story of 3 Golden Fishes: A Comedy of a Man Who Was Always Lucky — Especially in Marriage" which were published in Cosmopolitan and Nash's Magazine. For the third story GM may have been considering the revised version of "A Flood" (see A57-n1) or possibly "Christina Harford and Her Divorce" (M14 below) or "A Lost Masterpiece" (M15 below), but in any case the projected volume was never published.

Chicago, 1931. When questioned, Mr. Gertz could not recall the source of the information linking GM's name with the dramatization, but it very likely came from *My Life and Loves*, by Harris, where he says, "A little later Moore wrote to me, asking my permission to turn the *Modern Idyll* into a play, and I believe he did it with Arthur Symons, under the title of *The Curate's Call*, or something of that sort."

10. "Hail, My Farewell! By George Moore (in an interview)" in T-P's Weekly, 12 November 1927.

M14

Christina Harford and her Divorce

In a letter to Lady Cunard[11] GM mentions a long short story, "Christina Harford and her Divorce," apparently completed and ready for publication, but no further reference to it has been located. Some details of its plot are given in the letter, and from these it seems possible it might have become a part of the uncompleted *Madeleine de Lisle* (M16).

M15

A Lost Masterpiece

In a letter[12] "August 4th, 1930" GM wrote to A. J. A. Symons, "Ever since I saw you I have been trying (vainly I am afraid,) to write the opening pages of the story I spoke to you about to be called 'A Lost Masterpiece.' A country house didn't prove a suitable surrounding for the telling of the tale, and Tonks's studio didn't turn out any better. This morning I threw a week's work into the wastebasket and attempted a new opening in the house of a great book-collector like shall I say Mr. Wise. Johnson Creswell, another collector, was to have come to dinner at eight o'clock, but he has not arrived, and to pass the time the host, Mr. Ogleby, leads his guests round the shelves, and I need a few lines here giving the names of the books he would be likely to show them. I think he would choose, for the sake of the ladies, first editions of Shelley and Keats and writers of that period. He mentions Landor, & I wish you could supply me with a dozen names and a few accidental remarks that he might make, perhaps. He then leads his guests into the dining-room and the conversation continues about books, and at the close of the dinner Creswell arrives, apologizing for his late appearance and hinting that he has a story to tell. When the dinner is over and they go into the drawing-room he tells what has happened to him." From further remarks in the letter it appears that the story he has to tell deals with the discovery of a lost masterpiece by Landor, but no further details can be located regarding the story, which probably was never completed, and is possibly the same as the one called "The Houseparty" in GM's correspondence of the period.

11. Tentatively dated "May 1929" by the editor.
12. Original in my collection; two brief excerpts from it are quoted (p 43) in *A. J. A. Symons: His Life and Speculations*, by Julian Symons, London, 1950.

M16
Madeleine de Lisle

At the time of his death GM was working on a new book, *Madeleine de Lisle*, and some of its proposed story line, which apparently kept changing almost from day to day, can be found in Hone's *Life of George Moore* (pp 439 and 443); the article with letters, "George Moore: Letters of His Last Years, with notes by V.M. Crawford," in THE LONDON MERCURY AND BOOKMAN, December 1936; and in *Escape with Me*, by Osbert Sitwell, London (pp 19-20), and New York (pp xxxv-xxxvi), 1940.

Postscript

Compiling this bibliography has been in many ways a collaboration with numerous scholars, collectors, librarians, book dealers, and others who, with but a few exceptions, have been courteous and cooperative in answering questions, supplying information, and loaning books for examination. I am most grateful to them all, and my gratitude is none the less because space forbids no more than a perfunctory listing of the many who generously have given assistance. A few have been singled out for special mention in the course of this bibliography, and others must be noted here for help unstintingly given during an extended period of time.

In dedicating this book to Allan Wade I have attempted to acknowledge his invaluable trans-Atlantic help from 1950 to his sudden death in 1955 which deprived me of his interest and helpful advice regarding both specific and general problems. I am particularly grateful for the extensive lists of periodical material which he had meticulously noted while doing research for his bibliography of W. B. Yeats; for the loan and gift of books, clippings, photostats, and other pertinent material; and for the use of his unpublished "Notes for George Moore's Bibliographer."

I am also greatly indebted to Mr. Wade for introductions by mail to some of GM's Irish friends, including P. S. O'Hegarty, Dr. James S. Starkey (Seumas O'Sullivan), and William K. Magee (John Eglinton), each of whom generously supplied me with useful bibliographical information. In addition Mr. O'Hegarty kindly loaned me volumes from his collection[1] and also transliterated and translated a number of Gaelic titles.

Particular appreciation must be noted for the assistance given by Sir Rupert Hart-Davis, editor of *George Moore: Letters 1895-1933 to Lady Cunard* (A65), who for nearly twenty years has been my mentor, offering encouragement, displaying patience, checking items in England, locating particular copies of GM's books for my collection, loaning books from his own collec-

1. Now in the Special Collections department of the University of Kansas Libraries at Lawrence, Kansas.

243

tion, and urging completion of this bibliography. Sir Rupert's interest has continued through the final stage of preparing it for publication, and he has assisted in the reading of proofs, for which I am especially grateful.

Another who was kindness itself was the late Frank Fayant of Fort Plain, New York, a friend of GM during the Irish author's last years, who had an extensive collection[2] of GM's works, including many presentation copies, some of which had been reinscribed to him. On several occasions he extended his hospitality and permitted me unlimited use of his library. He also answered many questions and generously presented me with several duplicates from his collection. It is with his permission that I quote in the final section an inscription by GM disclaiming any part in compiling a book sometimes attributed to him.

I am also indebted to another collector, Dr. Ulrich Middeldorf, who, while chairman of the art department of the University of Chicago, kindly permitted me to examine his GM collection and who presented me with a number of items for my own.

A special word of thanks is due John Carter for a detailed and painstaking criticism of an early draft of this bibliography and also for suggestions regarding the use of the "degressive principle" in making cuts in an expanded version. Many of his suggestions have been adopted, although it has not been possible to eliminate all of the rightly objected-to uncertainties and "weasel phrases," nor have I been able to make this the contribution to publishing history that he suggested it should be.

Helmut E. Gerber, editor of *George Moore in Transition: Letters to T. Fisher Unwin and Lena Milman, 1894-1910* (A66), has freely shared GM information with me, for which I am extremely grateful. In addition, a further section originally planned for inclusion in this volume, listing books and articles about GM and his writings, has been made unnecessary by the extensive annotated bibliography of such material issued in ENGLISH FICTION [more recently LITERATURE] IN TRANSITION,[3] edited by Professor Gerber.

Among the many satisfactions in compiling this bibliography has been the pleasure of corresponding with a number of scholars who were working on particular phases of GM's writings. Three of these are Dr. John Denny Fischer and Dr. E. Jay Jernigan, whose dissertations are noted in the Preface, and Dr. Jack Wayne Weaver, whose 1966 University of North Carolina dissertation, "A Story Teller's Holiday: George Moore's Irish Renaissance, 1897-1911," traces GM's involvement in the Irish literary scene during a pivotal decade of his life. Another is Dr. Charles Burkhart, who has permitted

2. Now in the Rare Book Department of the Cornell University Library at Ithaca, New York.

3. In Volume II, Number 2, parts i and ii, 1959; supplements in Volume III, Number 2, 1960, and Volume IV, Number 2, 1961; with additional items listed in several succeeding numbers.

use of his 1959 University of Maryland dissertation, "The Letters of George Moore to Edmund Gosse, W.B. Yeats, R.I. Best, Miss Nancy Cunard, and Mrs. Mary Hutchinson." All have freely given assistance, for which I am grateful.

My gratitude also goes to Dan H. Laurence, bibliographer of Henry James, Robert Nathan, and George Bernard Shaw, for calling to my attention many periodical appearances and other Mooreana noted in his meticulous search for Shaw items.

I am also grateful to Prof. Malcolm Brown, whose book, *George Moore: A Reconsideration*, Seattle, 1955, has been helpful in suggesting the genesis of several books and stories.

Kathleen Cohalan, librarian of the American Irish Historical Society in New York, graciously permitted me to examine the GM volumes in the L. S. Goldsmith collection in the society's library, which contains a number of editions not readily located elsewhere, and she later was cooperative in answering questions regarding specific books in the collection.

Professor Joel Ergerer, bibliographer of Robert Burns and curator of the Fales Collection of the New York University Libraries, and his assistant, Edward L. Ochsenschlager, were helpful in granting me access to the GM items in their charge and in answering subsequent questions about some of them.

Albert J. Phiebig of White Plains, New York, a book dealer specializing in foreign publications, has been particularly helpful in locating a number of otherwise unprocurable translations and editions for my collection.

I am grateful to Colin Kilpatrick of T & A Constable who kindly supplied me with copies of their original invoices to the publishers of several of GM's books, from which it has been possible to establish the number of copies printed of *Impressions and Opinions* (A15-a), the 1895 edition of *Vain Fortune* (A16-c), *Celibates* (A21-a), *Memoirs of My Dead Life* (A29-a), and *Poor Folk* (B7-a).

Florian J. Shasky, special collections librarian of the Richard A. Gleeson Library at the University of San Francisco, has generously shared information regarding a number of variant issues in his personal collection of GM items.

Others to whom I am indebted include Ben Abramson; G. T. Banks; Nicolas Barker; Roderick Benton, Lillian Biegel of the education division of the Columbia Broadcasting System; Mrs. Edith Bleezarde; Dorothy W. Bridgwater and Barbara D. Simison of the reference department of Sterling Library at Yale University; Prof. Bradford Booth; Dr. Thomas R. Buckman; Prof. Samuel C. Chew; Prof. Milton Chaiken, author of a number of studies on the French sources and influences in GM's early works;[4] Stephen

---

4. "The Composition of . . . *A Modern Lover*" in COMPARATIVE LITERATURE, Summer 1955; "Balzac, Zola and . . . *A Drama in Muslin*" in REVUE DE LITTÉRATURE

Cipperly; William A. Clark, Charles B. Cohn; Miss Edith Coignon; G-P. Collet, author of *George Moore et France* (B58); Miss Grace Cranston of William Heinemann Ltd.; Mrs. Edna C. Davis of UCLA's Clark Memorial Library; Alan Denson; R. L. DeWilton; Miss Susan Dick; James H. Drake, Marston E. Drake, and R. A. Leland of James F. Drake, Inc.; K. D. Duval; Frances Edwards; Miss Luella D. Everett; Lew D. Feldman; Mrs. Aileen Felter; Lewis Ferbrache; Frances-Jane French; Elmer Gertz; Prof. Royal A. Gettmann; Norman Gullick; Henry J. Haldeman; Norbert Halliwell; James Harrison; Laine Harrison of Charles Scribner's Sons; George H. Healey; Richard Hecht; Kenneth Hieber; Fred H. Higginson; Miss Gertrude Hill; John J. Horton; Mrs. Thelma Ingle; George M. Jenks; Jack Kennedy of Conde Nast Publications; James F. Kuhn; Donald L. LaChance; Edward Lazare; Max Leavitt; Prof. Roger Lhombreaud; Liveright Publishers.

Also John L. Mayfield; Prof. John McClelland; John M. McConnell; Arthur Meeker, Mrs. Jeanne Minhinnick; Man-Hing Mok; Robert Molnar; Howard S. Mott; Percy H. Muir; John M. Munro; Jerrold Nedwick; Jeremy North; Henry H. Noyes; Patrick O'Mahoney of Mitchelstown, County Cork, Eire; David Mitchell; Miss Lucy Eugenia Osborn, former curator of the Chapin Library at Williams College; Miss Ida Ostrow; F. Press of the first editions department of Argosy Book Store, New York; A.E. Popham; Charles Retz; Arthur Richmond; Paul H. Rooney; Harlow Ross; Dr. Stanley Ross; Bertram Rota; Mrs. Dorothy Ritter Russo; Margaretta M. Salinger; Dr. Marilyn B. Saveson; G. W. Skinner; S. R. Shapiro; Dr. Ray Small; Vincent Starrett, editor of *Et Cetera: A Collector's Scrapbook* (B20); Charles W. Stearns; Lulu Stine of Baylor University Library, Waco, Texas; John Stokes; Mrs. Daisy Stouter; T. Tyler Sweeney; Mildred Lund Tyson; Martha E. Valentine; Glenn E. Veach; Mildred Ware; and Mrs. Richard Wetmiller.

A special word of gratitude is also due the many anonymous librarians, particularly those of the Library of Congress, book store clerks, and others whose names I never knew, but who briefly helped in many ways, with a word of apology to any who should have been listed, but whose name inadvertently has been omitted.

A final word of appreciation must be bestowed upon my friends and family who for so many years have borne with a bibliographical enthusiasm which they did not share or understand, and a particular note of thanks for her patience must go to my wife, Elizabeth, who discovered she had married a bibliography as well as its compiler.

Edwin Gilcher

COMPARÉE, October-December 1955; "A French Source for . . . *A Mere Accident*" in MODERN LANGUAGE NOTES, January 1957; and ". . . *A Mummer's Wife* and Zola" in REVUE DE LITTÉRATURE COMPARÉE, January-March 1957.

Index

INDEX